PATTERNS OF LITERARY STYLE

YEARBOOK OF
COMPARATIVE CRITICISM

VOLUME III

Patterns

of Literary

Style

Edited by

Joseph Strelka

THE PENNSYLVANIA STATE
UNIVERSITY PRESS
University Park and London

CONTENTS

CONTENTS

PREFACE

SAINTE-BEUVE'S FAMOUS REMARK THAT THE ONLY THING IMMORTAL IN literature is style stands as one of the prime testimonials to the importance of style analysis in literary criticism. It is by no means the only one. Speaking about the aesthetic circle of a literary work of art, F. W. Bateson stated that we are nearer to the working of the creative imagination on the level of style than we are on the linguistic level. There is hardly a work on the subject of style which does not quote the words of Buffon, "Le style c'est l'homme même," from which it is not far to the development of the Munich School of Voßler and Spitzer and their methods of showing the personal language system of an author as the expression of his personality. Helmut Hatzfeld once wrote that it seems rather clear that an epoch can be defined only by its style. Statements like this could easily be multiplied.

Another well-known quotation is from Dámaso Alonso, according to whom style is the only subject of literary criticism, and knowledge of it the real aim of literary history. Sentences like these show the wide range and numerous possibilities for applications of the term.

First of all there are the usual meanings of the term "style" as the expressive system of a literary work of art, of an author, or of an epoch. Besides that one might also speak about style as the style of a genre or of the style of literary art in general, in which case the death of the style would mean the death of art.

Literary style cannot be made a mere subdivision of linguistics, as Charles Bally attempted to make it. "All devices for securing emphasis or explicitness can be classed under stylistics," as René Wellek put it, "metaphors, which permeate all languages, even of the most primitive type; all rhetorical figures; syntactical patterns. Nearly every linguistic utterance can be studied from the point of view of its expressive value. It seems impossible to ignore this problem as the 'behavioristic' school of linguistics in America very consciously does."[1]

It was also René Wellek who pointed out the obvious dangers of stylistic analysis in concentrating on the peculiarities of style, i.e., on traits differentiating it from the surrounding linguistic systems. The dangers might be overcome—even if not too easily—if one remembers that a work of art is a whole, as well as style in itself is, and represents a whole entity. Therefore critics have been right in advocating again and again that style is more than the "how" in the form of language since the "what" is inextricably contained in language, or as David Daiches defined it, "Style is the continuous maintenance of the symbolic expansion of meaning through appropriate devices of language and arrangement."[2] In other words, style as an expressive system embraces the internal structure and world of a work or a group of works as well as the power of its words and the aesthetic efficacy of rhythmical interplay.

Some of the problems of stylistics in general belong to practically all human speech, but the style of a literary work of art has to deal with some additional, difficult problems. These are the problems of a particular kind of language, a "second language" in addition to the usual language of communication or of science on an empirical level. This "second language," as Wladimir Weidlé called it,[3] or this "expressive language" or "depth language," as Philip Wheelwright called it,[4] creates its own problems of special difficulty and sublimity.

"The lord whose oracle is at Delphi" said Heraclitus in regard to Apollo, the god and symbol of wisdom as well as of poetry, "neither speaks nor conceals, but gives signs."[5] It is done in the same way by his followers and fellow-poets. Wheelwright applies this gnomic utterance to "indirection" and "soft focus" alike of the "expressive language," and it leads him to the appreciation of the plain fact that not all facts are plain in expressive language, and this means in literary language.

It is rather difficult for stylistic analysis to cover the entire circumference of the literary expressive system in its full scale. Many studies which treat only certain elements and currents of style and which are not written with an awareness of their partial character give an impression, as though (to paraphrase Nietzsche) the Eroica Symphony were scored for two flutes. The essays of this book either treat single features and currents of style or deal with particular problems of style. In most cases they do not contradict each other but according to the basic idea of this yearbook complement each other, either looking at the problem of literary style from different perspectives like personal or period style, or analyzing single features and currents like linguistic, semantic, or rhetorical elements of style.

Unfortunately the present collection is far from being complete, not only in the sense that total completion cannot be reached at all in this endeavor, but also in the sense of rather obvious gaps which remain in the coverage of the subject presented in this collection. A comparative analysis of the treatment of time and style in the critical work from Günther Müller and Emil Staiger to Georges Poulet, a treatment of the relation of literary style to sociology, and especially one of the relation of literary style to the sociology of language were all solicited of various scholars, but for different understandable and excusable reasons these scholars were unable to finish their contributions on time. I most regret the lack of the contribution which Professor Hugo Kuhn (Munich) originally promised to write about stylistic parallels in different arts.

The question of style is, however, such a central and essential one, that sooner or later another volume of the *Yearbook* will be devoted to it. Both volumes together, then, may give a cross-section of the most important problems and possibilities which never could have been presented by one volume alone.

Finally, I should like to thank the Department of German of The Pennsylvania State University and its head, Dr. Stanley R. Townsend, for the continuing support of the *Yearbook*.

JOSEPH P. STRELKA

Notes

1. René Wellek and Austin Warren, *Theory of Literature* (New York, 1956), p. 178.
2. David Daiches, *A Study of Literature* (New York, 1964), p. 35.
3. Wladimir Weidlé, "Die zwei 'Sprachen' der Sprachkunst," in *Jahrbuch für Aesthetik und allgemeine Kunstwissenschaft*, Vol. 7, No. 2.
4. Philip Wheelwright, *The Burning Fountain* (Bloomington and London, 1968), pp. 3, 73–101.
5. Cf. Philip Wheelwright, *The Presocratics* (New York, 1966), p. 70 (Fragment No. 18).

Roland Barthes

ACTION SEQUENCES

EARLY ANALYSES CENTERING ON THE STRUCTURE OF THE NARRATIVE HAVE
shown that a short story consists of a systematic chain of events which
are distributed among a small number of characters, the function of
which is identical from one story to another. While analyzing several
hundred Slav short stories, Vladimir Propp succeeded in establishing
the constancy of their elements (characters and actions) and the constancy of their rapports (action links) which definitely constitutes the
form of the popular short story. With Propp this form nevertheless
remains a *schema*, a syntagmatic pattern which resulted from abstracting
the progressive development of the action in different short stories.
Levi-Strauss and Greimas, supplementing and correcting Propp's work,
have tried to structuralize this process by linking the actions of the
narrative sequence, separated in the course of the short story by other
actions and a certain distance in time, but linked to one another by a
correspondence of opposing paradigms (e.g., *default sustained by the
protagonist/restitution of this default*). Bremond, finally, has examined the
logical correspondence of narrative actions, to the extent where this
correspondence refers to a certain logic of human behavior, bringing
to light, for instance, a certain invariable structure in *intrigue* or in
deception, both of which occur frequently as episodes in the short story.[1]

This is to be a contribution to the problem which is absolutely
fundamental to the structural analysis of the narrative while examining
action sequences, and this time no longer in the popular short story,
but in literary narrative. The examples to be quoted here have been
taken from the short story "Sarrasine" by Balzac, published in *Scènes
de la Vie Parisienne*, and are not concerned with a discussion on the art
of Balzac, or even on the art of realism: the topic will be narrative
forms exclusively, not traits concerned with history or the perormfance
of the author.

As a point of departure it may be appropriate to make two general observations. The first is as follows: The analysis of short stories has extricated objectively important events, primordial manifestations of the story—i.e., commitments, tests, or adventures experienced by the protagonist; in literary analysis, however, once the important events have been outlined—supposing this were easy—there remains a host of events of secondary importance which on the surface appear frequently trifling or mechanical (*knocking at a door, starting a conversation, granting an appointment,* etc.). Are these secondary events to be regarded as a kind of insignificant background, and should they be excluded from the analysis with the excuse that it is *automatic* for the text to mention them to connect two principal actions? Definitely not, for this would mean to pass advance judgment on the overall structure of the narrative, to force this structure into a sole, hierarchic mold; on the contrary, we believe that *all* the events of a narrative, unimportant as they may seem, must be examined and integrated into a sequence which is to be described; in the written text—in contrast to the oral narrative—no turn of a phrase is insignificant.

The second observation is the following: To an even greater degree than in the popular short story, the action sequences of the literary narrative are chosen from an abundance of other "details," of other factors which in no way constitute *actions*; they are either psychological pointers denoting the nature of a character or of a locale, games of dialogue by means of which the partners try to agree, to convince, or to deceive one another, indications given by the text to set, to delay, or to solve riddles, general thoughts evolving from special knowledge or sound judgment, or, finally, devices of language—such as the metaphor—which analysis ought to integrate ordinarily into the symbolic sphere of the work. Not one of these factors is "spontaneous" or "insignificant." Each one receives its authority and liberty from a systematic combination of "outlooks," i.e., from repetitions and collective rules, or even from an overall cultural pattern: psychology, the sciences, prudence, rhetoric, hermeneutics, etc. In this multitude of additional signals, the behavior of the characters—inasmuch as it can be linked to coherent sequences—enhances a particular pattern, a logic governing the events, which, while it structures the text profoundly, gives it its appeal of being "readable," its appearance of rationality called by the ancients its *verisimilitude*. Still, this logic is far from occupying the entire meaningful surface of literary narrative: throughout several pages it is quite possible that *nothing happens,* i.e., no action is described, and, on the other hand, a following act may be separated from its antecedent by a considerable mass of signals deriving from patterns other than the motivating pattern. Furthermore, one ought not to forget that actions can be described indirectly by "hints" as to the nature of a character, e.g., "he was in the habit of . . ."; they are then linked to one another by an accumulative process, not by logical sequence, or, at least, the logical principle to which they refer is of a psychological and not of a pragmatic nature.

Aside from all this (which makes up the lion's share of literary narrative), in the classical text—before the caesura made by the modern period—there is just as much of a certain number of current data which are connected to one another by a rule of logic and time, i.e., the *latter* following the *former* is also the result of the former; hence these current data are organized in the form of closely linked sequences: 1. *arriving at a door*; 2. *knocking at this door*; 3. *seeing someone appear there*; the internal development of which—if it overlaps with that of other parallel sequences—assures the story its flow, and turns the narrative into an organic process as it approaches its "end" or "conclusion."

What are we to call this general pattern of narrative actions where some appear important and intensely charged with novelesque features, e.g., *assassinating, carrying off a victim, declaring one's love*, etc., while others seem trifling, e.g., *opening a door, sitting down*, etc., in order to distinguish them from other cultural patterns which permeate the text? (Obviously this distinction is only relevant to analysis, because the text features all patterns mixed and *interwoven*.) Referring to a concept of the Aristotelian vocabulary—Aristotle is, after all, the father of literary and structural analysis—I have suggested calling this pattern of narrative actions a *proaïretic pattern*.[2] Establishing the science of the action, or *praxis*, Aristotle in fact precedes it by a related discipline, *proaïresis*, or man's ability to deliberate in advance the result of an act, to *choose* (this is the original meaning) from two possibilities the one which is to be developed. At each crossroads of the action sequence, the narrative —it is more appropriate to focus on the narrative, and not on the writer, because our topic is narrative *language*, not the performance of the storyteller—chooses between several possibilities, and this choice involves at any given moment the very future of the story; obviously the story will change according to whether the door on which one has knocked will open or remain closed, etc. (this structural alternative has been the object of a special study by C. Bremond). It goes without saying that, where an action is faced with an alternative—having this or that consequence—the narrative invariably chooses that from which it profits, i.e., that which *assures its survival as narrative*. Never does the narrative record anything—implied or real—which would snuff out the story, bring it to an abrupt ending. To a certain extent the narrative possesses a true instinct of self-preservation which, from two possible results, implied by a stated action, always chooses that which provides the story with a "come-back." A study of this simple truth has actually met with little scholarly interest, and it might be useful to mention it at this time, because narrative *art*—the performance and the application of a pattern—consists precisely of endowing these structural determinants (the only concern of which is the "well-being" of the narrative, not that of this or the other character) with the security, i.e., the alibi, of variables which are usually of a psychological, moral, or intensely emotional nature, etc. Where the narrative in fact opts for its own survival, it is the character who appears to choose his fate; narrative thriftiness—just as stringent as monetary thriftiness—is sublimated into human free will. Such, then, are the implications of this term *proaïretism* which I propose to apply to any narrative action involved in a coherent and homogeneous sequence.

It is difficult to pinpoint what makes up the essence of these sequences, and to decide that an action belongs to one sequence and not to another. In fact, this essence of the sequence is closely linked to its nominal purpose, and, inversely, its analysis is connected with the unfolding process of its theme or label. For the simple reason that, under the general heading of *travel*, I may spontaneously infer a variety of actions such as *leaving, making a journey, arriving, staying,* the sequence takes on consistency and individuality—in contrast to other sequences and other themes; inversely, since practical experience gives me some reason to believe that a series of acts such as *suggesting, accepting, honoring* usually underlies the theme of *time or place of a meeting*—suggested by the text in one way or another—I cannot help but observe the schema of sequence. To separate the sequences (from the significant body of the text already defined as irregular in character) is to array actions under a generic label, e.g., *meeting, travel, excursion, assassination, abduction,* etc., while to analyze these sequences is to break this generic label down to its components. That simple labeling should suffice as criterion for the essence of the phenomenon to be observed may seem easy enough, left, as it were, to the altogether subjective and, to be truthful, not very "scientific," discretion of the analyst. Does this not in fact mean that we tell each sequence: You exist, because I give you a name, and I name you thus, because such is my pleasure? To this one must reply that narrative as a science, if there is such a thing, cannot obey the laws of the pure or applied sciences; narrative is a function of language—which endows it with literal or symbolic meaning—and it

is in terms of language that this function must be analyzed. Labeling
a sequence, then, is for the analyst an operation just as legitimate and
in keeping with his aim as measuring is for the land surveyor, weighing
for the chemist, and looking through a microscope for the biologist.
Furthermore, the label put on the sequence—constituting its essence—
is a systematic witness evolving from the vast classifying process of
language; if I attach the label *abduction* to a certain sequence, it is because the language itself has classified, summed up the diversity of
certain actions in one concept which it transmits to me, the coherence
of which is incontestable. The concept of abduction which I compile
from a variety of thinly strewn actions in the text coincides, then, with
all the abductions I have read previously. The label is the true copy,
irrefutable, as unquestionable as a scientific fact, of something *already
written*, *read*, and *done*. Thus, finding the label is by no means the work
of my imagination, left, as it were, to my fancy alone; to find the proper
label is to find this *already* which constitutes the pattern, to assure the
communication of this text and all the other texts which make up the
whole of narrative language, since linguistic or symptomatic study must
always focus on discovering the *connection* between the total past of
language and the specific present of the text. Finally, in labeling the
sequence, the analyst merely reproduces, more astutely and more
methodically, the very exercise of the reader, and his "expertise" takes
root in the study of the phenomena of the reading process. To read a
narrative continuum is in fact to arrange it— at the quick pace set by
the reading material   in a variety of structures, to strive for concepts
or labels which more or less sum up the profuse sequence of observations. To read is to prepare in one's own mind —that very moment as
one "devours" the story—for adjustments in concept, and constantly
to reduce the novelty of what one has just read to familiar concepts
which, in turn, have resulted from the vast pattern of previous reading.
When certain indications bring to mind the label of *assassination*, my
reaction to the story is in fact a *reading process*, not the simple perception
of phrases where I might understand the linguistic meaning, but not
the narrative meaning. To read is to classify, and this is why one could
go so far as to say that to read is to write, at least with reference to
certain modern texts.

Without intending to cover in detail all aspects of the logical principle which governs actions, and foregoing any claim that this principle
might be the same in all cases, let us try to reduce several proairetic
sequences to a small number of simple rapports in order to gain an
initial idea of the certain rational appeal of classical narrative.

1. *Consecutive*   In narrative, and this is perhaps its hallmark, there is

no simple or neat succession. Logic immediately pervades the notion of time: that which *follows next* is at the same time *the result*,[3] i.e., that which comes *after* appears to be result of that which was *before*. Nevertheless, as certain movements are broken down into their components, one draws nearer to the unadulterated notion of time; thus, in the awareness of an object, a painting, for instance, *looking around/noticing the object*. The faintly logical nature of these sequences—infrequent elsewhere—is easily recognized in that each expression, on the whole, merely repeats its antecedent, as in a series (which is not a structure): *leaving a first locale*, e.g., a room, *leaving a second locale*, e.g., the building which contains this room. Still, the element of logic is very close in the form of an implied coherence. In order to "enter a room," one *must* first "enter the building"; this rationale is even more obvious if the movement implies a return, i.e., *"excursion," "lover's walk."* Due to its fundamental nature, the structure then appears very vague, as that of *going away and coming back*; still, we are justified in assuming that an expression is not to be construed as a measuring stick for the logical upheaval which the narrative might suddenly support. The *journey without return*—for the simple lack of a better term for this sequence— is one of the most important devices on which the narrative can draw.

2. *Consequential* This is the classical rapport between two actions where one determines the other—but here again, symmetrically and inversely to the above rapport, the causal link, more often than not, influences the notion of time. The enumeration of sequences is obviously one of the most valuable devices, because it supports to some extent the "liberty" of the narrative; depending on whether a consequence is positive or negative, the fate of the story is changed completely.

3. *Volitive* An action, e.g., *getting dressed*, is preceded by a word denoting intention or will, e.g., *wanting to get dressed, deciding to get dressed*. Here the coherence may vary, will and accomplishment may be disrupted, e.g., *wanting to get dressed and not doing it*, if an event from a second sequence interferes with the logical development of the first; relevant for us is the fact that this event is always mentioned.

4. *Reactive* An action, e.g., *touching*, survives in the form of its reaction to it, e.g., *crying out*. Here we have a variation on the consequential schema, although the example is more of a biological nature.

5. *Durative* Having indicated the beginning or the duration of an action, the discourse denotes its interruption or end, e.g., *bursting with laughter/breaking off, hiding/coming out of one's hiding place, meditating/being roused from one's day-dream*, etc. Once again, it is that very banality of these sequences which is significant, for if the narrative should acciden-

tally fail to describe the end of a state or of an action, the result would be catastrophic. The description of an interruption appears to be a genuine checking device of narrative language, or, transferred to the level of discourse, even one of the *obligatory categories* mentioned by Jakobson in his discussion of language.

6. *Equipollent* A small number of sequences—reduced to the essence of their nucleus—merely perform the role of lexical opposites, such as *questioning/answering,* or *asking oneself a question/examining that question.* The two terms are certainly linked to one another by a logical rapport of simple implication—one replies, because someone has asked a question—but the structure is that of an explicit *complement* as it is found in pairs of lexical antonyms.

In action sequences there are certainly other rapports of logic, and the six rapports mentioned can undoubtedly be narrowed down and formulated to an even greater extent. Important, for the purpose of analysis, is not so much the *nature* of the logical link as the necessity of its being expressed. The narrative *must* mention the two terms of the rapport unless it is to become "unreadable." Now then, if the logical link seems less relevant than its expression, the logical principle to which the narrative refers is none other than that of the *already-read* type. The concept of stereotype—the product of a secular culture—is the true motivating force of the narrative domain, entirely founded on the impressions which experience (much more bookish than practical in nature) has left on the mind of the reader, and the memory of which constitutes its essence. One might equally say that the perfect sequence —namely, that which provides the reader with the most convincing assurance of logic—is the most "cultural" sequence where one immediately recognizes a host of previous reading and conversation patterns. In the short story of Balzac, the sequence *"career"* is a good example of this type; *going to Paris/entering the employ of a well-known master/leaving the master/winning a prize being exalted by an influential critic/leaving for Italy.* How many times has this sequence not been impressed on our mind? It must be realized that narrative logic is nothing else but the development of the Aristotelian concept of the *probable,* i.e., general opinion and not scientific truth. Hence it is not surprising that, in the attempt to establish this logic firmly in the form of aesthetic restraints and values, it is still an Aristotelian concept which the first theorists on the essence of narrative put forth during classical times: that of *verisimilitude.*

As yet we have not mentioned the ways in which the action sequence is expressed in the text.

The preceding analysis has outlined a few fundamental aspects of logic, and it could well lead us to believe that the sequences, subject, by definition, to a syntagmatic principle, have a binary (paradigmatic) structure, but this would be an illusion created by analysis. If one accepts as the criterion of the sequence its capacity for reduction to a label, i.e., to be summarized by a generic term resulting from the cultural vocabulary, one must necessarily admit sequences where the number of terms is not fixed. When the sequence describes a trivial, futile operation, generally its terms are not very numerous; the exact opposite occurs when it refers to a prominent novelesque pattern, e.g., *lovers' walk, assassination, kidnapping,* etc. Moreover, in these prominent sequences different structures may overlap; the discourse, for instance, may blend the description of "real" events—in the logical sequence of time—and ordinary concepts of rhetoric *dispositio*, i.e., announcement, divisions, résumé, which prolong the sequence without dispersing it. The discourse may also establish two or three principal—and different —themes and repeat each one several times, changing their meaning: a character caught in a certain situation may *hope, be disappointed, make amends*, but hope, disappointment, and amendment are revealed several times by means of personal reflections and the flashback. Lastly, one must not forget that the repetition of terms (effecting the expansion of the sequence) can have a semantic value—as repetition it is endowed with a content of its own. This is the case in such sequences as *danger* and *threat*, where the multiplication of the same expression, e.g., *courting a danger, being exposed to a threat*, conveys the impression of dramatic suspense.

Generally, the structural analysis of narrative does not classify the actions (called *functions* by Propp), before they have been specified by the character who determines or is determined by them. From this point of view, analysis ought to point out that a sequence is nearly always determined by two or three characters; in a sequence such as *acting/reacting*, there are obviously two distinct participants, but this is an aspect of analysis which does not concern us at the moment. In terms of simple structuralization—which is our present concern—it is legitimate, and undoubtedly profitable, to consider the action-governing factor as a verb divorced from any personal process, and, quite on the contrary, confined to its true significance as a verb. (Furthermore, the meaning of some verbs already implies two agents, e.g., *to meet*).

A sequence, when it is of more than average length, may contain additional sequences inserted into its overall development as "subprogrammes" ("bricks" in cybernetics). The sequence *narrating* may, in a given set of circumstances, contain the term "meeting" (meeting to tell the story). This term may, in turn, contain a sequence, e.g., *asking for an appointment/accepting it/refusing it/keeping it*, etc. The action network consists essentially of the principle of substitution, which may have an expanding or a reducing function, depending on the circumstances. Occasionally the discourse *breaks down* a term, thus producing a new sequence of actions; in other instances it condenses several events in one word: this freedom of oscillation is peculiar to articulate language as opposed to screen language, where it is kept under much closer surveillance.

When a sequence appears to be inconsistent, mostly one only has to detach oneself temporarily from analysis and proceed to certain fundamental substitutions in order to restore the sequence to its rationality. If a "lacuna" appears between the telling of the story and the effect of this story on the person who has listened to it, it is because the act of narrating, without being mentioned explicitly, is represented by the text of the story itself. The missing term, then, appears in the guise of the whole story, signaled as such by the quotation marks of the opening statement.

These substitutions or, better, "restitutions," come to mind because it is well known that in classical narrative the sequence tends to cover as completely as possible the event described. There is a kind of narrative obsession to corroborate an event with the largest possible number of supporting data. "Narrating," for instance, will be preceded by both *conditions* and *causes* of the act of narration. The event—or the action nucleus in which it is expressed—is endlessly prolonged by its preceding events, the most typical example being the flashback. From the point of view of action, the principle of narrative art one could say, its ethics—is the *complement*: it is a matter of producing a discourse which best satisfies the demand for *completeness* and leads the reader away from the "horror of the vacuum."

These few observations focusing on a certain level of narrative (which, incidentally, comprises many others) aim at introducing, in the form of a kind of preliminary inventory of available evidence, a concise problem: what is it that makes a piece of narrative "readable"? Which are the structural factors that determine the "readability" of a text? Everything that has been said may well appear to be "obvious," but if these narrative-determining factors seem "natural," it is because there virtually exists, deep down, an "anti-nature" of the narrative, the new expression of which is undoubtedly found in certain modern texts. In pointing to the fundamental logic of action sequences, one approaches the *limits* of narrative, beyond which begins a new art—that of narrative transgression. The sequence of actions is to some extent the privileged depository of this readability: It is through the pseudo-logic of its action sequences that a piece of narrative seems "normal," i.e., "readable." This logic, as we have pointed out, is empirical. It cannot be attributed to the "structure" of the human mind. What is important is that it assures the sequence of the events to be described an *irreversible order* (of logic and time): *it is this irreversibility which makes for the readability of classical narrative*. Thus it is understandable that narrative undermines itself as it intensifies the attempts at reversibility in its general structure. The reversible level par excellence is that of the symbols —the dream, for instance, is exempt from the demands of logic and time. As a romantic work, the text of Balzac to which we have occasionally referred occupies a historical place at the crossroads of action and symbol. It is a perfect example of the *transition* from simple readability, characterized by a stringent irreversibility of actions (of the classical type), to a complex readability (precarious), subject to the forces of dispersion and to the reversibility of symbolic elements which destroy both time and logic.

Notes

1. Cf. especially: A. J. Greimas, "Eléments pour une théorie de l'interprétation du récit mythique," *Communications*, Vol. 8 (1966), pp. 28–59; C. Bremond, "Le message narratif," *Communications*, Vol. 4 (1964), pp. 4–32, and "La logique des possibles narratifs," *Communications*, Vol. 8 (1966), pp. 60–76.
2. In a work dedicated to the structural analysis of "Sarrasine," to appear shortly at du Seuil, Paris.
3. Cf. "Introduction à l'analyse structurale du récit," in *Communications*, Vol. 8 (1966).

Manuel de Diéguez

BRIEF BIOGRAPHY OF AN IDEA: THE EXISTENTIAL PSYCHOANALYSIS OF STYLE

A Letter to an American Friend

YOU HAVE ASKED ME TO LET YOU KNOW, AS A CONTRIBUTION TO YOUR *Yearbook of Comparative Criticism,* what has been happening to my idea of "existential psychoanalysis of style" since 1960. I had in mind to send you a very weighty memorandum on this very weighty matter. In it, "existential psychoanalysis of style" would have been an illustrious figure in my thought, reigning supreme at the center of all critique. Unfortunately, one little word—"existence"—has prevented me from carrying out this momentous project. Nothing induces humility more than "existence": not even "existential," or "psychoanalytical," or even "of style."

Moreover, existence is something that flows along of its own accord, of which we might say that it goes its own sweet way. Even "existential psychoanalysis of style" is doomed to submit to the authority of existence. This is why I ask your permission to talk about the vicissitudes of critique in existence in the form of a letter. For any letter is by nature existential in that it is in fact addressed *to* someone—and this, today, has become a great luxury for the writer.

Besides, we can say things through the mail that are extremely difficult to understand, and even terribly dialectical, because in writing a letter it is against the rules to stop partway: we have to maintain the pace, and this is good for our processes of reflection. And finally, when I consider that all this is going to be translated into a language which, although admirable, is beyond my comprehension, and that I shall be unable to recognize what I have written and be obliged to take the word of those who tell me I have indeed written this or that, I confess that I look to you as to a witness, one solitary witness to whom I can attach my discourse as to a buoy.

Without wishing to exploit this letter-form to discuss myself, there is nevertheless one thing I must say at once, because of a certain reference work[1] in which I read that "Diéguez's critique is neither psychoanalytical, nor existential, nor stylistic." Splendid! If my work consisted of the "application" of "psychoanalysis," "existentialism," and "stylistics" to critique, literary existence would cease to pose insoluble problems to anyone. It would be enough to "apply" history, and sociology, and medicine, and morals, and religion, and psychoanalysis, and existentialism, and so on and so forth, to critique in the same way that we apply a dressing to a sore foot. But if such had been my intention I would still have had to *choose* from among the countless categories of science that add luster to our culture and that constitute that city-symbol of our civilization that Nietzsche called *"die bunte Kuh."*

For there are many varieties of psychoanalysis: had I decided in favor of Freud, Adler, Lacan, or Jung, my books would be blossoming as from the tomb—the tombs of *schools* of psychoanalysis. Psychoanalysis has greatness, the schools of psychoanalysis are mortal. Bachelard's *La Psychanalyse du feu* has become unreadable because the kind of scholarly psychoanalysis it uses as a systematic framework for interpretation has aged dreadfully. For a good thirty years now, fire has ceased to symbolize the male organ: what a catastrophe for the hundreds of works of literary criticism that set out so valiantly, armed with the panoply of the "compleat psychoanalytical explorer" (umbrella, staircase, walking cane), to conquer sex in works of art. But sex has become metaphysical and, with Lacan, transcendence now opens up to the vast spaces of *nothingness* a subject in search of a symbolic father! And "existentialism"? Ever since St. Augustine there have been as many kinds as there have been philosophers; for with what, I wonder, do philosophers concern themselves if not with existence, even if they turn their backs on it? Varieties of stylistics are also innumerable; they are grounded in varieties of metaphysics that decide in advance the level of their observation and hence their field of action. So I would have been hard put to it to base my critique of style on existentialism as such, and on stylistics as such, assuming I had ever had any such foolish intention.

As it happens, my position is quite different. I believe that literary criticism should occupy a position in the vanguard of thought; if it had nothing to teach psychoanalyses, existentialisms, and stylistics, it would be merely one more genre and, as such, dependent on the literary sensibility of an epoch. It would then become a branch of the sociology of letters, and it would be sociology that would have to be advanced in order to obtain a better understanding of criticism as a "running commentary" on literature.

The fact is, however, that my reflections on *freedom* in poetic *literary language* which formed the basis of my very modest research on "existential psychoanalysis of style" have become much more intelligible since the entry of Lacan into the public domain, with the result that it is psychoanalytical research that has joined forces with my intuition of the essence of poetic language. But, beyond what I call the Galileoism of Lacan,[2] the works of Michel Tort, for example—which finally refute the implicit, hence unthought, metaphysical foundations of the Freudian theory of pulsions (and even the concepts of an "outside" and an "inside" to the psychism)— confirmed the avant-garde role of all psychoanalysis which the "philosophy" of styles should occupy. *Sed de his plura mox.* I merely want to make clear that my critique is concerned with what we do not yet know and not with what we do know.

Merleau-Ponty once said: "I don't like Christians: they *always already know.*" I fear that psychoanalysts also believe they already know the nature of psychoanalysis, and stylisticians the nature of stylistics. Fortunately there remain the philosophers, who know that fresh discoveries modify the whole field of knowledge, and that even the definition of an *unfinished science* is an extrapolation. Scholars who define their science from its inception are like the Roman soothsayers who cut a space out of the sky in order to found a city. Philosophers *do not already know* what existence is. This makes them truly "existentialists." And if we do not know what existence is, how are we to know what psychoanalysis and stylistics are? Definitions, like people, ought always to see themselves in terms of the future.

The second confession I am bound to make in order to render intelligible the rather difficult things that are to follow is that I am not a true literary critic: I am only a philosopher who has presumed to take a closer look at certain writers. Needless to say, the critics have spoken of my books as critiques, and I am very grateful to them. They could accord me no greater praise—for in so doing they have acknowledged that the philosopher was not apparent in my books; consequently I could not be accused of philosophical aggressiveness. As for the old philosophers, the critics, believing they were concerned with literary criticism, have not read them, for which I am likewise very grateful, for they might have tried to convince me that their masterpieces were but shadows on the walls of Plato's cave. Nevertheless, I made up my mind to write books of philosophy for the sake of philosophers, and I have sent you the first one;[3] before the year is out I shall be sending you another,[2] over six hundred pages long, dealing with the philosophy of the sciences. A third has been announced that will deal with Descartes, the unintelligibility of the physical world, and the new *cogito*. All this fills me with great hope and a renewed naïveté, for I am hoping for the birth of a new genus of critics who will be high-powered super-philosophers, and of a new genus of philosophers who will also be critics because they will search for the essential in the exceptional, instead of looking for it, as did the rough-and-ready philosophers of the past, in everything that bears the imprint of the mass. But this brings me to what style can teach us, to what neither psychoanalysis, nor stylistics, nor anthropology, *already knows*.

You have asked me to elaborate on the period that begins with "L'Ecrivain et son langage." I wrote this essay in 1958 and 1959. The famous dispute between Sartre and Camus was then quite recent; minds were still inflamed by the question of deciding whether or not the writer should be "engaged." The whole affair, of course, was dominated by terror—it would have been an act of terrorism to say that Shakespeare was much more engaged in history through having given birth to his theater than some beardless militant member of the Communist Party. For "existence" had been defined in advance as "historical"; and the historical defined in advance as "political"; and the political defined in advance as "revolutionary"; and the revolutionary defined in advance as "truth"; and truth defined in advance as "justice"; and justice defined in advance as the "dictatorship of the proletariat." Thus fear remained the sole master of the game; it divided the innocent from the guilty in a manner which from the very outset confined literary quarrels in the arena of punitive thought. On this wheel of history, then, the mass learns, by dint of clever schooling, to fear itself, and we only increase this fear by pointing it out. This is how history has managed to erect veritable mental systems of fear. These systems proceed to coagulate in men's minds in such a way that no light whatsoever can pierce the hard shell of the human spirit. In spite of this I have tried to counter the self-coagulation of thought.

The blindness of every hell vis-a-vis itself immediately divides the philosophic race into three natural species: those who do not see the hell; those who stand aghast and open-eyed as they face the fires; and those who tell themselves that the true light is bound to be much more visible in the thick darkness of hell than in the twilight. These are the ones who, like Diogenes, go looking for man with a lantern. Is not this lantern "style"?

For two very different men can utter the same words, yet these words liberate one person and enslave another. Nietzsche and Hitler appear sometimes to say the same thing, for example: "Woman, what is there in common between you and me?" One man is a prophet, the other a savage. The words "force" and "superman" have precisely opposite meanings when used by both men. Bonhoeffer shows that the notion of superman is essentially Christian. If we were truly awakened to the profound style of human beings, we would know why Zarathustra is as free as the Gospel and his "disciple" a slave like Caesar, and why Bonhoeffer let himself by killed by the Nazis as "disciples" of Nietzsche. Plato is free when he speaks of freedom; but how many millions of men today let themselves be enslaved while surrounded by a *unanimous* language of freedom? So we see that it is not necessarily words—or even men's belief that they think with the aid of their words—that make for freedom, but the light of their language; and this light is their style.

I was battering at an open door here. Valéry went into ecstasies long ago over Bossuet's style, while still considering his ideas absurd and inconceivable. Yet he proclaimed the freedom of his style as one of the highest freedoms of our literature. Hence, said the poet, the form is more durable than the content. But why is this so? If form was durable, it was necessary to explain why it was durable, and it seemed to me that there must be reasons for this other than those "of form"— unless, that is, the idea of form is understood at an entirely different level of depth. Valéry explained the preeminence of form by the pre-eminence of the musicality of language—the ultimate authority— which would be anterior to the *meaning* of the discourse and sometimes dictate its content. Proust in turn invoked something he called an "*au-delà des mots,*" a "transcendency of words." These conclusions seem to me to be mainly composed of undefined presentiments. Vagueness and invocation reigned here. We must take a new look at the very nature of man (his *existence*) if we want to understand *who* is speaking as a slave, *who* is speaking as a freeman. Recourse to verbal explanation is the fundamental trap of thought. Words fabricate a cincture of fetishes such as "form," "aesthetics," "beauty," "style." How can we

know what such words mean if we don't know which man, which freedom, are expressed by "form," "aesthetics," "beauty"? Vocabulary is
also a standard-bearer: colors are unfurled by preference in the street;
but since the true writer demonstrated his sovereign freedom in his style
and not in the street, freedom did not run through the streets. In fact
it remained very secret and hidden, just like the secret of style. The
simple fact of having "existence" all around one, of finding oneself
immersed in existence: Is it not precisely this plethora of existence that
is free, and is it not precisely this free existence that escapes the scrutiny
of the masses?

The men of old were lucky. Buffon said: *"Le style est l'homme même."*[4]
But where does man himself *hide*? Did Buffon believe that "man himself" is manifested in full daylight? That he is immediately recognizable,
from whatever distance we see him? But tyrannies, even those that are
diffuse and insidious, are the veritable paradise of philosophical reflection since they lend an invincible power to the fact that "man himself" is invisible and hidden. Tyrannies beget depth because freedom,
which eluded display in full daylight, where it is only pretence and
indifference, suddenly becomes the rare commodity, barely visible to
the naked eye, that it always was. It is only bondage that becomes
instantly recognizable and everywhere apparent. Then the philosopher
says to himself: since everything that until yesterday seemed free has
now changed its appearance and stands revealed as never having been
anything but the disguise and ornament of the mass, we shall have to
ferret out freedom with the aid of thought, i.e., with the lantern of
Diogenes.

At this point I would like to call upon Ghelderode: the more this
great man saw of people, the unhappier he became and the more he
lost his power as a writer, because in his eyes human beings had become more lifeless, more bereft of destiny, than objects of art. So the
poet surrounded himself with *things*, bearers of light and mystery and
depth: a wooden horse escaped from a carousel, a flamboyant bronze
eagle, puppets charged with silence, an ancient and intriguing mirror:
from these objects fraught with destiny, i.e., with style, he drew an
enormous, life-proclaiming theater. For the philosopher, objects that
cry aloud are the memorable footprints of freedom.

But how shall we learn to make an infallible distinction between a
free pen and a pen in bondage? I need hardly say that I lack any such
prodigious gift. We may well envy the saints, those extraordinary
psychoanalysts. "The mystery that I sense beneath the semblance of
an object displayed on a table has left me a profound understanding
which, *at the first word I hear*, perceives spiritual persons and things,"

are the words of Angelo de Foligno as quoted by an obscure monk.
Had I been able to arrange styles like objects on a table, their freedom
or their bondage would still not have become visible to my blind eyes.
But then, once again, there came to my aid that beneficent despotism
of vengeful and punitive thought which at the time encompassed the
earth and in the midst of which the style of the great writers burst
forth as "spiritual persons and things." Miraculously, prisons reveal
themselves thus at pen-point: Faces are deceptive; the pen betrays the
bondsman. At the very core of the great freedoms where styles expand
like suns, what was the freedom of man?

In my attempt to descend into the abyss of language and man, I
needed a speleological technique—a psychoanalysis of unfathomable
existence *in its relation to a form*.[5] I attempted this through humble
obedience to that night which is philosophy's own.

For philosophy, poetry, and mysticism share a common nocturnal
beginning; they are the three nocturnal instances of man: waiting for
understanding, waiting for song, waiting for grace. Philosophy is an
asceticism of thought, a powerful *via negationis* carved out by reason, a
preparatory destruction, a preliminary annihilation of all impure
knowledge and all facile certainty; hence an inauguratory call to the
desert for a second birth of clarity of the spirit. For what is the systematic doubt of the Cartesian genius if not the basic démarche of all
authentic metaphysics, whose mission is to make a *tabula rasa* of the
visible and crudely recognizable world? Philosophy is a search for the
dawn along the road of nescience, of unknowing. It was therefore necessary to obey, as far as possible, a certain "demon" peculiar to philosophy—a Cartesian *malin génie* inhabiting philosophy—in order to celebrate the marriage between style and freedom.

It seems to me, therefore, that the poet, like the mystic and the
philosopher, does not speak first to the world, does not respond to the
mass of things in this world: his foundation and his asceticism are hidden from view. The word, like thought, demands first of all the void.
Nothingness is its first domain. A style is a formal act—hence, in a way,
cosmic—whose "natural" abode is limitless space and which would prefer to maintain itself in its "absolute" gesture, and in its deserted habitat, without ever encountering a single terrestrial object. There is no
opposite number to being. For being is at the mercy of nonbeing, of
nada, where it vainly strives to capture its own "being" in the form of
image and appearance, thus surrendering to the eternal snare of the
mirror. The temporal confines of style are also its downfall. Every great

style has its beginnings in a blessed nothingness. In this Valéry was right: a musical curve is "expression" itself; it takes priority over any "impure" content in the word.

The men who accede to this demiurgic freedom of gesture—or sustain the impact of that power of freedom—are the men of Genesis of whom Chateaubriand writes that they "begin Creation anew." But what an exhausting euphoria: "to tear ideas from the night and words from silence," as Balzac says. And Stendhal: "I have come to grips with nothingness."

So we see that, out of the depths where the movers of heaven and the poets of earth are born, style emerges as an original "gesture" of the soul: we have called this gesture "cosmic" in order to signify that its scope is on the scale of a silent "cosmos" untroubled by any star; a gesture neither delivered up in advance to an object nor already sprung from the world; neither a proposition confinable in its essence by rational syntax or the logical checking of cognitive propositions, nor anything in the necessary order of objects. As a cosmic act, style amounts to a kind of meta-physical behavior symbolized by a pure form. This form interprets the most basic intuition of man, like breath as yet voiceless, like an act without content. It is, if I may so put it, an ontological form: If this freedom is going to "begin Creation anew," it is going to bend it to its own ontology as lived.

In order to understand it, let us choose the "cosmic gesture" of one language among others. Of 3328 sentences enumerated by Jean Mourot in *Mémoires d'Outre-tombe,*[6] 2700 (i.e., more than eighty per cent) obey the following demiurge: short and swift ascent, then an expansion in slow flight; speeding arrows, impatient to reach their apogee, and magnificent descent, interminable dying. We might speak of an ascending falcon whose upward surge, sharply broken off, anticipates a sovereign fall; or of a pebble falling in skillful rallentando, beauty taking its revenge by lingering over all that perishes. *"Par un chemin plus lent descendre chez les morts,"** said Racine.

"Dans les bruyères armoricaines, | elle n'était qu'une solitaire avantagée de beauté, de génie et de malheur."†

"L'heure viendra que l'obélisque du désert, | retrouvera sur la place des meurtres le silence et la solitude de Louxor."‡

---

* "By a slower path, to descend among the dead."

† Among the heathers of Armorica [Brittany], / she was but a solitary figure favored by beauty, by genius, and by misfortune."

‡ "The hour will come when the obelisk of the desert, / will find once again on the place of murders the silence and solitude of Luxor."

This strange punctuation was in common use during the eighteenth century. Chateaubriand gives it a romantic import; he makes use of it to shorten to the utmost degree the first part of the sentence, and to make the second part inordinately long. Highly conscious of his method, he makes this comment on his diction:

"*Je dis, comme aurait déclamé Talma: 'Vieux chêne!* . . . *avec un repos; puis, tout à la suite et tout d'une haleine: 'le temps a fauché sur ta racine jeune fille et jeune fleur.'*"* Sainte-Beuve was perfectly aware of this alternation between a brief challenge and a surging toward the infinite: "*Il peint d'un trait et comme d'un son,*"† he wrote. Flaubert instinctively imitates him in his homage: "*Dans ce sépulcre bâti sur un écueil, | son immortalité sera comme fut sa vie déserte des autres et tout entourée d'orages.*"‡

But is not sentence structure of this kind "existential" at the deepest level? For here we have a man who rises to his feet, contemplates the expanse before him, takes measure of his brief destiny, and strives to slow down the inevitable. This is what Romanticism is all about, you may say. But that is just it: Romanticism, like all great forms of freedom, resorts to a "cosmic gesture" in writing, i.e., to a certain original exercise on the part of the writer in that particular work. Here, as always, form takes precedence, of course, over content, but it "takes precedence" by applying a kind of preliminary "formative process" to the things of the world; the *mundus* will be summoned to repeat at all times, in all places, that man is this swift, violent ascent and this arching, gradual descent.

It might be countered that this linguistic structure necessarily models itself on eloquence—because the orator needs to fill his thoracic cavity with a sharp intake in order to arm himself with one long breath.[7] Chateaubriand made of this compulsion in oratorical style a funerary lament. Cicero also often spoke in this way. But Romanticism invented a sepulchral Christianity. A thousand-year-old structure employed in public verbal usage sets out to express a new revolt in the face of death: that of the saints who would pity themselves. "*Saint Augustin, | regardant son argile tomber. . . ,*"**says Chateaubriand. In this sentence structure St. Augustine pities himself, although Chateaubriand salutes him for

---

* "I say, as Talma would have declaimed: 'Old oak!' . . . with a pause; then, all at once and all in one breath: 'Time has mown down above thy roots both young girl and young flower.' "

† "He paints with one stroke and as if with one sound."

‡ "In this sepulchre built upon a rock, / his immortality will be as was his life, solitary and surrounded by storms."

** "St. Augustine, / watching his clay fall."

his *indifference* to human clay. For this form denies the Augustinian content of Christianity.

It might also be objected that all life is inevitably composed of a sudden rise of sap, a youthful cry, followed by interminable death-throes. Each of these interpretations is accurate at its own level; but all that interests philosophy is the deepest truth of all, the kernel from which everything springs. This kernel is revealed by a "metaphysics of gesture."

I have sketched the structure of Chateaubriand's style here merely to give an example of one "cosmic gesture" among other gestural possibilities of basic freedom, hence of language. Good examples are also to be found in Rabelais[8] or Pascal.[9] Pascal's style is constructed on a logic of tautology characteristic of Euclidian geometry. This can be easily demonstrated first of all by Pascal's brief *Traité des ordres numériques*, in which a certain mathematical proposition occurs that Fermat had discovered at the same time. Pascal acknowledges him as follows: "This same proposition that I have just reviewed in a number of ways has already occurred in the mind of our celebrated counselor from Toulouse, Monsieur de Fermat; and the admirable thing is that, without giving me the least inkling of it, or I him, he was writing down, in his province, the very thing I was inventing, hour by hour, as witness our letters written and received at the same time." It is from this that Pascal draws his entire philosophy of reason. Here is the final sentence of the *Traité des ordres numériques*:

> The ways of turning the same thing are infinite . . . for if one does not know how to turn propositions in all directions, and one uses only the first bias that comes to mind, one will never get very far: it is the variety of routes which open up new consequences and which, by means of various enunciations on the subject, connect propositions that had no relationship within the terms in which they were first conceived.

Pascal's style is an "application" of this seminal discovery: that it is new formulations that lead to the discovery of new things, i.e., relationships between propositions that seemed irreconcilable. The result: "Words differently arranged have a different meaning, and meanings differently arranged have different effects." Or: "Let no one say that I have said nothing new; the arrangement of the subject is new. When we play tennis, we both play with the same ball, but one of us places it better. I had as soon it said that I used words employed before. And in the same way if *the same thoughts in a different arrangement do not form a different discourse, no more do the same words in their different arrangement form different thoughts!"* *

In discovering that truth is always *implicit*, Pascal understood that reason unveils that which is already contained—although hidden—in the discourse, which is also the basic discovery of psychoanalysis.

Beginning with a "cosmic gesture" embedded, as it were, in the gyrations of a discourse that is transposing its propositions—propositions already invisibly contained one within the other—Pascal strives for the freedom bestowed by the thunderclap that will lift him off the ground. The kaleidoscopic logic of internal equivalences excludes the compenetration of immanence by transcendence: grace will be a veritable atomic explosion of the *mundus*; and grace and charity will be "of a completely different order." God will no longer test the mechanism of the stars, as Chateaubriand has it; He will be a stranger to the "wonders of Nature." Pascal's "cosmic gesture" nails you to the platform of the "body of the discourse"; it is a treading of the tautological roundabout of logic and a waiting for God within those wearisome confines. Here man does not first emerge, in youthful animal ardor, and then watch himself perish; he *remains* within the spiritual stupor and suspension of his earthly body, to be broken. Here the motion is provided by the roundabout—in its gyrations, earthly madness is the launching pad of repetition from which the rocket will burst skyward. Other "gestures," other freedoms.

But what does this freedom teach? To establish a fact is not to understand it. The writer who deploys the ideal curve of language as a *characteristic*—this characteristic being his own particular support, like a scale held in perpetual suspense, both in Chateaubriand's thrust and in Pascal's roundabout—who was this writer? How can we get to know him? What meaning are we to give his strange practice? The "pilot of the abyss" who ties up at the quays of "reality," or the dogged collector of tautology who is engulfed in the mystery of The Word: what are their agonies, their ecstasies, their metamorphoses, their bondages, and what, finally, becomes of a word suspended from itself, a word that begets its own curve and occupies a space without support?

In order to approach this mystery we must first try to outline the relationship between writer and his word structure: i.e., to try to see

* Pascal, *Pensées*, Nos. 23 and 22 respectively. As translated by W. F. Trotter in *Thoughts*, Collier (New York, 1910). [*Transl.*]

the profound and symbolic existence contained entirely within the highly significant gesture of a language. In style, the structure of a being is of foremost importance, but this structure has no biological antecedent; the style gives the world, and in its "gesture" gives the world to itself; the world obeys the injunction of verbal structure. The poet Michel Deguy points out[10] that the word "symbol" means "to throw together" ($\sigma\upsilon\mu\text{-}\beta\alpha\lambda\lambda\varepsilon\iota\nu$)[11] That which is "thrown together" is *the being with its stylistic "gesture,"* in such a way that the original poet is already identical with the *form of his initial act.* This encounter of the writer with the revelatory *sign* of his being is existential: it is the encounter of his "ontological" freedom, *not* the encounter of some freedom of action that may be given him externally and hence is borrowed, but with the symbolic freedom of his writing. The writer is free within the *act of breathing* of a certain style, because the form (or "structure") of this style is already "action," initial demiurge, symbolic genesis. The freedom of the sentence is already a form of the being, and a being of the form.

Inasmuch as he expresses his formal totality, the writer becomes identical with the symbolic structure of his style; he pours "his own self" into the mold of this style—but this "form," in turn, constitutes an act of "placing in verbal structure" of the world. There can be no immobility for the writer structured by his language: the writer is always subject to this *formal movement* where he *moves* primordially within a style. Since style symbolizes an *active* structure, this structure is necessarily that of a *sentence of the being.* The writer begins to move in order to forge *his* world *onto the mode of his sentence.* There is no such thing as "arrested" writing, and for good reason! If the writer is always about *to become,* and *forming himself* through his verbal structure, it is because the sentence is in motion; it is only structural when deployed in time, a moving form on the path of its "gesture." This is why being and style are "thrown together" on their course; this is what I wanted to signify by my use of the letter-form, which is also in motion, and in which you see me in motion within it. But style can also *suggest* immobility, as with Pascal: This is the possibility I wished to avoid by being in motion myself.

Style is the genesis of being. The writer is fulfilled in this genesis. This is why Zarathustra said: "Man is a bridge between the animal and the superhuman; a cord stretched across the abyss; the arrow of desire toward the other bank." So what exists below the cord is not man but animal. Man begins with the stretched cord that *is* "being." Man *becomes* man or *does not become* man according to whether or not he achieves his "reality," his active symbol, the essential act of being a symbol in motion.

It is not surprising, therefore, that freedom did not run through the streets: most men are at the mercy of the world, not of their inauguratory gesture. That which runs through the streets is the word already in bondage to the world. The world is therefore nothing but the word of others: the "styled" word, not the style; hence "styled" man rather than "styler," hence the masters of the world who have given the world its earthly tonality. And when the masters of earthly tonality happen to be also the masters of fear, they imprint on the languages of the whole world the tone of their own bondage—the tone of men's enslavement through their bondage to their own fear. Whoever penetrates this language is at the mercy of the fear experienced by the masters in their innermost selves. The masters of the world have begun by giving voice to their fear of being in the world—hence, in speaking the language of their terror themselves, they subject humanity to terrorized language.

As a result, it is always in their language that men are first enslaved. They are the bondsmen of a bondsman. For language in bondage is itself that bondsman of which men are the servants. In tyrannies it is the mass of speaking men who show that the original bondage is that of the false word. So we must look at freedom among men of a different word and ask ourselves what constitutes the word of the great writers if we wish to rediscover the nature of freedom.

But how are we now to consider the man of the cosmic gesture? What, under the critic's gaze, will happen to that word which obeys in advance the structure it will give to the world? Who is this strange being armed with the symbolic act and in turn grounded in it, and what will he do with his freedom? What will be his conscience? Is *conscience* to be observed only in the man who strives for the verbal inauguration of the universe? Man of baptism, man the predecessor of the earth: but what will he do with his power, and what have we to say of this latter-day priest, of this, as it were, cosmic condenser who has appeared at the very heart of the unfolding of language?

I thought I had my eye on him, the deepest and truest man, the man of the greatest freedom, the man of style; I thought I could perceive "human nature" in his demiurge and his madness. But what is his littleness, what is his grandeur? Is it a fullness? Is it an empty form,

a vain structure of discourse and of himself? What is the good of filling
a sovereign word with his challenges and his downfalls? What significance have these songs of glory and ruin, these sepulchres built high,
these empires cast into the ditch? I had to penetrate more deeply,
observe in turn the spectacle of this superior spectator who gesticulated
superbly with thrones and tombs and mingled his memory with the
bones of humanity. Why achieve freedom in this way? Why identify
with the age itself? "I am no more than chronos," said Chateaubriand. This is no mean feat! "I maintain an obituary index of the
dead." This is not easy, and it requires assistance. What obsessions,
what powers, what prodigies bewitch his pen when his freedom culminates in such desire for immortality on earth, in such interminable
regret at man's return to dust?

And furthermore, what does he do with men with that style of his,
the wrecker of genius? He casts them into nothingness with visible ex-
ultation. Speaking of Bossuet, Chateaubriand writes: "How he sweeps
the world with his gaze! He spans a thousand leagues at a time. . . .
He passes with the speed and majesty of the centuries. Clasping the
staff of the law, he drives Jews and Gentiles pell-mell before him into
the grave; *finally he himself brings up the rear of this procession* of so many
generations and, leaning on Isaiah and Jeremiah, he strides ahead,
raising his voice in prophetic lamentation above the thunder and
lightning and the debris of the human race." Clearly this is his own
"cosmic gesture," throwing memorable ashes over the empires and
nations sung by the poet through a Bossuet who is so representative of
René. "Ceaselessly preoccupied with the grave, and as if leaning over
the chasms of another life," Bossuet "loves to let fall from his lips those
grand words of time and death that reverberate in the silent abysses of
eternity." For Chateaubriand, the "Eagle of Meaux" is already the
romantic who "flings himself down to drown in incredible abysses, in
inconceivable sufferings." Who was this man so obsessed with the
tomb?

In "L' Ecrivain et son langage," my goal was a *tabula rasa* so that the
word might show itself free of its terrestrial bonds. In my eyes, style
was a miracle comparable to that celebrated maiden whom laborers
working on the Appian Way in April, 1485, discovered in a perfect
state of preservation and aglow with youth inside her sarcophagus. An
oil lamp is said to have been still miraculously burning when the body

was exhumed. Pope Innocent VIII caused this living mummy to be transported by night and buried on waste ground outside the Pincian Gate. A link was thus allegedly restored between the present and antiquity because twenty thousand Romans came to see the phenomenon for themselves, and the Renaissance was compared to the dawning awareness of a civilization which then strove to resuscitate and transfigure the maiden.

This legend has fascinated me ever since my childhood. In it, the theme of the Renaissance found its appropriate symbol. The lamp that was still burning was obviously the poet's lamp. But a renaissance must not kill what is sacred; on the contrary, its mission is to revive it. If style was buried in waste ground, at the gates of the city of men, it was because criticism stifled it beneath its own papacy. Later on, when I studied Rabelais—after Anatole France the skeptic—I found my belief confirmed that freedom is transmitted by writing, of which Rabelais was a giant, comparable to a verbal Niagara pouring over the top of lifeless objects and transforming them into "living stones." But how are we to outline the relationship between the style and resurrection of a culture if we do not know the relationship between a style and the resurrection of a man? Styles were superb cosmic mummies—how were they to be given life? Somewhere an Orpheus has said that the maidens of language are called Eurydice, and that they must be sought at the bottom of Hades, symbol of all tombs. But Diogenes's lantern threw no light on such things, and Rabelais himself churned his famous "Diogenes tub" in vain.

So I found myself at a loss before the mummy and its sarcophagus, because Chateaubriand's "cosmos" was in itself a kind of sarcophagus in which René's style resuscitated no one. In it was a kind of invincible immobility of soul and word, gestural though they might be. To populate itself with its own witnesses and, in a way, its own demonstrators, his language went around and around, treading a magnificent tautology but tragically deprived of ascending motion. Certainly his style did launch a freedom on its course—but then it became gyratory in the poet's secret exhaustion as he strove to participate in the great lift-off of Things, in the capture of the world on the wing of flame, while still remaining unable to shake the eternal fixity of the universe and still not really moving within the repetitive immensity of his own circle. So I wondered what pulsion might animate the mummy doomed to a revolving freedom and engendering its own gyration. I had to advance still deeper into poetic life, since the verbal power of baptizing the earth by breath led no farther toward that other life where the poet might be captured. Was there no built-in motion in man that would prevent him from turning in vain on the wheel of time?

Orpheus being the god of poetry, perhaps he had something to teach us about poetry. Why not seek him out and question him as to his own motion? What are we to make of these words of Chateaubriand: "The genius is a Christ; misunderstood, persecuted, beaten with staves, crowned with thorns, placed on the Cross for and by men, he dies in bequeathing them the light, and on rising again is worshipped"? Would the poet instinctively seek out Christ-Orpheus, he who descended into the night of death, hell, or Hades, and who returned as a bringer of light? "I died and rose again with my casket of spiritual jewels," said Mallarmé.

But if the man of language, the man of motion and becoming, the man of freedom and symbol, is the one who "dies" and "is born again," what is this "dying" and "being born again"? What can all this convey to a man of common sense? Mallarmé wrote to his friend Cazalis: "I am no longer the Stéphane whom you knew, but a certain aptitude of the spiritual universe to see and recognize itself through what I once was." And Chateaubriand, seeking his "other self" among the ruins of Rome, cried: "The times to which I belong will be fulfilled in me." To which "times" does the poet belong, and what is meant by the fulfillment of the "times"? Mallarmé says that he *was* (that he *no longer is* the man), and that he *is* an "*aptitude* of the spiritual universe." And Chateaubriand: "The times to which I *belong*." Both speak in the present, in a kind of fascinating immobility—and yet, in this immobility, they seem to have acquired a mysterious motion in that they are subject to the Orphic cycle of descent into the grave and rising anew in song. Hence the salutation of the earth achieves a kind of mystical immobility: "Poetry, Orphic *knowledge* of the earth!" writes Mallarmé.

Hence it is as *knowledge* that poetry comes face to face with its eternal present, the present that causes it to say: "I *am* an aptitude . . ." or: "The times to which I belong . . ." What is this "knowledge"? And why does literary criticism not concern itself with such words? Either they are truly essential, in which case we should give the study of them priority over all others since, surely, the essential enjoys a right of absolute priority; or they mean nothing at all, in which case we must show that they are of no account.

First, the strange cycle of symbolic death and of resurrection into the light of the earth: I had to verify that this was evident in the innermost being of every poet, like a kind of ontological cyclothymia. My first attempt was with Mallarmé.[12] J. P. Richard had just published *Pour un tombeau d'Anatole*, in which the poet sings a song of lament for his son, dead at the age of eight. Mallarmé's Orphic orchestration was so evident and so profound that all his poetry was illumined by it. Might not thematic critique find in the study of "creative cyclothymia," if I may use this term, a *significant* ordering of *themes*? I was struck by the fact that, when we enumerate the circles, hairs, azures, conches, combs, feathers, and clouds in Mallarmé, we are finally left with a puzzle whose deep meaning escapes us. If we do not know how to orchestrate these themes; if we lump them all together in a heap or in the misleading order of some ready-made nomenclature—in order of their appearance, or in alphabetical order!—we efface the traces of poetry's profound life. But if instead we place the themes in relation to the poetic soul's fundamental experience, we give thematics a spiritual framework and gain the possibility of working out a *philosophy* of themes without which thematics is as blind vis-a-vis the poet's *act* as current biographical critique is vis-a-vis Marxism or as ready-made psychoanalyses are.[10]

I pursued my researches by closely examining the Orphic cycle of Chateaubriand.[14] I tried to show what a deceiving Eurydice it was whom the poet vainly sought in Hades: History herself, elusive mistress who delights in her own funeral ceremony, mistress whose tombs and ruins are at once both adornment and mockery. All this opened up perspectives on the relationships between poetry and the "temporal." Is it really possible to "rise again" in the noble transparency of poetry by sounding the trumpets of the epic? What is the dialogue carried on by poetry with the "glories of the earth"? Michelet also saw his Eurydice in history: to him she appeared with the features of a pale, beautiful young woman, at the point of death, who had to be revived. Clio, muse of history, was his Eurydice. The young Roman girl of the sarcophagus was present everywhere—but *who* was this maiden? Since it was a case of symbolic life in poetry, it was hard to dodge the question of the relationship between the symbolic and the spiritual. For there are many Eurydices: there is Beatrice, there is Quixote's Maritornes. And if Orpheus brings a dead girl back to life, to spiritual life, i.e., "resuscitates" her, then poetic life, insofar as it is symbolic, begins through Orpheus to speak essentially of "Life" and "death."

From there I extended my enquiry to Pascal, Bossuet, and Claudel.[15] It would be presumptuous to offer a résumé of this work here. But since you have asked me to give you an exact account of the "path" taken by my reflections, let us say this path included a number of wayside

inns at which I took on supplies of food and water; and if I failed to
point out, in passing, these wretched imaginary inns of mine, what
follows would be unintelligible, for you would not understand how I
could always set out again for that desert of my ignorance stretching
endlessly ever farther ahead of me.

I also examined the poet's alternating death-throes and resurrection
in Dante, Petrarch, Ronsard, Rilke, and a number of others, although
with no notion of publishing this evidence. I even drew up a "short
Orphic history" of all French poetry, from its origins to today, that
might have found a place in my *Essai sur l'avenir poétique de Dieu*. But
the book would have assumed still more discouraging proportions; the
editor was wise enough to spare the reader.

The sole aim of these researches was to establish the facts irrefutably.
But what interested me much more than the facts was the very meaning
of the cycle of the "life of the soul" and its relationships to objective
knowledge of the world.

Yet if varying "cosmic gestures," i.e., different structures of freedom
and the world, corresponded to Orphic cycles which themselves varied,
what were the place and value of the "rational"—i.e., "explanatory"
—contents of the universe? What happened to the world-systems that
were founded on objective knowledge? Was not the living destiny of
freedom wholly subjective if experimental classifications of the earth
held the exclusive monopoly of "verifiable truth"?

It was in order to approach this problem that I based the study of
"cosmic gestures" in my *Essai sur l'avenir poétique de Dieu* on the four
great apologists of the Christian religion in French literature: Bossuet,
Pascal, Chateaubriand, and Claudel. Two of them, Pascal and Chateaubriand, based their glory on the "defense and illustration" of
Christianity; Claudel is the giant who, a century after *Le Génie du
christianisme*, carried René's "poetic theology" to its most formidable
position of power; and Bossuet, alone among our four celestial muske-
teers, dared to take the place of Heaven itself and speak as God the
Father. If there are men whose objective vision of the world ought to
be identical, these four should be the ones, if only because they de-
fended, all of them with one heart, the same religion.

Well, that's not how it is at all. Bossuet wrote a learned treatise on
anatomy of which the ignorant scientific postulates—the "unthought"
assumptions of his "rationale"— today bring a smile to the lips of the

anatomists of "objectivity" that philosophers initiated in Lacan's psychoanalysis have meanwhile become.[16] Pascal was the scholar we know him to be; he believed the human spirit to be endowed with Euclidian *lumières naturelles* to which the natural order was supposed to correspond, resulting in a wondrous ontological harmony between the functioning of our spirit and the laws of the universe. And yet everything that to our logical eyes seemed "absurd" was not absurd, for that wondrous "proof via the absurd" guided us instead to the truth. Today this logic of "common sense" has become a "cosmology of the street,"[17] although structuralists such as C. Lévi-Strauss still believe in a mythological harmony between "natural reason" and the "reason" of nature. For the French have remained arrant Cartesians, and the physics of "evidence" is still their greatest consolation. Chateaubriand was for his part an out-and-out "Galilean," just as Lacan and any number of post-Einsteinian scholars are to this day: He proved God by the "logic of the spheres"; in *Le Génie* he sang the praises of those Jesuits who set out valiantly for the court of Peking armed with telescope and compass, to explain to the "astonished mandarins" the "true course of the stars and the true name of Him Who directs them in their orbits." Only Claudel, the Nietzsche of poetry, used a triumphant "poetic reason" in refusing to "grovel before the locomotive" in the manner of the scholars—but it would be useless to look to him for a solid critique of scientific reason. He was not a philosopher.

So the outcome was the following paradox: Although belonging to the same religion, these four defenders of Christianity turned out to be all different, not only in their "cosmic gestures" and "Orphic cycles," but also in their scientific cosmology. If there are as many cosmologies of the "rational" in the same religion as there are styles among the great poets, as many structures of "dying" and "being born again" as there are "explanations of the world," of what value are the world's "objective" classifications? And how do they propose to give intelligibility to their recordings of the dromomania of matter? What leads man to believe that this motion is intelligible, and what is the arcane language to which the man who believes this clings?

I chose four great Christians because it was the best way of showing to what extent our scientific explanations of the world are, in fact, religious. What held the scientific cosmologies of Pascal, Chateaubriand, Bossuet, or Claudel upright was their "scientific" concepts, of which the most fundamental are "force" and "cause." Now the concepts of "cause" and "force" are manifested in the mythical constructions of our minds: baptismal operations based on vocabulary; religious

ideas—"religious" in the bad sense of the word because "reassuring."
But true religion has never reassured anyone, least of all the saints.
Today every serious mathematician places the word "cause" in quota-
tion marks—which is not reassuring.

Hence "existential psychoanalysis of style" leads the mind to an
analysis of the psychological foundations of the concept of the intelligibility of natural "laws." Why does the objectivity of our scientific
observations, becoming ever more detailed and accurate, suggest to us
a kind of comprehensibility of matter launched into space, as if motion
found its own explanation in repeating itself regularly? It is because
constancy reassures us, and because the coded replica of constancy
seems to us to be "explanatory" of the original. To fabricate speaking
likenesses out of all the regular happenings around us, and to believe
we understand a thing as soon as that thing repeats itself and thus becomes predictable, is quite clearly a thoroughly animal behavior of
the mind. Animals also believe they understand what is occurring
repeatedly around them, because this reassures them and renders their
world usable to them. We do this a little better than they do, but we
do not change our "order" for all that, as Pascal said. I live in a little
house buried in the country; my dog is my field of experience when it
comes to philosophy of the sciences. I observe how and why he thinks
he understands continuity, and why he has his own explanation for
everything that moves regularly around him, and how he becomes
frantic when matter ceases to divide time into predictable slices. My
dog is a veritable nuclear center of metaphysics.

Who speaks within us when we make strange deities speak, animators
of motion, when all we ever see from our observation is blind sequences
of phenomena separated by nothingness, without the action of one
phenomenon on another ever being comprehensible in itself? For it is
this very "comprehensibility" that demands the intervention of ridiculous, wholly conceptual little gods (cause, force, structure). This basic
mythology of our reason corresponds in itself to a "style": to utilize
the regularity of the world in order to give it meaning is to give a style
to the world—it is to declare that this regularity constitutes a *meaning*
(*sens*) because it is guided by hidden personages, by "master workmen,"
by "laws" animated by "spirits"—Cause, Force, and other magic and
intangible entities. But who has ever seen a cause? All we ever see is
another event, and science is gradually discovering more and more of
them while accomplishing nothing but the taking of pictures that then
pass for explanations because equational photographs are of necessity
condensations of motion, by very reason of the regularity of nature—

so handy for our calculations. It follows that regularity furrows mental grooves within us and fabricates common sense or "sense of evidence" —but it is the meaning (*sens*) that subsequently appears magically evident to us, not the motion, which alone is evident.

From Hume to Lacan, critique of the concept of the intelligibility of the fruits of experience has always stopped at a simple demythologization of the "ontological" rationality of the mathematical legality of the universe—i.e., at a demythologization of induction, without ever ultimately arriving at an analysis of this very concept of *meaning* that seduces us into believing that constant and repeated happenings will eventually explain themselves because of their regularity! But what, in terms of style, does this mean, to place the universe in equation, i.e., to believe we are making nature intelligible by means of a certain equational doubling—a mathematical microfilm, a coded image, a "speaking" mirror? On what hidden discourse is this belief in meaning founded? On the discourse of motion in the void. The man who *speaks* in science and who desires to *pass for* intelligible, is not the man but motion itself. In terms of style and "cosmic gesture," therefore, science is reduced to the act of making the headlong rush of things in nothingness speak, to making them embrace the discourse of their course. In modern science this behavior is basically the same as that of primitive peoples who cause the moon or the sun to speak—all we have done is reduce objects to their motion, and it is their motion that we cause to speak by the intervention of our explanatory idols, allegedly rendered comprehensible by regular circuits. What is the secret of this style? Who is the man who renounces speech for himself and desires motion to speak in his place? For, needless to say, we do not escape language; we merely pretend to make things speak of their own accord when we believe we can renounce speech for ourselves.

The "cosmic gesture" to which the man of science proceeds is to establish a base on the mass of matter in motion. Through a confusion of being with the intelligibility of being, the man of science rests on the cosmos, saying: "This revolves regularly, hence this is explained by the fact of regularity that I establish, as the herald of constancy." This gesture is "style," a style of halted motion, because it reveals what is implied, for man, in coming to a halt. Confronted by the universal course of matter, man dreams of coming to a halt, and he comes to a halt by resting on the mathematical duplicate of motion.

However, what "existential psychoanalysis of style" allows us to demythologize is, at the core of philosophy, the fundamental perversion of the *very quest for meaning* when that quest takes as its starting-point *being*—i.e., the "real" existence of the world. This search for *meaning* obeys the meaning of direction (also *sens*), i.e., the word that asks only: "In which direction has this weathercock turned—toward the south or north, toward the east or west?"

But is the *sens* (direction) of being, the same as the direction of roads? Or: if we look for *sens* in all "directions," is this not precisely because science is concerned with motion, i.e., with the direction of matter in the void, and so predicts by equation the universe of direction? Once we demythologize this concept of *sens*, then the motion of being, as revealed by style, becomes once more a motion that is entirely foreign to space. And, indeed, the Orphic cycle itself is not a motion in space. If the *sens* of man is not within the motion of matter in space but within a "spiritual" motion of "death" and "resurrection" into which the freedom of cosmic gestures of style initiates us, then the monopoly of "truth" would no longer be the property of the scientific replicas of the headlong rush of things in the void, because this replica would itself be a cosmic gesture of man.

More recent philosophical intuitions are of disarming simplicity. Unfortunately, a good deal of time is required to elaborate their dim light, and somewhat more time for it to be accepted. Twentieth-century philosophical enlightenment stems from the fact that matter has ceased to be regular on the scale of elementary particles; in other words, it is being discovered that belief in the intelligibility of motion is derived from its regularity—but that *regularity is in itself just as mysterious as irregularity*. That which *time* becomes in a science in which the "hour" can no longer be used to predict—and in which all science then strives merely to render the hour predictable again instead of reflecting on the *very nature* of time—leads once again to the instant, and to the being of the instant, whose fire changes into a symbolic "gesture" of language and a spiritual cycle of death and life.

This time I really had to desert literary criticism for philosophy. I spent two years rewriting my just-published book *Science et Nescience*[2] four times. It would be an abuse of your patience, my dear Professor, and that of your readers were I to explain the contents of this work to you. I shall merely indicate, in passing, the basic metaphysical intuition from which will later emerge a philosophical anthropology: i.e., a new frontier between man and animal. For the only thing dividing animal manner of observation from human manner of observation is a distinction that is entirely different from that hitherto separating animal instinct on the one hand from man's "science" on the other; and unless modern theology finds this new line of demarcation, it will experience neither anthopological awakening[18] nor any new exegesis of death-agony and resurrection.

Truly human observation is that which desires to see man and never can, because man is always outside his re-presentation and struck by the distance between his "self"—which is beyond his grasp—and the image in which he vainly tries to delineate himself. Consequently he becomes entangled with his own image, with the lure of the mirror. For all he sees is his εἴδωλον. I have tried to give a résumé of scientific anthropology and "transcendental" or philosophical anthropology to show how the peculiarly human method of observation is one of progressive de-relictio vis-a-vis the physical world, and why the re-ligiosus desires to connect (relier) the animal of de-relictio with nature and its images; the ontologically disconnected (dé-relié) being, the deserter from zoology.[19]

But you will ask, what is the style, what is the cycle of the de relictus being? Here it is, cut off from motion and no longer in search of meaning in the various directions of roads; detached from the course of matter and capable of seeing how it attempted to rest on the cosmos, then making for itself a coded photograph of the universe, a recording on film, with the aid of replicas, facsimiles, or microfilms as unintelligible as the originals. But when a spirit is freed from a specular doubling that is supposed to be explanatory, what unity will it find? For you will tell me that we cannot yet clearly see the indissoluble bond linking the "cosmic gesture" with the "Orphic cycle," and that there is no explanation of the diversity between "dying" and "being born again" unless they are articulated on the diversity of "cosmic gestures," i.e., the initial freedoms of the symbolic word. How are we to confirm the alliance of language with "life" and "death"? How do Orpheus's lyre and his descent into Hades, and his climb back to earth in the song of a musical Eurydice, make one and the same being? And if this unity between lyre and cyclic life is not achieved, where is the poet's spiritual unity, since he would be seen to strive for freedom of style on the one hand and to submit to the tyrannical law of Orpheus on the other, in a mysterious rending of his flesh and song—perhaps like the rending of Orpheus being torn apart by the Maenads?

But it so happens that the harmony between cosmic gesture and Orphic cycle is perfectly evident. For the style characteristic of Chateaubriand's discourse derives from symbolic "death" and "resurrection" *among the "ruins of Rome."* Why is this so? Because history is indeed the chosen spectacle of sudden upsurgings of the spirit followed by gradual descent to the ruins where stone will tell the time. Alexander, Napoleon, Caesar, rise into the air like savage falcons, brief predators —then in the memory of men their death becomes immemorial. It is because Chateaubriand's style is built up on the lyricism of an arrow shooting to its zenith, and slowly dying, that he could find no more obvious natural terrain of "dying" and "being born again" than that of the history of armed glory: Alexander, Napoleon, Caesar—briefly we wrench them, helmeted, from Hades, and we lift up their names into the air like brief fires each time we celebrate them. The structure of historic time consists of rapid ascents and dying falls, of invocations of the dead and abandonments to oblivion. The "cosmic gesture" of upsurge and regret could not "be born" and "die" except on the scale of history.

With Bossuet, Claudel, and Pascal, this harmony between the structure of a style and the structure of *their Orphism* is no less easily demonstrated.[15] In the case of Pascal we have already discovered how his style of embedding himself in the Euclidian roundabout of propositions, and the logic of tautological permutations of discourse, prepare the way for amazement in the face of the Infinite and for a mystical waiting, where only the lightning flash of grace can ensure a lift-off into the light: Orphic cycle in a broken line, where the long romantic moan and the suspect accommodation to earthly harmonies are invoked by the modesty and brevity of a language enclosed within its circuit. However, everything takes place as if the *raptus* of the mystics, the overpowering transports of delight when God addresses His creature, were only possible when emanating from the tortured and revolving style of ontological dereliction. The roundabout of a style, the treading within its own circular confines, is symbolic of the temporal knot, of obsessional labor, of the grinding fatigue of repetition. Pascal is indeed the man of science, that is to say, of tireless motion in the void, of the sterile recording of the dromomania of things in an expanse. Does not his style illustrate the very essence of blind knowledge in search of its cosmic abode?

We might say, therefore, that a style constructed at its deepest level on the tautological genius of the rational simultaneously reveals the basic bond between the temporal and the rational—the rational being that fathomless tautology of the temporal forever embedded in its own headlong rush. Everything in the Pascalian style predestines him in some measure to the "atomic" Orphic cycle, where the creature will be thunderstruck in The Word_(Fire! God of Isaac and of Jacob . . .) from the moment of its embeddedness in mathematics.

In the Pascalian Orphic cycle, "death" is the "desert island" onto which we are herded by an obscure butcher who slaughters us one by one. How are we to sing the "wonders of nature" and pretend that "the moon is a proof of God" on that island of dereliction? "The final act is always bloody, however fine the comedy of all the rest. Earth is thrown on one's head, and that is all for evermore." Chateaubriand had the right comment for these words: "What bitter indifference in this short, cold history of man." But Pascal did not know of René's feigned indifference. He makes no parade of interment; his is a tragic genius, waiting for the lightning flash. The genius of the "cosmic gesture" in his style is precisely that of a man attaching himself to the cosmic soil and stubbornly knotting his writing to a blind astral round-about in order to receive the saving omnipotence that is beyond all the obstinate mechanics of the universe. His is not the magnificent style of Chateaubriand confronted by the wonders of nature (in the tradition that reaches from Dr. Nieuventyt to Teilhard de Chardin by way of Bernardin de Saint-Pierre and Rousseau), which will never lead to frenzied mystical transports! What is needed for that is a style cut off, as it were, from God, a thirsting style, expressing the terrestrial prison in its very essence, its revolving rationality, its repetitive tautology. Here again, the "gesture" of a style is articulated on the Orphism that it demands.

So, in the profound harmonies between the "gesture" of being and the "cycle of the soul," we rediscover symbolic man, in his inalienable individuality—the man of δυμ-βαλλειν. With what are we concerned if not to tear man from the sclerosis and rigidity of a Pascalian cycle that is unique and universal yet exhausted by ritualism, the way it appears when the sacred becomes weary? And have we not been living in this weariness since Nietzsche? But if the man endowed with a style, that of the most intimate freedom, is, *by this very fact*, subject to a *living* Orphic (or Pascalian) cycle; if this man "dies" and "is born again" in ontological harmony with the structure of his *own language*; if, then, there are original styles, hence true individuals, we have some chance of rediscovering human freedom as well as the divine freedom lying beyond the universe of bondage to the word of others. Is it not our task to break the Caesarian discourse of submission to a world manipulated by the masters of fear?

So much for "existential psychoanalysis of style," linking the original gesture of style to the Orphic nature of life, an attempt to rediscover the basic exigency of truth that brought it into being during times of despotism. But are those times at an end? Literary criticism is beginning to pose the problem of the universal bondage of language.[20] How much longer will it be able to invoke reflection on values?

For what is the profundity of Chateaubriand's "creative cyclo-thyma"? What is poetry when the poet pities himself at the level of a laughable renown or a bloody epic? When he wishes to extract an Orphic song from the games of the sword? "Before Homer, there is Orpheus," declared Mallarmé. And finally, what is the "Homeric" idol of the human creature—this εἴδωλον with which psychoanalysis is *beginning* to concern itself as with the basic lure of man caught in the trap of his own image?[18, 21] Are this image and this trap a kind of world arena where matter is launched into the void and into time—a course flanked by its blind mathematical replica and peopled by mythological divinities such as Energy, Force, Cause, of whom we are beginning to see who it is that is making them speak: our will to knot space to itself, and to knot ourselves to it—our fear of being outside the world, *de-relecti*?

But that is just it—"we are not in the world," says Rimbaud. Deep words, and the key to poetry. To what extent is the poet, like the mystic, passive? And not linked (*re-lié*) to the deepest, most unperceived εἴδωλον? What is the clarity of "poetic cyclothymia" when it is at the mercy of Homeric song, of the historic weight of the universe? Is it silence, because in us the word itself is Tantalus deprived of the fruits of the spirit and the water of the earth? An Orpheus "torn apart by the Maenads"? Or shall we find Dionysus appeased, Nietzsche's Christ-like Dionysus at the end of the quest for truth? Well, here is another mystery, a desert awaiting the plowshare of the critique of *existence*.

For my modest part, when I consider the dead maiden in her Roman sarcophagus, I would so much like to help her to revive by lifting now and then the somewhat heavy name—"Existential Psychoanalysis of Style"—with which she was baptized, and to give her back, secretly, the simpler name of Truth.

[*Translated from the French by Leila Vennewitz*]

Notes

1. *Les Chemins actuels de la critique* (Paris, 1968).
2. *Science et Nescience,* Bibliothèque des Idées (Paris). In preparation.
3. *De l'Idolâtrie* (Paris, 1969).
4. From his address on being accepted into the Académie Française, Aug. 27, 1753.
5. Form or structure. "Structure" is merely another view of "form," sometimes more *precise* and sometimes more confused.
6. "Le Génie d'un style. Rythme et sonorité," in *Mémoires d'Outre-tombe* (Paris, 1960).
7. See my article, "Le Style de Chateaubriand," in *La Table Ronde* (February 1968).
8. *Rabelais par lui-même* (Paris, 1960).
9. "Style et logique chez Pascal," in *Esprit* (July 1962).
10. "Poésie et connaissance," in *Modern Language Notes,* No. 3 (1966), pp. 255–269.
11. From βαλειν, to throw.
12. "Jean Pierre Richard et la critique thématique," in *Critique* (June 1963).
13. "Critique et méthode," in *Critique* (November 1964).
14. *Chateaubriand ou le poète face à l'histoire* (Paris, 1963).
15. *Essai sur l'avenir poétique de Dieu* (Paris, 1965).
16. Or rather, already "post-lacanian."
17. Lichnerowicz.
18. *"Lettre sur l'angélisme,"* in Esprit (March 1969); "une passion transtombale," N.R.F., May 1970.
19. *Sur Erasme,* to appear in Editions de l'IIerne, with a translation of the *Disputatiuncula de taedio et pavore Christi* by Erasmus.
20. George Steiner, *Language and Silence* (New York, 1967).
21. "La Raison, l'orthodoxie et le sacré," in *Esprit* (October 1965).

Eugene H. Falk

STYLISTIC FORCES
IN THE NARRATIVE

THE TASK OF THE SCIENCES HAS BEEN TO DISCOVER THE SECRET OF THE order that governs the phenomena of any field to which man has turned his attention, first in wonderment and later with increasingly sophisticated observations, hypotheses, tests, and classifications. In the course of their growing intellectual mastery of the worlds outside and within us, the sciences have sought to understand the cohesion of phenomena as self-contained units, as well as the mutual interactions of these units. They have studied various phenomena from the point of view of their development, functions, cause and effect relationships, their similarities and differences, and they have taught us to recognize the cohesion of any self-contained reality as the cohesion of a whole, governed by natural laws.

To the extent to which literary scholarship has turned to the study of the cohesion of individual works as whole and self-contained structures, as well as to the study of their mutual interactions, it has evolved a science of literature. If we recognize that style governs the cohesion of individual works, we may conclude that what may be called "stylistic force" is the counterpart in literature of natural law in the sciences. Obviously, natural law is operative regardless of whether the emergence of a phenomenon is seen to be the result of chance occurrences, or of coincidental conditions, or of human experimentation. A work of literature *is* a creation, and therefore its cohesive wholeness is the result of a formative intention, of an application of stylistic means and patterns by which the parts are linked together and unified. As in the world of natural phenomena, this is true regardless of the degree of consciousness with which that intention is carried out.

Here I am concerned exclusively with style in prose narrative, and only with that aspect of style which we may consider as the structure of composition. For purposes of clarification, I shall be using the term "coherence" throughout this essay to designate the connections which exist between individual parts of a work, whereas the term "cohesion" will be used to refer to the totality of connections which exist among all parts within the whole.

Regardless of considerations of "point of view," regardless of the degree to which the presented subject matter agrees with existing reality, regardless of the intellectual and emotional attitudes which inevitably inform a narrative, the structure of its composition reveals certain features that manifest the *manner* in which the parts are linked. The basic component part in a narrative is a statement of words *in a context*. The statement is a carrier of a meaning; thus we may term the statement as it occurs in the text a *motif*, while referring to its contextual meaning as a *theme*. Motifs, then, are textual elements revealing states of mind, feelings, actions, or environmental settings. What binds motifs into coherent clusters is their thematic significance i.e., the meaning which emerges from the context. Hence the theme is not only the signification conveyed by motifs in context; it is also the underlying force, the principle, which governs the coherence *within* the various motif clusters which compose a work.

The relationships between motif clusters are likewise determined by the force of thematic coherence. This coherence may be achieved in different ways. In what E. M. Forster called the *story*, thematic coherence is effected by a *probable sequential coherence* of incidents (motifs). Here we grasp and accept incidents as sequentially probable if we can conceive of them as possibly relatable—in time and circumstance—to their antecedents.

We should ask, however, by virtue of what criteria we are willing to accept incidents as sequentially probable. We appraise the probability of the order in which motifs occur in terms of a logic derived from experience. That is, a given succession of incidents may appear plausible to us as long as this sequence conforms to our experiential notion of verisimilitude. Not that the incidents represented, or their order, need be actually derived from our own experience; indeed, the incidents themselves may actually be far removed from our known lived reality. In this case, the basis for our acceptance from experience of the sequential order of motifs as probable lies in the thematic coherence[1] which governs the incidents.

In the story the motifs carry themes of the moods or states of mind, and their transitions from one stage to another, which invest the actions of characters and affect conditions and situations. Here, regardless of the particular incidents, we perceive attitudes and moods which are common to all men; thus, these states of mind appear probable to us, both in themselves and in their development. It is this thematic coherence on the level of the story that accounts for what we consider and accept as the probable sequence of motifs. Obviously, this fact does not explain the process of imaginative creativity, as it does not account for the source of the particular incidents an author uses to convey his themes; an iconological approach would be needed in the attempt to solve such a problem. This fact does, however, explain why a certain incident is a fitting constituent part in a probable sequence of motifs. Thus an author's conscious or intuitive recognition of the necessity for thematic sequential coherence is one possible stylistic force effective in the composition of a story.

Another type of thematic relationship is based upon a *necessary causal coherence* of motifs in what Forster called a *plot*. Here we *understand* (rather than merely *grasp*) and accept the relationship between incidents in the light of causal necessity. We allow ourselves to be persuaded that one event or action is the necessary consequence of another event or action, or of instinctual, spiritual, or environmental conditions. We apprehend motifs in the plot with reference to motivations which engender them and purposes they fulfill. These motivations and purposes form the themes of the plot, and we recognize from our own experience their logical and necessary effects. Hence an author's conscious or intuitive recognition of the exigencies of causal coherence serves, in addition to his awareness of thematic sequential coherence, as a stylistic force, one which is operative in the composition of a plot.

Although sequential and causal thematic coherences are the most frequently used structural principles, they are not the only stylistic forces which may determine the design of the composition of a narrative. There is yet another type of thematic coherence which I have called the *generic coherence of themes*. Generic coherence is independent of both the sequential and causal coherence of motifs. Although generic coherence may be found in narrative compositions wherein story and plot are clearly discernible, it may also occur in the absence of either story or plot, and thus may serve as the only principle of structural coherence.

Our daily lives consist largely of fragmented experiences the relatedness of which is often discernible only in retrospect. Our involvement in seemingly disparate incidents causes life to appear to us often as disconnected, chaotic, and therefore devoid of meaning. When we attempt to master the disparateness of our lives, when we try to establish coherences between various incidents, we may recognize the relatedness of certain occurrences. We also have such a recognition when we encounter disconnected incidents in literature. In this case, it may even be said that we experience a tension between certain incidents, a tension which is only partially resolved when we have recognized their sequential and causal coherence. However, we have traditionally been conditioned to assume that such a recognition exhausts the whole potential of a work's coherence.

When an author aims to represent man's experience of disparateness and fragmentation, he may do so by intentionally disrupting the probable sequential order of incidents or by omitting any causal coherences. Thereby he hopes to set the reader on a course of emotional and intellectual exploration that leads to an apprehension of different interrelationships between phenomena, culminating in an essential vision of correspondences beyond time or cause. The stylistic force which is necessarily operative in this case is the author's desire to establish a generic coherence of themes. The stylistic means by which such a generic coherence is achieved differ significantly from those used to establish sequential and causal coherences. The difference lies in the manner in which motif clusters are linked: rather than being linked by probability or necessity of succession, motif clusters are interrelated in accord with their thematic affinities.

We may find, for instance, the same motif clusters repeated at different points of the narrative. In this case we speak of *materially identical* motif clusters. (In making these distinctions, I use the term "materially" to refer to the *Stoff* of a given motif cluster.) *Materially similar* motif clusters may describe various incidents which exhibit some similarity, but in which the characters or circumstances differ, or in which certain details are modified, omitted, or added. *Materially different* motif clusters are those which exhibit no material similarity at all. It stands to reason that materially identical motif clusters will carry the same theme, and that materially similar motif clusters will carry similar themes, though probably with variations. Materially different motif clusters, however, need not carry different themes; in fact they may carry similar or identical themes. In the same way, materially similar motif clusters may, by virtue of some modifications, carry contrasting themes. It is thus possible to conceive of a narrative which exhibits neither sequential nor causal progression on the motif level, but is structured almost entirely on the principle of generic coherence. In such a case, we may actually detect a thematic development which parallels that of a motif progression in a story. An excellent example of the extended use of such a generic coherence is Sartre's *La Nausée*.

One of the stylistic devices frequently used when the generic coherence of themes is to be brought forcefully to the reader's attention is the so-called "leitmotif." It is possible to establish existing generic coherence even between motif clusters which are widely separated in the text. However, such devices prove particularly useful when the reader needs to recognize thematic correlation between materially different motif clusters, especially when these clusters are textually not contiguous. Since the nature and function of leitmotifs differ, I have introduced new terms to distinguish them. The *repetitious label* is a recurring leitmotif, usually a gesture or a phrase, used to underscore some particular trait of a character. Strictly speaking, the repetitious label is not a leitmotif—i.e., it is not a thematic link. It recurs in order to emphasize a characteristic trait, and thus its function is epithetic. The *linking phrase*, by contrast, does serve the function of establishing thematic relatedness between textually separated motif clusters. Its recurrence points to the correlative quality (by virtue of similarity or of contrast) of the themes of those motif clusters with which it is associated. The *linking image* likewise serves as a thematic link, but the manner in which it relates themes differs: it reflects in a perceptual manner, as an image, not only the theme which it carries, but also those themes carried by other motif clusters which it links. In contrast to the linking phrase, the linking image does not recur every time in connection with all motif clusters whose themes it mirrors. Rather, it is placed focally so that it serves to draw together the themes of various motif clusters regardless of their disposition in the text.

These stylistic devices help the reader to establish the existence of generic coherences between individual constituent parts of the text, and thereby facilitate the reader's apprehension of at least certain aspects of the thematic cohesion of a narrative. The frequent use of leitmotifs as thematic links on the part of numerous authors provides convincing evidence that generic correlation of themes is a consciously or intuitively chosen stylistic force in the shaping of a significant structural feature in the narrative.

An understanding of the various types of thematic coherence as stylistic forces helps us to recognize the cohesive and self-contained structure, the *Gestalt*, of the narrative as an art form. As we have seen, this thematic cohesion may remain intact even if the story as an account of events has "no ending," or if certain cause-effect relationships are not followed up. Thus even the omission of such essential features in the story and plot need not disrupt the total structural cohesion, so long as generic coherence is preserved. In the light of this realization, we find it necessary to modify certain or our traditional critical assumptions. No longer need we seek to establish the indispensability of all motifs within a text. Rather, we accept as given the existing motifs in any narrative, and seek only to ascertain their functions. However, this approach will be valid only insofar as we attempt to establish the functionality of motifs from the point of view of all three types of thematic coherence.

The stylistic forces of thematic coherences are not merely arbitrary methods for the shaping of a narrative. This needs to be particularly stressed in reference to generic coherence, since its consistent application may result in the disruption of story and plot as structural substrata. This breakdown of story and plot is a useful technique for the modern author, as it enables him to prevent his reader from finding the represented experience too orderly, simplistic, and therefore contrived. Hence generic coherence is an indispensable stylistic force, as it alone provides a means of representing the disparateness of lived reality, while at the same time ensuring a cohesive structure of meaning.

We may, as already noted, apprehend such a structure of meaning in lived reality only in privileged moments of eidetic vision, either in retrospect or in the course of an intentional distanciation in the very process of our involvement. Represented reality, however, does afford us an opportunity for involvement and simultaneous distanciation. The representation of disparate motifs is a singularly effective technique for inducing such a distanciation, because our involvement in apparently unrelated incidents is checked by an inevitable questioning about their meanings. The process of distanciation is presumed when the generic coherence of themes is applied as the primary stylistic force. During this process, we direct our awareness away from an involvement in the represented incidents themselves, toward an effort at understanding the reciprocal relatedness of motifs by virtue of the correlation of their themes.

Only thus do we perceive each motif cluster in its multiple connections determined by progression, causality, and the generic affinities of themes. To do so is to achieve an essential vision of the complex totality of meanings in a self-contained world. As long as we remain emotionally involved in individual incidents of represented reality, as if they were lived reality, we fail to apprehend their thematic relevance. Such a failure implies that we do not view motifs in the larger context of their interrelationships, which define motifs according to their nature and function. In the process of a distanciated vision, however, we may succeed in transcending the limited and limiting immanence of individual experiences, and thereby attain an eidetic vision based upon our perception of a work's total cohesion.

We have established the three types of thematic coherence as stylistic forces operative in the composition of a narrative, and we have noted that they may coexist within the same structure, each exercising a more or less decisive degree of control upon that structure's *Gestalt*. In any given narrative, one type of thematic coherence may be predominant or one type may be so underemphasized as to prove incidental. Thus it may be said, broadly speaking, that narratives are classifiable into three main categories, according to the *type* of thematic coherence which governs them. Within each type of thematic coherence, however, one may distinguish certain *patterns* peculiar to that type. For example, within the sequential coherence of themes, we may find different patterns based upon the textual configurations of such devices as time-shifts, acceleration of pace, and parallel progression, confluence, or interlacing of separate story lines. Similarly, within the causal coherence of themes we may find patterns based upon the confluence of various "forces maîtresses"—to borrow Taine's terminology—and the simultaneity of mutually reinforcing or conflicting motivations and purposes.

The range of patterns of thematic structure within the generic coherence of themes remains as yet largely unexplored; however, we may here point out a few identifiable configurations as examples of the variety of patterns possible. For instance, a pattern similar to that of counterpoint in music may be perceived in the case of thematic correlation of materially *different* motif clusters. However, whereas relatively distinct melodies may be heard simultaneously in a contrapuntal arrangement, materially different motif clusters are necessarily perceived separately, even in the case of textual contiguity, and despite the fact that they carry correlative themes. Thus, within a narrative, an approximation to counterpoint may be achieved only on the thematic level. Here the theme lingers on in our awareness beyond the range of the motif cluster which carries it, and may combine or blend with another similar or contrasting theme. Such a contrapuntal pattern may be reinforced by the use of leitmotifs, and it becomes particularly effective when supported by a linking image. This is true, in the first place, because a linking image is less obviously a device than a linking phrase, and secondly, because the associative quality of its theme is more far-reaching, and may encompass a whole sequence of motif clusters.

A generic coherence of themes based upon materially *similar* motif clusters scattered in the text may lend itself to the development of a pattern which we know in music as "theme and variations." In this case, materially similar motif clusters recur with continually varied modifications as the narrative progresses. Some of these "theme and variations" patterns of composition are based upon the perspective of presentation. We know that the thematic signification of any motif cluster is derived from that cluster's contextual meaning. One aspect of that contextual meaning is determined by the particular focus from which a represented phenomenon is perceived. If a given phenomenon is presented from various points of view, its thematic meaning is correspondingly varied. Consequently, the device which we may call *multiple focusing*—the representation of a single object from different perspectives—is a means whereby the thematic signification of a given phenomenon can be diversified in order to reveal a complexity of meanings.

Multiple focusing may be achieved either by the use of the same narrator at different points in time, or by the use of two or more different narrators. When a single narrator is used, we may find the same phenomenon perceived by him at different times, with changed attitudes, and hence with different predispositions for intellectual and emotional apprehension. An excellent example of such a pattern may be seen in Robbe-Grillet's *La Jalousie*, in which the variations in themes that result from such modifications convey increasing emotional tensions in the narrator's consciousness, tensions which mark the stages of his progression from initial uncertainty to compulsive hallucinations. Here, then, we have a case of a narrative in which, although there is no story on the motif level, the thematic pattern itself traces a linear development.

When, however, multiple focusing is achieved through the use of several narrators, the different perspectives may produce kaleidoscopic variations upon the same phenomenon in which thematic configurations, carried by materially similar motif clusters, follow each other in more or less contiguous units. This pattern is one which is frequently used by Proust.

We may conclude by reemphasizing the fact that types of thematic coherence are recognizable stylistic forces, which govern the composition of a narrative as natural laws govern our physical world. In the past, critical attacks were frequently leveled at the narrative genre for what was considered to be its essential formlessness. Even though now the novel has come into its own, critics are often put on the defensive in trying to establish the existence of formal qualities peculiar to the narrative. The traditional critical emphasis upon poetic and dramatic theory has given rise to frequent misapplications of the formal tenets of drama and poetry to the narrative art. Because critics have often approached the novel with critical preconceptions based upon other genres, they have tended to confine their stylistic investigations to a search for the formal qualities which prevail on the motif level of the narrative. They have therefore failed to recognize certain formal aspects of the narrative which *do* govern its structure—i.e., the stylistic forces of thematic coherence which we have just described.

Just as a scientist must work within the limits imposed by the laws of nature, so is a writer of narratives bound by the structural exigencies of the three types of thematic coherence. Within these bounds, his freedom lies in the possibility of choosing the types of thematic coherence which will govern his composition, and the varieties of patterns he wishes to explore. Even on the motif level, his choices must be shaped by the requirements of these stylistic forces. In the narrative therefore, as in other genres, art is always *difficulté vaincue*.

Note

---

1. For complete definitions of the critical terminology used here, and for a thorough analysis of thematic structure, see my *Types of Thematic Structure* (Chicago, 1967).

Wilhelm Fucks

POSSIBILITIES OF EXACT STYLE ANALYSIS

BY "EXACT STYLE ANALYSIS" WE MEAN THE ANALYSIS OF WRITTEN TEXTS by the use of mathematical aids, in the same way that these are applied to the exact natural sciences, to physics, for example.

Let us begin with two introductory remarks about the problem of mathematical analysis of literary style. First: the efforts of literary scholars to devise exact style typologies are of a purely descriptive nature and have nothing whatever to do with normative stylistics. This makes possible the use of mathematical aids to arrive at greater accuracy. Second: the concept of literary style, whether it be style of a particular work, author, or period, always expresses a kind of totality, an artistic totality in which the form corresponds to the outward manifestation of a specific statement just as it shapes the content into a specific structure. Mathematical analysis requires that these interlocking components of the totality be taken apart that they might be more easily examined separately and their interrelationships observed. But this should not disguise the fact that the end result must once again be sought in a synthesis, and that each totality of style amounts to more than the sum of its parts, and is, in fact, more of an integration.

We can only grasp this totality by carrying out the appropriate analytical and functional study of that totality, not by the examination and comparison of some of its extrinsic form elements alone. However, mathematical analysis necessarily restricts us to the analysis and establishment of typological properties and common features of individual traits and elements of style. We are concerned with the quantitative analysis of the formal externals of a text's structure, and it makes no difference whether the texts under examination are works of literature —i.e., statements existing logically on an aesthetic level—or statements belonging to the empirical level. The text of a travel guide or a political speech, of a lyric poem or of instructions for the use of a razor, can all be subjected to identical methods of quantitative analysis. Neither the specifically *literary* element nor its aesthetic reconstruction (the most important levels in the complexity of literary cognitive theory) fall, first of all, within the scope of quantitative analysis. But even when poetic literature alone is examined, individual traits of style do not necessarily tell us everything about a totality of style, since those same traits may, in the most varying functions, go to make up all kinds of totalities.

This is not as discouraging as it may sound, however. On closer inspection, and taking into account the necessary methodological assumptions of literary scholarship, we find that mathematical analysis and the computer offer us undreamed-of possibilities of accuracy which, in certain areas, may completely eliminate those sources of error which originate in the fact that earlier studies often had to rely on emotional impression and uncertain memory. In the examination of style traits, the precision of mathematical analysis can be of the utmost importance: not only does it enable us to establish style typologies but, in style analysis, it can also be of seminal significance in questions of authenticity or authorship. It is in these points that the precision of an exact science of literature is attainable.

The question has been raised as to whether an exact science of literature will ever replace or oust traditional approaches and methods in the way that the exact natural sciences, for instance, have largely ousted the preceding philosophical approaches to the cosmos. This will never be the case with the exact science of literature. The reason is very simple. When a stone drops, or a planet revolves in a certain manner around the sun, or an atom emits a radiation quant, we do not, as human beings, have the ability to identify ourselves, anthropomorphically speaking, with what the stone feels when it drops, or what the atom feels when it emits a quant. In other words, what happens in inanimate nature is inaccessible to the understanding and empathetic interpretative process, in contrast to man's cultural creations. Interpreting and evaluating therefore continue to remain essential to literature, as well as to all other artistic creations. Even in classifying groups of texts that we wish to analyze from a common point of view, we must call upon the traditional methods of literary and artistic research. So we see that exact sciences of the arts can only evolve in teamwork.

Yet another question is whether we will be able to find objective and definitive solutions to controversial problems of authenticity. For the unsatisfactory situation exists, in literature as well as in painting and every other field of art, that questions of authenticity can often only be answered, more or less inconclusively, on the basis of highly subjective reasoning. Let us reply by offering an illustration from chemistry. Chemists can now exactly identify chemically complicated substances and distinguish them from other equally complicated substances; this was not remotely possible in the early stages of the evolution of chemistry. A similar development will take place in the exact science of literature.

The basic difficulty confronting us in questions of authenticity is that an author may alter his style considerably, and that there seems to be no such thing as a literary fingerprint. That would be a test which, first of all, would distinguish every author infallibly from every other author; next, would not change throughout the author's entire lifetime; and finally, would be easily accessible. During the roughly fifty years in which Thomas Mann wrote, the mean value and standard deviation of frequency distributions of the length of his sentences increased almost exactly by the factor of 2. The mean value and the standard deviation of these distributions in *Buddenbrooks*, for instance, and *Königliche Hoheit* are farther removed from each other than the mean value and standard deviation of the *Gospel According to St. John and Revelation*. (A small standard deviation indicates that the main part of the distribution is closely grouped in the region of the mean value; a large standard deviation indicates the contrary.)

ASSOCIATION OF TEXTS IN TEXT SOCIOGRAMS

Even very simple characteristics of literary style lead to an association of groups of texts written by certain authors ("text sociograms"). Figure 1 illustrates such a text sociogram.

In Fig. 1, two groups immediately emerge. Let us call the upper group "writers" (in the sense of essayists, historians, scientists, etc.) and the lower group "authors" (playwrights, poets, novelists, etc.). There are only two exceptions: Chaucer is in the writers' field, and Carlyle is in the authors'. The relevant works studied are listed in Table 1. We find all the prose authors in the area of shorter words and largely in the area of shorter sentences. Figure 2 provides an analogous picture of a number of German writers. In this diagram we have outlined two additional fields: in that of prose authors, a "Goethe field" containing a

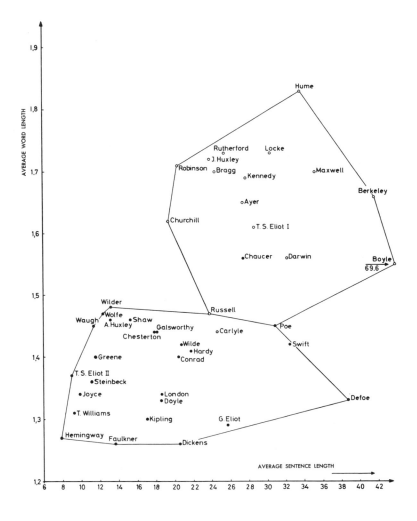

FIG. 1. Scattergram of works of "authors" and "writers," by average word length (average number of syllables per word) and average sentence length (average number of words per sentence).

TABLE 1. Works Analyzed for Fig. 1

Author	Work
Ayer, A. J.	*Language, Truth, and Logic*
Balzac, H. de	*Contes Drolatiques*
Berkeley, G.	*The Principles of Human Knowledge*
Boyle, R.	*The Works (1)*
Bragg, W. L.	*The Crystalline State*
Carlyle, T.	*The French Revolution*
Chaucer, G.	*Troilus and Cressida*
Chesterton, G. K.	*The Man Who Was Thursday*
Churchill, W.	*Great Contemporaries*
Conrad, J.	*Almayer's Folly*
Darwin, C.	*The Origin of Species by Means of Natural Selection*
Dickens, C.	*Christmas Stories*
Doyle, A. C.	*Sir Nigel*
Eliot, G.	*The Mill on the Floss*
Eliot, T. S. (I)	*The Use of Poetry and the Use of Criticism*
Eliot, T. S. (II)	*The Cocktail Party*
Faulkner, W.	*As I Lay Dying*
Galsworthy, J.	*The Forsyte Saga*
Greene, G.	*The Power and the Glory*
Hardy, T.	*Jude the Obscure*
Hemingway, E.	*A Farewell to Arms*
Hume, D.	*Enquiries Concerning the Human Understanding*
Huxley, A.	*Brave New World*
Huxley, J.	*Man in the Modern World*
Joyce, J.	*Ulysses*
Kennedy, J. F.	*Profiles in Courage*
Kipling, R.	*The Jungle Book*
Locke, J.	*A Letter Concerning Toleration*
London, J.	*The Call of the Wild*
Maxwell, J. C.	*A Treatise on Electricity and Magnetism*
Poe, E. A.	*Complete Works (vol. 3)*
Robinson, D. S.	*The Principles of Reasoning*
Russell, B.	*The Analysis of Mind*
Rutherford, E.	*Radioactivity*
Shaw, G. B.	*Immaturity*
Steinbeck, J.	*Tortilla Flat*
Swift, J.	*Gulliver's Travels*
Waugh, E.	*Decline and Fall*
Wilde, O.	*De Profundis*
Wilder, T.	*The Bridge of San Luis Rey*
Williams, T.	*Four Plays*
Wolfe, T.	*Look Homeward, Angel*

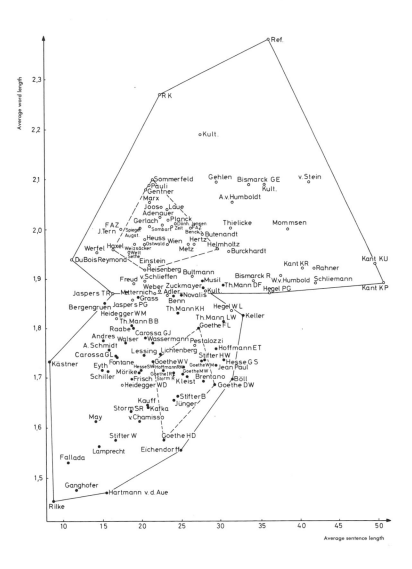

FIG. 2.   Scattergram of works of German "authors" and "writers," by same criteria as in Fig. 1. Also outlined is a "Goethe field" in lower area and a "physicists' field" in upper area. "Ref.," at top of diagram, is explained in text.

large number of works by Goethe. Many people might have expected Goethe's prose to have made use of a far wider range of possibilities in the German language than our Goethe field indicates, but the graph shows that this is not so. In the area of fact writers we have outlined a field containing the works of numerous German physicists. In the upper field we also, of course, find many texts by journalists, politicians, and scientists and scholars of other disciplines. As we see, Kant's writings lie at the extreme outer edge of sentence length.

Without seriously deviating from our principle—neither to interpret nor evaluate—it is nevertheless permissible for us to speak of verbal turgidity in the case of extremely long words, and of sentence-turgidity in the case of sentences containing an extremely large number of words. Here the symbol "Ref." at the top of Fig. 2 catches our eye: it denotes a lengthy treatise entitled *The Reform of the German Secondary School System*, signed by a large number of prominent exponents of culture. Figs. 1 and 2 tempt us to draw conclusions as to the quality of a style; but two sets of figures cannot possibly suffice to substantiate reliable judgments on the quality of style characteristics of even a purely formal nature.

It might be objected that the associating of prose authors and other writers in our diagram resulted merely from the selection made and that, as more and more texts are added, the differences will become blurred. This assumption is contradicted by Fig. 3, in which the centers of gravity of "writers" and the centers of gravity of "authors" have been calculated according to length of sentences, using a constantly increasing number of works. As we take in, without bias, more and more works, we see that the distance between the centers of gravity ultimately becomes more or less stationary.

Figure 4 is a further example of a text sociogram. The point of departure here was the frequency distributions of sentence lengths among numerous texts by German authors. The two most important characteristics of these distributions—mean value and standard deviation—have been entered horizontally and vertically, so that each text sample appears in the diagram as a point. From some texts only one value has been entered, shown as a solid square. For others, three samples have been taken; these are indicated by solid circles. This allows us to obtain at least an approximate idea of the size and character of the area within which the author writes.

Here again, groups of writers immediately stand out in our sociogram. In Fig. 4, for instance, a number of texts that some literary scholars would classify as minor works are to be found in an area of

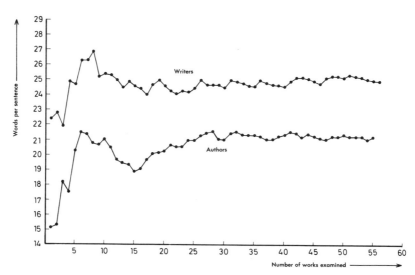

FIG. 3. Centers of gravity of "writers" and "authors."

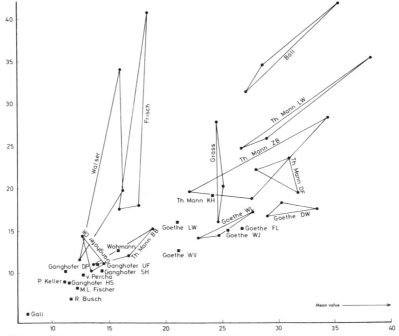

FIG. 4. Mean values and standard deviations in distributions of sentence lengths, for German authors. For explanation, see text.

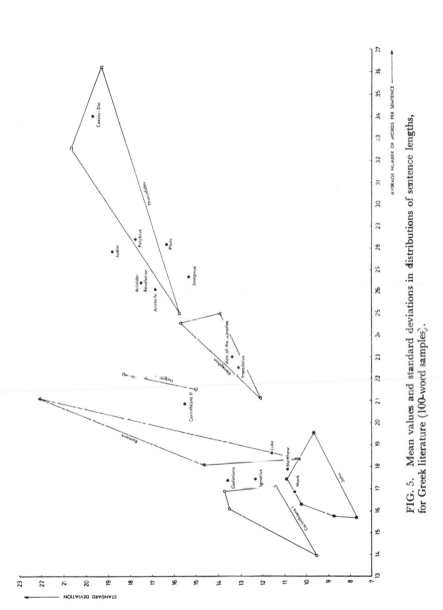

FIG. 5.   Mean values and standard deviations in distributions of sentence lengths, for Greek literature (100-word samples).

low standard deviation and low mean values (lower left, in the diagram), a very dense area. This becomes especially clear when we see how the works of Thomas Mann developed during his lifetime from areas of low standard deviation and mean values in *Buddenbrooks* (lower left) to very high values in *Königliche Hoheit* (upper right).

What strikes us particularly in this sociogram is the configuration of three samples each from the works of Walser, Frisch, Grass, and Böll. In Grass's *Die Blechtrommel*, the average length of sentences in the samples differs very little. Similarly, in Frisch's novel *Mein Name sei Gantenbein*, the mean values of the sentence lengths in the three samples do not differ very much, and the same applies to Walser's novel *Das Einhorn*. But the standard deviations of sentence lengths as compared to their mean values are noticeably high. The three samples from Böll's book indicate high mean values in sentence lengths as well as high standard deviation values. These examples from modern authors become quite clear when we compare them with Goethe's works as shown in Fig. 4. The differences in the lengths of sentences used by the modern authors as compared to Goethe, and also as compared to some of Thomas Mann's works, are pinpointed quantitatively in the diagram.

Figure 5 offers an analogous picture of Greek literature. Here we discover a grouping of the Greek texts of the New Testament largely in the left half of the diagram. The Gospel literature (Matthew, Mark, Luke, and John) in particular is located in a comparatively small area of low standard deviation and mean values of sentence lengths. We find the Acts of the Apostles in the same area as the works of Xenophon and Herodotus. The book of Revelation, in terms of sentence lengths, is found in the area of classical Greek literature—which is not to say, however, that the same applies to this book's segmentation and articulation or to its distribution of word lengths, for when we look at these three values we find they all fall into the same areas as those occupied by the other Gospels.

IS THERE AN ATTRACTION BETWEEN SENTENCES?

Are there such things as reciprocal effects between sentences, that might be described as forces, and if so, can the potency of these forces and their effective range be numerically defined?

We can approach this problem from any of the various style traits of a sentence: its length (indicated by number of words or number of syllables); its segmentation (reduction into component parts); its articulation (the extent to which the component parts are interdependent); its syntactical characteristics; and so on. For the sake of simplicity we will take the sentence-length approach here, this time measured by the number of syllables in each sentence. If we take successive sentences in the order in which they appear in the text and write down the number of syllables, we arrive at a series of numbers. These numbers extend from 1 to around 1000, in the case of some works of modern and even classical philosophical literature.

With the aid of the computer it is now quite a simple matter to calculate the correlation of neighboring sentences as well as that of more widely separated sentences, and thus to draw some conclusions as to the effects of sentences upon each other in terms of their lengths. Let us adopt a very simplified approach. We will distinguish between only two types of sentence: longer, or l, sentences, and shorter, or s, sentences. In any text, we can call one half of the sentences longer and the other half shorter, thus arriving at two equal quantities of sentences, so that each sentence in one group is longer than each sentence in the other. In this way, every sentence in every text can be defined as an l-sentence or an s-sentence. Needless to say, a sentence that is an l-sentence in one text can be an s-sentence in another. The median will generally differ in value from work to work.

So let us take the particular work that interests us and count in it, first, how often an l-sentence is followed by an l-sentence; second, how often an l-sentence is followed by an s-sentence; third, how often an s-sentence is followed by an l-sentence; and finally, how often an s-sentence is followed by an s-sentence. We have now arrived at four figures according to the following schema:

$$\begin{bmatrix} ll & ls \\ sl & ss \end{bmatrix}$$

If we imagine the end of the text to be cyclically joined to the beginning of the text, we find, on the basis of our premises, that ll equals ss and sl equal ls. If we know the total number of sentences, we need only determine one of these four figures by actual enumeration; this automatically establishes the others.

As a concrete example let us take a sample from Balzac's novel *Père Goriot* in French. Our schema then looks like this:

$$\begin{bmatrix} ll & ls \\ sl & ss \end{bmatrix} = \begin{bmatrix} 152 & 98 \\ 98 & 152 \end{bmatrix}$$

The sample contains, as we see, 500 sentences, and we have 152 cases in which a longer sentence is followed by a longer one, and an equal number of cases in which a shorter sentence is followed by a shorter one; further, 98 cases of a longer sentence followed by a shorter one, and an equal number of cases in which a shorter sentence is followed by a longer one.

From these figures we calculate as correlation coefficients the very simple formula $(ll-ls)/(ll+ls)$, which yields the value 0.28, or 28%. What does this value mean? The first thing we note is that it is positive —i.e., that the combinations ll or ss occur more frequently than the combinations ls or sl. We will call the former combinations "equal" and the latter "opposite." So we can say: "In the sample that we have examined, equal sentences attract each other more than opposite sentences do."

If we come upon a longer sentence in our sample, the probability of the following sentence being in turn a longer sentence is 28% greater than of its being a shorter sentence. Should we come upon a shorter

TABLE 2.   Correlation coefficients for selected texts

Author	Work	Coefficient c_1 (%)
Jean Paul	Titan; Flegeljahre	2
Camus	La Chûte	2
Hoffmann	Goldener Topf; Magnetiseur; Kreisler	2
Churchill	A History of the English-Speaking People	3
Voltaire	Candide	3
Brentano	Sänger; Godwin; Chronika eines fahrenden Schülers	3
Hume	Theory of Knowledge	4
Descartes	Discours de la méthode	5
T. Mann	Buddenbrooks	6
Adenauer	Erinnerungen	6
Sartre	Qu'est-ce que la littérature?	7
Goethe	Dichtung und Wahrheit	7
Russell	A History of Western Philosophy	7
Bismarck	Gedanken und Erinnerungen	9
Grass	Die Blechtrommel	9
Wetzel	Fischers Reise; Kleon	10
Stifter	Brigitta	10
A. Huxley	Brave New World	10
Kant	Kritik der praktischen Vernunft	11
Luther	Ob Kriegsleute auch in seligem stande sein können	11
Dickens	Christmas Stories	12
Grimmelshausen	Simplizissimus	13
Jaspers	Philosophischer Glaube	18
Luke	Gospel	19
Bonaventura	Nachtwachen des Bonaventura	21
Balzac	Père Goriot	29
Kleist	Die Marquise von O.	31

Correlograms of sentence lengths (syllables per sentence) in relation to median

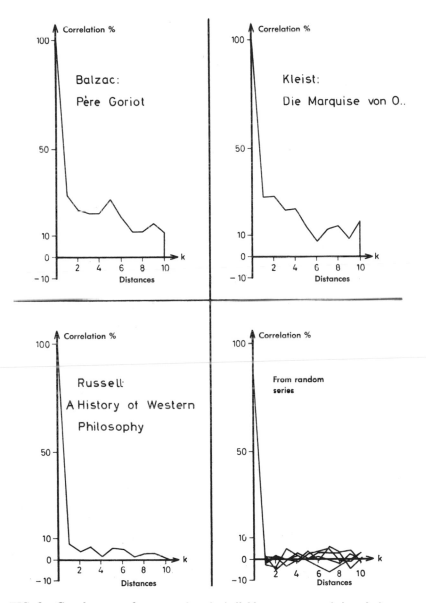

FIG. 6. Correlograms of sentence length (syllables per sentence) in relation to median, for Balzac, Kleist, Russell, and five random number-sequences.

sentence, the probability of the following sentence again being a shorter sentence is likewise 28% greater than of its being a longer sentence. If we had a coefficient with a negative sign the relationships would be reversed—i.e., opposite sentences would attract each other more strongly than equal sentences would.

Correlation coefficients of this type were calculated for numerous texts (Table 2). The coefficients increase from the area of 2 up to the value of 31, and all values are positive. In other words, in all texts examined, equal sentences attract each other more strongly than opposite sentences do. Of course, this need not apply universally, and especially not for short samples.

The force of the attraction varies greatly. The highest values were found, for samples of 2000 sentences, in Balzac's *Père Goriot* and Kleist's *Marquise von O.*—29% and 31%, respectively.

So far we have been dealing with attraction between neighboring sentences. Let us now repeat the same procedure between each sentence and its next-but-one neighbor, to see whether the sentences of a text exert any attraction in this situation. We then proceed to combine all these sentences with the third-next, fourth-next, fifth-next sentence, etc., each time calculating the applicable correlation coefficient.

Thus for Balzac's *Père Goriot*, Kleist's *Die Marquise von O.*, and Russell's *History of Western Philosophy* we obtain the three correlograms shown in Fig. 6. For Balzac and Kleist, the attraction is effective up to the area of the tenth-next sentence. In *Père Goriot*, for instance, the probability that a longer sentence will be followed by a longer sentence as tenth-next, or that a shorter sentence will be followed by a shorter one as tenth-next, is still 12% greater than the opposite possibility. So we see that, in Balzac and Kleist, the attraction has not only great potency but also great effective range. In Russell's *History of Western Philosophy* this is very much less true. The first value, which applies to neighboring sentences, works out at only 7%, and the potency of the attraction declines very rapidly with increasing distances between sentences.

In order to determine to what extent the effects thus established might have been the result of coincidence, analogous correlograms were drawn for five random number-sequences. The results are shown in Fig. 6, lower right. As was to be expected, here there are approximately as many negative values as positive values, and all the values are dispersed in what we might call a "gray" strip, which provides a yardstick for the extent to which the effects that have been established are significant or merely attributable to coincidence. We find that effects which exceed values of a few per cent do indeed represent significant effects. If we record the force of the attraction in per cent of maximal possible values vertically, and the effective range of the attracting forces in per cent of maximal possible values horizontally, Fig. 7 provides us with an over-all picture. The diagram speaks for itself and requires no further elucidation.

ESTABLISHING THE STRENGTH AND EFFECTIVE RANGE OF METRIC CONNECTIONS

Following the same pattern by which we determined the force of attraction between sentences, we proceed to determine the strength and effective range of metric connections.

Seen mathematically, metrics is concerned with more or less sustained periodicities and more or less skillfully constructed sysmmetries

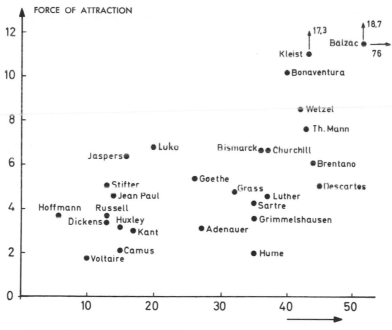

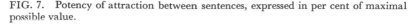

FIG. 7.   Potency of attraction between sentences, expressed in per cent of maximal possible value.

and asymmetries. Absolutely rigidly metric speech is virtually impossible. Conversely, even "prosaic" prose evinces certain vestiges of metric order. The texts range anywhere from very rigid to very random arrays of metric elements.

In terms of their metric order, poems may be compared to crystals. The atomic components of crystals show both close order and extended order. Like natural crystals, poems have dislocations that may, under certain conditions, be very attractive. Prose can be compared to fluids. In the latter, the atomic components show a very limited close order. The metric properties of some ultramodern poetry with more or less randomly distributed elements in the fields of words and sentences may be compared to certain physical properties of gaseous or partially gaseous systems.

To arrive at some precise conclusions, let us now consider a long poem such as Goethe's epic, *Reineke Fuchs*. Disregarding the line-structure of the verse form, we will instead imagine the whole poem to be written in linear sequence as if it were prose. Now let us look at the resultant sequence of syllables, in which we distinguish two stress elements—stressed and unstressed. Here again we have a sequence of dual-valued parameters, s and u. In contrast to the sentence lengths, where we had a parameter with the two values s and l, here ss does not equal uu and su does not equal us. Consequently, in this case the correlation must be based on the quotient derived from the difference between the two diagonal products and the square root of the product of the linear and columnar sums.

For a large number of texts we set up four-part matrices consisting of the elements ss, su, uu, and us, and determined the indicated correlation. At first we were concerned with neighboring stress elements. As with the sentences, the next obvious step was to consider the next-but-one syllable of each selected syllable, then the third-next, fourth-next, and so on. We carried this process as far as the sixteenth-next syllable following each selected syllable (because of the conditions obtaining in six-foot hexameters). This again produces correlograms, and these correlograms tell us the force and effective range of metric connections. If we standardize these two values in per cent of the maximal possible value in each case and give them equal weight, we can combine the two into a metrics index. The metrics index introduced here is therefore 100% if the effective range as well as the force of the metric connection has attained the highest possible figure.

Results of this study are shown in Table 3. In prose texts, the metrics index ranges from 5 to 12; in verse literature from 21 to 85, in terms of the values derived from the works examined here. The very low values that we find in St. Paul's first Epistle to the Corinthians, in Caesar's *De Bello Gallico*, and Adenauer's *Memoirs*, as well as in Bismarck, Marx, and Pushkin, are explained largely by the metric quality of the individual words. The higher values of 11 and 12, however, indicate

TABLE 3.   Metrics index in prose and verse

Author	Work	Metrics index (%)
	PROSE	
Paul	*Corinthians 1*	5
Caesar	*De Bello Gallico*	5
Adenauer	*Memoirs*	6
Bismarck	*Memoirs*	7
Marx	*Das Kapital*	7
Pushkin	*The Pastmaster*	7
Stifter	*Brigitta*	8
Goethe	*Theory of Color*	8
Kleist	*Die Marquise von O.*	8
A. Huxley	*Antic Hay*	8
Benn	*Prosa und Szenen*	11
Lenin	*The Development of Capitalism in Russia*	11
Kennedy	*Profiles in Courage*	11
Churchill	*Great Contemporaries*	12
Rilke	*Die Weise von Liebe und Tod des Cornets Christoph Rilke*	12
	VERSE	
T. S. Eliot	*The Cocktail Party*	21
Tyrtaios	*Elegies of War*	24
Harmann v. Aue	*Der arme Heinrich*	25
Grass	*Advent*	27
———	*Nibelungenlied*	29
Brecht	*Lehrgedicht von der Natur des Menschen*	32
Shakespeare	*Hamlet (German translation)*	33
Homer	*The Odyssey*	34
Virgil	*The Aeneid*	36
Ovid	*Metamorphoses*	37
Goethe	*Faust*	39
Goethe	*Hermann und Dorothea*	40
Schiller	*Wallenstein's Death*	43
George	*Vorspiel*	45
Shakespeare	*Hamlet*	46
Goethe	*Torquato Tasso*	50
Rilke	*Requiem für eine Freundin*	53
Pushkin	*Eugene Onegin*	53
Dante	*La Divina Commedia*	76
Byron	*Elegies*	85

a certain proportion of poetic attitude. We find these in Benn, Lenin, Kennedy, Churchill, and Rilke.

It need hardly be pointed out that, with classical Greek and Latin literature, it is not a matter of the syllables' stress but of their length. For purposes of calculation this makes no difference, of course. The highest values of the metrics index are to be found in Dante's *Divina Commedia* in Italian and in Byron's *Elegies* in English: 76% in Dante, 85% in Byron.

SOME REMARKS ON STUDIES OF AUTHENTICITY

Two problems relating to Biblical texts were chosen to see how effective our method was in studies of authenticity. We will confine ourselves here to a few short comments on these studies and discuss only one of the problems dealt with: the question of whether the book of Revelation and the Gospel According to St. John could have had one and the same author. Figure 8 shows the percentages in which the various word types occur in the Greek texts of the Gospel of St. John and Revelation. The Gospel of St. John was broken down into two samples, and in all three cases the samples were kept to a standard number of words. The graph shows that frequency percentages in which the various word types occur coincide very closely in the two samples from the Gospel. On the basis of word-type frequency, the Gospel of St. John may be considered as being very uniform in style. The frequency with which the various word types occur in Revelation varies very considerably from that with which they occur in the Gospel.

We can characterize these findings by means of an index of differences. This is arrived at as follows: We calculate the difference between the frequencies of the two works being compared, divide it by the sum, and add the results for all word classes. This yields for the St. John sample No. 1 as against St. John No. 2 an index of differences of 1.15; for St. John 1 as against Revelation, 5.58; for St. John 2 as against Revelation, 5.74—an average of 5.66, compared with 1.15 for St. John 1 as against St. John 2.

Transition frequencies occurring in the two works were also examined, and finally a comparison of the vocabulary was carried out with the aid of a new type of matrix. Analogous studies were also undertaken concerning the problem of whether the Acts of the Apostles and the Gospel of St. Luke might have the same author.[1]

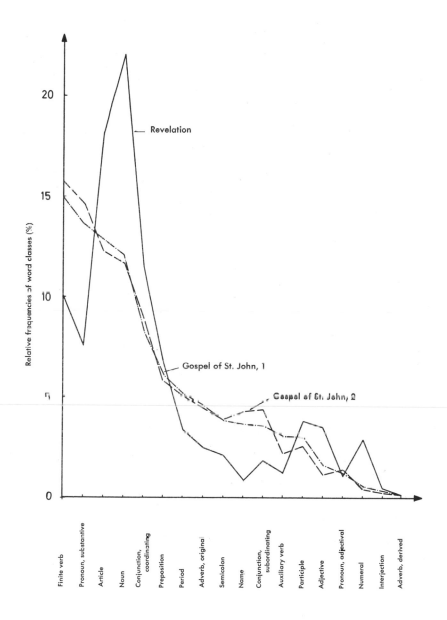

FIG. 8. Relative frequencies of word types in Greek texts of Revelation and Gospels of St. John (in per cent).

IN MIXING THE LENGTHS OF THEIR SENTENCES, DO AUTHORS FOLLOW MATHEMATICALLY FORMULABLE LAWS?

An approach to this question is shown in Fig. 9. These graphs show six distributions of the frequencies of various sentence lengths as they occur in texts from Goethe's *Dichtung und Wahrheit*, Stifter's *Brigitta*, Bismarck's *Gedanken und Erinnerungen*, Adenauer's *Erinnerungen* (Memoirs), Aldous Huxley's *Brave New World*, and Sartre's *Qu-est-ce que la littérature?*

The measurement values in the diagrams, depicted as corners of frequency polygons, tell us which fraction of the sentences contains 1–5 words, which fraction 6–10 words, which fraction 11–15 words, and so on. Each diagram also contains the mean value and standard deviation as well as some additional values to which we shall shortly refer. The question now is: "Can these and many other analogous distributions of sentence lengths be described by mathematical laws; and, if they can, can such laws be interpreted?" In other words, have they anything to tell us about what went on in the authors' minds, or what the authors did, when they produced the mixture of sentence lengths in their works?—in doing which, of course, they were no more aware of following a certain mathematical law than are objects in inanimate nature when they follow mathematically formulable laws.

When in any of the exact sciences we have a series of measurement points and are looking for a law, the *sequence* of measurement points is the first fact that we have to consider. If we succeed in finding a mathematical formula that significantly reproduces these measurement points according to the rules of statistical tests, we arrive at a second fact. The mathematical reproduction represents what is possibly a meaningful summary of the measurement points. But this is not unequivocally so. The same series of measurement points might possibly be significantly represented by other mathematical formulations as well. Having decided in favor of one of these representations, we still are not told anything about the causative connection of the relationships— e.g., effects and causes—contained in the series of measurement points. So we have to distinguish between three things: the series of measurement points, the mathematical representations of this series, and the causative connections on the basis of which we wish to explain the series of measurement points.

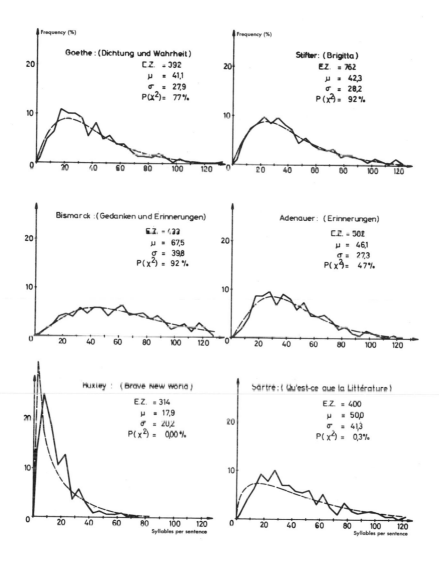

FIG. 9. Frequency distributions of sentence lengths in six works. See text for details.

For the first four frequency distributions of sentence lengths in our graph, a mathematical reproduction was evolved as follows:

$$\text{(A)} \qquad P(k) = \left\{ \frac{(1^0+d)(1+2d) \ldots (1+(k-1)d)}{(k-1)!} \left(\frac{t}{1+dt}\right)^{k-1} \right.$$
$$\left(\frac{1}{1+dt}\right)^{\frac{1}{d}+1} k > 0$$

This formula was derived from a well-known one developed by Polya, which is as follows:

$$\text{(B)} \qquad P(k) = \left\{ \frac{1^0 (1+d) \ldots (1+(k-1)d)}{k!} \left(\frac{t}{1+dt}\right)^{k} \right.$$
$$\left(\frac{1}{1+dt}\right)^{\frac{1}{d}} k \geq 0$$

We cannot take the Polya formula itself to solve our problem because, according to it, the argument zero would yield a functional value different from zero—that is, we would have to find a certain fraction of sentences that did not contain a single word or a single syllable, i.e., of sentences that cannot exist. The variation of the Polya schema as shown in Formula A has eliminated this difficulty.

Whether a mathematical reproduction of facts such as those before us may be accepted or must be rejected is something that can, as we know, be examined by applying various mathematical tests. The relevant test in this case, applied to Formula A, demonstrated its correctness in the first four illustrated frequency distributions as well as in a number of other ones. It must, as we have said, be borne in mind that the measurement points do not unequivocally determine the mathematical formulation. In the laws of physics, of course, we have exactly the same situation.

The next question is: Can we interpret the formula? Here we, can get some sort of picture if we visualize an approach by which we can deduce Polya's formula. We start out from the very simple and familiar Poisson distribution. This is a so-called single parametric distribution, since it is enough to give a single figure—that of the mean value, for instance—to determine the total distribution. However, for the frequency distribution of words in sentences, this simple formula does not suffice. A useful formula can be obtained by letting the mean value of the Poisson distribution be in turn redistributed according to a gamma function.

What does this imply in terms of our problem? Let us imagine that the author, in writing down concrete sentences of a certain length, dips at random into a great reservoir of sentences that is potentially available

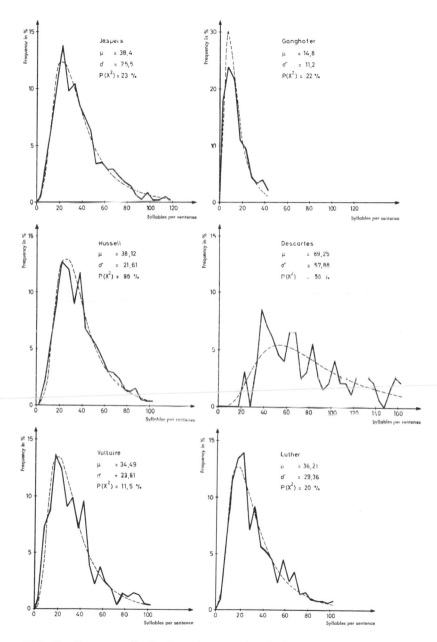

FIG. 10. Frequency distributions of sentence lengths for six additional authors.

to him for his work. Then we can construct the correct potential fund of sentence lengths, as follows. First we determine the sentence lengths according to a Poisson distribution, with a specific mean value. Next, while the author is at work we continuously and randomly vary this mean value, at the same time making sure that in total the variation of the mean value will result in a gamma distribution. So, while he is writing, the author is, as it were, "playing" in his fund of available sentences, with the mean value of a specific function in a specific manner. Thus our formula summarizing this observation tells us, in the case of the first four examples, exactly how the author is following certain laws in terms of sentence lengths without himself being aware of it.

Next comes the question of whether this quantitatively fixed result can now be interpreted at a still deeper level. Such may indeed be the case, but it is no longer the concern of an exact science of literature—perhaps rather of informational psychology.

It must be added that by no means all frequency distributions of sentence lengths are obliged to obey the formula indicated. The laws according to which authors mix their sentence lengths will, as is to be expected, vary. The last two examples in Fig. 9 show deviations. Huxley's *Brave New World*, for instance, deviates in a highly significant manner from the above formula (as do the analyses shown in Fig. 10); the same applies to Sartre's *Qu'est-ce que la littérature?* So, side by side with this mechanism which, if you like, follows certain laws, there must also exist other mechanisms—to recognize which is our next task. As is shown by the last graph in Fig. 9, which relates to Sartre's *Qu'est-ce que la littérature?* a different kind of reproduction has been achieved. The frequency distribution can be reflected in a highly significant way by logarithmic normal distribution. The latter, together with the Polya distribution used above, has been incorporated in the graph to show that one distribution offers a satisfactory reproduction while the Polya-type distribution does not. The corresponding values of the Chi-square test have likewise been included in the diagram.

It may not be that simple to interpret why in the case of Sartre's *Qu'est-ce que la littérature?* the logarithmic normal distribution offers a good reproduction of the frequency distributions of sentence lengths. In analyses of this kind it may be helpful to recall in which other problems the Polya distribution or logarithmic normal distribution has proved useful. Polya distributions prove interesting in the study of infectious diseases, in which, as in the Polya process, what happens at a given moment depends on what has happened before. They are also usefully applied to electron showers such as we find in high-altitude

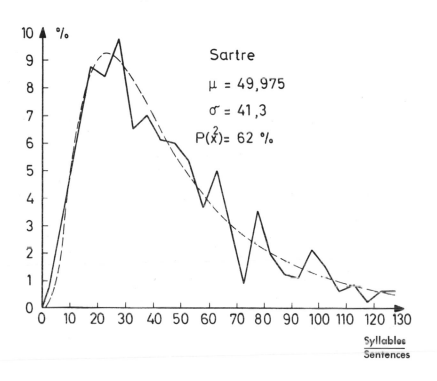

FIG. 11.   Frequency distribution, in the works of Sartre, of syllable:sentence ratios.

cosmic radiation. There have been many and varied applications of logarithmic normal distribution—among them, distribution of natural or ground rock sizes; distribution of a mineral at a site; income distribution; family expenditures; hormone production as dependent on growth; effects of certain drugs; hereditary traits; human height and weight; principal life-span of products and tools; and distribution of certain star clusters.

Whether and how we can proceed to more profound interpretations of the innate laws demonstrated by Fig. 11 is a matter for further study.

[*Translated from the German by Leila Vennewitz*]

Note

1. Details of these results are in my book, *Nach allen Regeln der Kunst* (Stuttgart, 1968).

Pierre Guiraud

MODERN LINGUISTICS LOOKS AT RHETORIC: Free Indirect Style

WE ARE WITNESSING A RENEWAL OF INTEREST TODAY—AFTER A LONG eclipse—in rhetoric in its dual form: a theory of style and writing, and a theory of literature that pluralizes "poetics," "dramaturgies," "the arts of the novel," "the structures of the story," etc. This is not the place to dwell on the familiar reasons leading to the discredit and decline of rhetoric, yet it is interesting to examine, if only in summary, those that have been the cause of this regeneration.

These reasons have their source in the profound renewal of linguistic and aesthetic thought represented by structuralism. Structuralism has identified itself all along by its opposition to nineteenth-century historical determinism, and in so doing was bound to rediscover the paths—or at least some of the paths—of classical rationalism; the interest, for example, of generative linguistics in Port-Royal and in grammar as a whole, and the interest of semeiologists in taxonomy and the universal languages of such philosophers as Leibnitz, etc., are merely the consequences of a formalist, rationalist, and essentialist concept of language. And structuralist-inspired criticism has a way of looking at literature today which is very close, in its postulates and concepts, to that of rhetoric. Both are based on three types of common criteria: formalism, structuralism, and functionalism.

Classical formalism is based on the notion of "figures," which is the foundation of rhetoric, and which is regaining its cardinal importance in modern linguistics now that the historical grammar and teaching methods stemming from it are placing the emphasis on "meaning."

Admittedly, this formalism is not structuralist in the modern sense of the term, and it will be contemporary neorhetoric's original contribution to restore the analysis of "figures" to its place within the perspective of a system. But rhetoric is already demanding a typology which, although pragmatic in origin, will nevertheless rapidly develop into a systematic method of grouping. By this method of *disposition*, or of the search for the order in which arguments are to be arrayed, it distinguishes between *exordium, division, confirmation, refutation*, and *conclusion*; whence are deduced—or rather induced—a natural order and an artificial order, according to the manner of commencement, continuing, and concluding. Thus one may begin with the beginning, the middle, or the end, and in each case one may open with a proverb or an example; in this way eight types of artificial order are obtainable. In the same manner, it is possible to enumerate nine types of *metaphor*; descriptions are classified of which the types vary according to whether one begins with the head, the body, etc. Lists are drawn up of *topoi* susceptible to literary development, which today we call "themes." With the troubadours and the Great Rhetoricians, the art of verse pursues to the limit this analysis of combinatory virtualities of a "system," even to the point, for example, of distinguishing as many as 115 types of rondeau! All these are things that today we call "models."

Now this deductive rationalism is the major methodological postulate of present-day linguistics, from Hijelmslev to generative and transformational grammar. In short, rhetoric and structuralism share a common functionalism.

Positivism is interested in the origin of phenomena; hence stylistics and criticism concentrate on the problem of historical sources and the author, whereas rhetoric is interested in form as it relates to its function; *genres* are defined as particular situations (song, narration, performance, etc.) aimed to instruct, move, convince, or amuse the listener or reader.

This point of view is preeminently represented by present-day analysis of communication and the functions proceeding from it. By showing that all linguistic form derives from the system of the values that enable it to fulfil this or that function, we arrive at rhetoric while at the same time showing that the traditional "figures" correspond to functions that implicitly subtend the genres.

Thus modern, formalist, deductive, and functional linguistics enters spontaneously upon the paths of rhetoric, but armed this time with concepts of structure and communication as well as a whole methodological apparatus capable of newly describing and defining genres and traditional figures. In other words, by emphasizing communication on the one hand, and form and function on the other, modern linguistics is rediscovering and rejuvenating the old notion of "figures of style." In fact, figures—of sound, word, construction, thought—are distinctions whose form is defined in relation both to the grammatical norm and to the genre—i.e., to the type of communication. In this regard, rhetoric is the art of choosing a specific form acting as subject and situation.

Bally's *Traité de Stylistique Française*, conceived as the study of "expressive forms" in contrast to "logical and intellective forms," already reemploys the old distinction between grammatical forms and rhetorical figures, the latter consisting of "a manner of speaking that is more vivid than ordinary language and aimed either at making an idea perceptible via an image, a comparison, or at commanding increased attention by its correctness or originality." But Bally's analysis places the facts in an entirely new perspective, showing that, far from being marginal forms, figures are directly rooted in language and that, as Valéry says:

> If I venture to investigate these usages, or rather these abuses, of the language that are grouped under the vague and general title of "figures," all I find is the abandoned vestiges of that very imperfect analysis which the old writers had attempted to make of those "rhetorical" phenomena. Now these figures, so neglected by modern criticism, play a vitally important role, not only in declared and organized poetry but also in that perpetually active poetry which plagues the fixed vocabulary, dilates or restrains the meaning of words, operating on them by symmetries or conversions, continually altering the values of that currency; and, at times through the mouth of the people, at times through the unforeseen needs of technical expression, at times by the writer's hesitant pen, begets that variation of language which imperceptibly turns it into something quite different. No one seems even to have embarked on the resumption of this analysis.[1]

Today Paul Valéry's wish has been fulfilled, and even if we do not yet have that exhaustive and systematic repertoire of figures, the "very imperfect analysis which the old writers had attempted" has been resumed, and often in highly precise terms; and above all we have come to recognize the expressive powers and literary functions not only of "figures" but of all grammatical forms and particularly of the most neutral ones, of those that appear to be the most empty, such as articles, genders, pronouns, etc. In redefining linguistic forms and exploring their functions, modern linguistics has brought the powers of language to light and recognized the nature of the effects which the writer has instinctively and more or less unconsciously always obtained from them.

A clear definition of the past-continuous tense, for example, and of the system of contrasts determining these values, enables us to understand why it is the preferred tense of classical *narratio* and, furthermore, to grasp the reasons leading to the adoption of the imperfect tense by realistic novelists and of the present tense by the "new novel" of today.

In *Le Degré zéro de l'écriture*, the critic Roland Barthes demonstrates this historic and historicizing value of the past-continuous as well as its relation to the pronoun *il*; and in exploring the idea of style he sees in this usage a "manner of writing," i.e., a form through which the author manifests his adhesion to a social ethic of the novel.

At this point linguistic reflection brings us not only to a subtler and more profound description of the form of a work but to a new definition of literature and its functions. Today, therefore, literary criticism is indebted to the linguist for new criteria and new models. Without doubt, no one has contributed more in this area than Roman Jakobson. His definition of metaphor as a figure of similarity, as opposed to metonym as a figure of contiguity, not only clarifies the nature of tropes, but, when extrapolated, shows that they correspond to the two great imaginative types that play a fundamental role in both literature and the arts. To contrast, for example, the metonymic imagination of the Romantics and the Symbolists is to throw a conclusive light on the history of contemporary poetry.

The role of the metonym in dreams and myths permits us to wonder whether the poetic function of this figure is not of much greater importance than the metaphor, the chosen object of critical thought. Armed with this criterion, we can now decipher the great metaphors described by Bachelard as metaphorized metonyms.

We will not discuss here the schema of communication as taken up again by Jakobson, with its six functions: referential, emotive, conative, poetic, phatic, and metalinguistic; it is well known. But it is important to point out that it has resulted in a complete renewal of the study of genres by showing that, far from being artifices, they correspond to specific and natural forms of communication.

There is, of course, nothing new in this—apart from the contrasting of similarity and contiguity—but the strictness of the analysis and the clarity of the definitions are enough to illumine and restate the old problem, to which the solutions had appeared exhausted.

Particularly fruitful in this regard is Jakobson's definition of the poetic function, conceived as "the projection of the principle of equivalence from the axis of selection upon the axis of combination." Or more simply: A relationship exists between the place of words and their form, their meaning, and their syntactical function. Again, nothing new here, of course; but the definition allows us to distinguish, formulate, and classify a whole ensemble of facts—parallelism, symbolics of sounds, rhythm, meter, etc.—of which we hitherto had but a shadowy intuition in regard to both form and functioning.

We find, for example, that the traditional figures of sound and construction in rhetoric correspond to this definition:

Antanaclasis, in which the repeated word alters the meaning.

Anaphora, consisting of repetition of a word at the beginning of several sentences or lines of verse.

Anadiplosis, or the repetition at the beginning of a sentence of a word occurring at the end of the preceding sentence. And so on.

Samuel Levin's *Linguistic Structures in Poetry* (Mouton and Co., The Hague, 1964) proceeds directly from Jakobson's principle, whence he derives his theory of "coupling" while at the same time giving a precise formula and an inventory of the different forms of coupling.

All these definitions, however, are more than a mere accommodation of old facts to the prevailing fashion beneath the plumage of modern jargon; this new formulation allows us to understand linguistic mechanisms, stylistic properties, and literary functions that until now we only saw in a glass darkly.

As an example of the linguist's contribution to criticism, I would now like to offer a stylistic analysis and literary interpretation of free indirect style. I propose to do this by starting with two new concepts: the "shift" and the "locutive."

Once again it is to Jakobson that we owe the concept of the "shifter," although, of course, we already find it in Jespersen and Benveniste, the latter calling it the "indicator"; but Jakobson gives us a clear description of the role of such words in communication and hence in literary texts.

"Shifters" or "indicators" are words that have no meaning of their own but indicate the functioning persons and things of the communication in which the latter are implicated. *Personal pronouns*, for example: "I" denotes "the person who is speaking." *Demonstrative pronouns*: "this one" denotes the person or thing that is "approached by the speakers." *Adverbs of time and place*: "today," "here." *Time*: the "present" is "the moment when the communication takes place," etc. The predicate phrase implies two times, two places, two series of persons: the time and place of the communication, the persons who are speaking or present in the communication; and on the other hand the time, place, and persons of which or of whom one is speaking.

These two levels of speaking and the spoken always exist in every predicate communication, assuming that the predicativity consists in speaking of, or in telling something to, someone. And when the "speaking subject" says "I," this "grammatical subject" is a spoken subject, and when he speaks in the present, the present of the person speaking is distinct from the spoken present.

So we see that there is a coincidence between the two subjects and the two times, since the two levels of communication are distinct when the speaking subject speaks of someone else, or speaks in the past tense.

This concept of levels of communication plays an essential part in literary expression, and particularly in the narrative genres which imply a narrator distinct from the person about whom he is speaking. Hence the importance—often pointed out by criticism—of the personal pronoun in the novel. For "I," "you," "he," etc., refer to two distinct entities: on the one hand the "speaking subject" and on the other the "grammatical subject":

"The three pronouns are projections of the speaker's thought; and the 'I' indicates a distinct and separate self which the *loquens* observes, thinks, and speaks and which he detaches from himself in order to endow it with time, space, and the modalities of its speaking existence. . . ." And since I have begun to quote myself, I may perhaps be permitted to recall what I wrote not long ago on this subject:

> There is such a thing as a narrative "I" that is not to be confused with the autobiographical "I" and the pseudoautobiographical "I" and that extracts the "I" from its history the better to place it in History, where the self contemplates itself. Michel Butor has given us a perfect demonstration of this game of novelistic mirrors and has put into practice the narrative usage of the pronoun. Take, for instance, the "you" in *La Modification*: it is a "you" of the character-narrator who is talking to himself and at the same time addressing the reader, whom he attracts and confines within this intimate dialogue. This "you" corresponds to the fictitious "I" but removes the narration from the narrator's time and places it in that of the reader.[2]

Roman Jakobson's analysis of "shifters" enables us to grasp and analyze the mechanism of these alterations of level within communication. These alterations become especially complex and subtle when—as often happens in the novel—the character is himself the narrator and the author introduces a narrative within his narrative. This, as we shall see, is the problem that is resolved by the use of three "styles": direct, indirect, and free indirect. But before embarking on this question we must say a word about *expressivity*.

We know that language corresponds to a dual function according to which it either indicates objectively the object that is being spoken about or expresses the feelings and emotions of the speaking subject. This idea—by no means new—is central to Bally's work; but the concept of *shifter* allows us to pinpoint and explore it while showing that semeiological indications and expressive connotations occur on two distinct planes of communication, the first of these referring to what is narrated, the second to the narrator.

Among all the distinguishing features—phonetic, lexical, syntactical—that form the basis for expressivity, a special place should be given to prosody and to what I myself have described elsewhere as "the locutive." A sentence develops along a twofold line: there is the predicative phrase, made up of a succession of signs whose relationships are defined by the rules of grammar and of such nature that a speaking subject places in the predicate a person or thing of which he is speaking; and then, on these grammatical signs, are superimposed prosodic, suprasegmental variations which, via the modulations of the voice, express the feelings and emotions of the speaking subject.

This is well known; what is perhaps less so, and what I have tried to show, is that the predicative phrase and the prosodic line constitute two distinct semeiological systems.

The imperative, the vocative, and "word phrases" such as "Fire!", "Excellent!", or "Oh, what a beautiful horse!", etc., do not belong within the system of normal sentences; hence the difficulty of finding a place for them in grammars. They comprise neither verb nor subject since they do not "tell something about someone"; they are acts in which the modulations of voice "express" the feelings of the speaking subject. When I exclaim: "Oh, what a beautiful horse!" I am not saying that the horse is beautiful: I am expressing the sense of beauty which I experience in the presence of that horse. This is why I prefer to substitute for the concept of "word phrase" that of the "locutive phrase," the latter being an autonomous statement and not a mere transposition of the predicative phrase. In other words, "the beautiful horse" does not mean: "this horse *is* beautiful" (the way it is usually expressed) but: "the speaking subject *experiences a sense* of beauty in the presence of this horse."

So we see that an ordinary sentence transmits two messages at once: a predicative message by means of which the speaking subject *says* something about someone, and a locutive message by means of which he *expresses* his feelings with regard to that statement. It is therefore effective at two simultaneous levels: that of the narrated, and that of narrator and narration.

Phaedra, for example, confesses to Oenone the love she had once felt in Athens for Hippolytus; and at the same time the form of this narrative and the tone of the recital express the pain, shame, and remorse she is feeling here and now in the very act of this confession.

We shall now see that the three styles are simply three types of relationships between the predicative phrase and the locutive phrase. Their purpose is to introduce a statement within a statement: the narrator says something concerning a character "being narrated," but this predicate attributed to the character "being narrated" is something that the latter says about a second person or thing being narrated, the object of a second statement. So there are two narrators and two narrations (two persons, two places, two narrated times), the second being subordinate to the first. In its simplest form, this statement-within-a-statement is expressed by a proposition subordinated by *that* to a declarative verb such as *to say, to think, to believe*. The predicative syntax defines these subordination rules, which consist in placing the tense and the pronoun in perspective—e.g.: "I am happy" becomes "he said that he was happy," and so on. The essential feature of this statement, subordinated in this way, is that it is of a purely predicative type and implies no locutive message. For the latter is linked to the voice of the speaker, and the secondary speaker does not participate in the communication: he has no voice. This accounts for the impossibility of transposing the locutive sentence into the subordinate. The secondary speaker has in fact been able to say: "How happy I am!", "I'm madly happy!", "What bliss!", etc.; but none of these variations is possible in the subordinate sentence, which is limited to the use of the construction: "He said that he was happy"; and although one might, at a pinch, say: ". . . that he was *madly* happy," the adverb loses its emotional intonation. This causes the indirect style to neutralize the locutive sentence, and the statement to lose one of its chief dimensions.

The solution lies in the direct style, in which the primary (and effective) speaker reproduces the statement of the secondary and absent speaker and lends him his voice: e.g., "*He said*: 'how happy I am!' "

But now a new dilemma arises, for if the primary speaker delegates his voice he no longer possesses it and loses the capacity to express the emotions and feelings that he experiences himself with regard to both the statement and the secondary speaker. For example: John tells Jim that he has been ill, although the form and intonation of the sentence express the feeling of self-pity he experiences in this situation, something like: "I've been as sick as a dog!" Jim has received this dual message, but he is not convinced of the gravity of John's illness, and he finds this self-pity slightly ridiculous. There follows a communication from Jim

to Paul that aims at implying three messages: predicative (John's illness), locutive No. 1 (John's self-pity), and locutive No. 2 (Jim's
sarcasm). But Jim cannot convey both locutive messages at once; he
has to choose between the direct style that allows him to lend his voice
to John, or the indirect style that permits him to state a subordinate
proposition with a sarcastic intonation but does not report John's feelings about his own illness.

Free indirect style provides the solution to this problem in that it
superimposes the primary speaker's voice and the secondary speaker's
voice; or rather, the primary speaker's voice and the secondary speaker's words. In grammatical terms, it is a mixed form: it suppresses the
subordination *that* (the essential feature of indirect style) but preserves
the transposition of tense and personal pronoun:

He was ill, he said.

John arrived late; he had been ill.

He was quite pale; he'd been as sick as a dog!

Such statements permit us to superimpose both intonations: the
primary speaker can reproduce the whining tone of the secondary
speaker; and, by caricaturing it or by combining with it some skeptical
or sarcastic modulations, he can also express his own feelings.

For purposes of simplification, we have so far been analyzing the situation in terms of prosodic variations, but these represent only a particular
case of a group of "expressive" signs that also comprise lexical forms
and syntactical constructions. Both of these latter, side by side with
prosody, play an important part in the manipulation of the three styles.
One of the most frequent forms of free indirect style, for example, consists in reporting the words of a secondary speaker in indirect style but
in adopting his vocabulary—scholarly, dialectic, slangy, etc. This is a
systematic process in Zola's *L'Assommoir*: "He had a laugh like a badly
oiled pulley, nodding his head, his eyes resting fondly on the apparatus
for getting drunk. By Jove, she was a beauty! In that big fat copper pot
there was enough to keep your whistle wet for a week. . . ." It is
expressions such as "that big fat copper pot" and "keep your whistle
wet" which indicate that the statement is reported in the language of
that particular character.

But the process remains the same: the placing of tenses and pronouns
in perspective is the mark of the indirect style that makes self-expression
possible to the author; and "freedom" (i.e., absence of subordination)

is the mark of the direct style that makes self-expression possible to the character to whom voice, vocabulary, and syntax have been partially restored.

The use of the conditional in free indirect style corresponds to the same mechanism. Proust displays this admirably in his pastiches of Flaubert: "They would travel, they would see unknown countries, would experience a new life. . . ." In this sentence the "conditional" superimposes and combines both temporal values and the modal value. In other words, the conditional is a future as it relates to a moment in the past. In direct style, the lovers said: "We will travel . . ."; and in indirect style the author reports these words by putting the future in the perspective of the past: "They said that they would travel . . ." But the conditional tense can also be a mode, and in that case expresses the speaking subject's conception of the action as an unrealized hypothesis: "They would travel if they could: but in actual fact they will not travel."

Now the free indirect style combines both these values; the words "they would travel" refer to both speaking subjects. The characters offer us this journey as a project, but the author lets us know that it will not come about, thus projecting a nostalgic and compassionate look at the illusions of his hero and heroine.

The function of free indirect style is to combine and superimpose the words (voice and linguistic forms) of the narrator and his characters. The importance of its role in the novel is obvious.

Flaubert is the master of this process, a process that is the key to that subjective realism which permits him, as his narration flows along, to espouse the projects, dreams, remorse, hopes, and regrets of his characters while at the same time maintaining the perspective of a gaze that observes and judges them. Let us see how he tells us of the encounter and conversation between Frédéric and Monsieur Arnoux at the beginning of *L'Education sentimentale*:

> The gentleman in the red boots gave advice to the young man; he advanced theories, told anecdotes, using himself as an illustration, and he reeled off all this in a paternal tone combined with amusingly depraved ingenuousness.
>
> He was a Republican; he had traveled, he had inside knowledge of theaters, restaurants, and newspapers, and he knew all the celebrities of the entertainment world, whom he called familiarly by their first names; Frédéric soon confided his plans to him; he encouraged them.

The first paragraph places Jacques Arnoux under the objective gaze of the author (and the reader), who describes his vulgar glibness. The second paragraph is a report of his conversation, but in free indirect style so that Flaubert and Arnoux are both speaking at the same time. It is Flaubert speaking, inasmuch as he does not exactly reproduce his character's words, for the latter did not say: "I am a Republican, I have traveled, I have inside knowledge of theaters . . ."; ridiculous, vain, and naïve though he may be, this is not the way he talks. But it is Arnoux speaking inasmuch as the author superimposes on the indirect sentence the direct intonation of his character. Flaubert says: "He was a Republican" with the naïve intonation of Arnoux proclaiming: "As for me, you know, I am a Republican."

Thus the statement is offered simultaneously as a sample of this conversation and as expressing the character's childish vanity; but it is a selective sample, a caricatural imitation expressing the author's irony.

Frédéric's encounter with Madame Arnoux (a little farther on) carries on with the same process but in a manner even more complex, since here we see Flaubert listening to Frédéric listening to Madame Arnoux: listening and looking, for here three styles of description correspond to the three styles of the discourse:

> When he had moved a little farther away, on the same side, he looked at her.
> She was wearing a wide straw hat whose pink ribbons fluttered in the breeze behind her. Her smooth bands of black hair. . . .

The heroine, seen by the author, is simultaneously subjected to the observation of the characters in the novel: Flaubert and Frédéric observe as one; then the narrator's gaze detaches itself and stands aside in order to watch Frédéric watch Madame Arnoux, and at the same time he is listening to the thoughts passing through Frédéric's mind:

> He gazed at her workbasket in astonishment, as if it were something extraordinary.
> What was her name, where did she live, what were her life, her past? He longed to know what the furniture in her room was like. . . .

But now we shall hear Madame Arnoux speaking:

> A Negress with a silk kerchief around her head appeared, holding by the hand a little girl who was quite tall for her age. The child, whose eyes were brimming with tears, had just woken up. She took her on her knees. "This young lady was not a good girl, although she would soon be seven; her mother wouldn't love her any more; she was too often forgiven for being naughty." And Frédéric rejoiced to hear these things, as if he had made a discovery, an acquisition.

The key to this passage is the report in free indirect style of the mother's words.

In direct style, the sentence is stylized by substituting the third person for the second: "This young lady is not a good girl" (i.e., "you are not a good girl"), and it is a manner of speaking of which the element that Frédéric finds touching is preserved by free indirect style. The description goes on:

> He assumed her to be of Andalusian origin, Creole perhaps: had she brought this Negress back with her from the Islands?
> A long, violet-striped shawl was draped behind her over the brass rail. Many a time, during damp evenings at sea, she must have wrapped herself in it, covered her feet with it, slept in it! But now, weighed down by its fringes, it was gradually slipping, was about to fall into the water; Frédéric sprang forward and caught it.
> "Thank you, Monsieur," she said.
> Their eyes met.

What is described here is not the shawl but Frédéric in process of looking at the shawl and, in free indirect style, the thoughts inspired by that sight. Then the author resumes the description for his own account by inserting at that point Madame Arnoux' words in direct style. And the faithful reproduction of the words: "Thank you, Monsieur," enhances their triteness and Madame Arnoux' indifference, which are further underlined by the next words—the husband's—still in direct style:

> "Are you ready, my dear?" cried Monsieur Arnoux, emerging from the companionway.

Here[3] direct style turns the sentence into a simple object in which the contact between the two characters is broken, whereas the free indirect style of "This young lady is not a good girl . . ." shifts the communication onto Frédéric and is conveyed through him.

The three styles define the form of a secondary statement within the principal statement; the author is reporting the words or thoughts (silent words) of his character. But it is noteworthy that, by using the same mechanism, the same processes may be applied to description and, like words spoken by two voices, the spectacle unfolds beneath a dual gaze. There again Flaubert knows just how to look over the shoulder of his character: at Emma's window, at the rail on Frédéric's ship; or, on the other hand, to move back in order at one moment to watch them looking, and at the next to make them merge in the general scene.

So we see how and why the choice of one of the three styles, or a mixture of them, constitutes one of the basic criteria of the novel. Linguistic analysis shows that tenses, modes, genders, numbers, parts of speech, tropes, constructions, etc., correspond in turn to functions that determine their usage in narrative, drama, lyric poetry, and so on. "Figures" cease to be conceived as anomalous forms, all signs appearing as figures whose form and place in a system of structural contrasts determine values and their usages. In the same way, genres, in addition to purely normative rules, appear as specific forms of communication; hence every text depends on a semeiology of literature that makes use of new models. In this way conditions have been created for a neorhetoric in which linguistics and literary criticism are from now on jointly engaged.

[Translated from the French by Leila Vennewitz]

Notes

1. Paul Valéry, "Questions de poesie," in *Variété*, Vol. 3, p. 45.
2. *La Syntaxe du français* (Paris, 1962), p. 101.
3. I must say "here," because in this case we are dealing with a particular sense that might be entirely different in some other context.

Fritz Martini

PERSONAL STYLE AND PERIOD STYLE: Perspectives on a Theme of Literary Research

---

IT IS TYPICAL OF THE VITALITY OF TODAY'S LITERARY RESEARCH THAT basic methodological trends and positions change rapidly and before long acquire a certain historicity. The prevailing methods of, say, fifteen years ago as applied both to existential observation, and to the intensive interpretation centering on the immediate self-sufficiency of any one literary work, are certainly not obsolete. With their findings and results they have become part of the literary scholar's methodological equipment. At the same time they have been subjected to a critical discussion that curbed those claims to scientific exclusiveness commonly associated with each new breakthrough in methodology. Immanent interpretation, for which the real object of literary research was the autonomous literary work, and which regarded the understanding and interpreting of such a work as its primary task, has lost nothing in importance, especially as a pedagogic approach to the obtaining of scholarly literary insight. But we have now moved away from making it central to the study of literature or allowing the latter to be determined solely by it. The methodological outlook has returned to a historical understanding of literary works as they exist within the network of their historical situation—to a synoptic view of each work and its historical basis which, although never entirely forgotten, had been pushed aside by the claims of immanent interpretation. Immanent interpretation taught, in greater differentiation than before its application, that the study of literature is a science of the art of language (in all its forms, not merely in terms of "poetics" and "literary art"); the countermovement, in resuming the path of a literary work's historicity, has brought home the extent to which the study of literature is a study of history and society.

However, this did not imply a return to an ideohistorically-oriented literary research. This approach, after its groundwork had been laid by Wilhelm Dilthey and others, found general acceptance in the second decade of the twentieth century and has yielded important clarifications and insights; for it created, or at least confirmed, those broad classifying concepts that gave intelligibility to the history of thought in its contexts and influences up to and well into the first third of the nineteenth century and caused each era to stand out as an intellectual entity.

Nevertheless, ideohistorical research failed to cope satisfactorily with a number of aspects. Not without a certain abstracting constructivism, it linked each creative artist to broad epochal, intellectual, and idealistic trends of a general historical nature, to the point where the laws governing his very existence and giving his work its specific character became indistinct and even indistinguishable. It caused the element of individuality to be swallowed up in general movements and trends that gave priority to the intellectual physiognomy of over-all historical situations. Furthermore, it led to the practice of a literary work's being examined primarily on the basis of its general perspectives on life, its historical, idealistic, and stylistic category. This meant that a work was examined not for its own sake but as a mirror and example relating to broad associations whose sources and reality lay outside its own. The ideohistorical method led to alienation from a work as a specific structure subject to its own laws; while at the same time, in its tendency toward type-forming constructivism, in its interpretation of history as an immanent intellectual development governed by type-laws, it led to alienation from concrete historical conditions and determinants in their constantly self-renewing and shifting individuality. And finally, for the sake of large-scale syntheses the ideohistorical approach led to a forfeiting of accuracy in terms both of the work itself and its specific historical background; and its opposition—ultimately and unmistakably rooted in Hegel's philosophy—to the positivism of literary research that had preceded it meant that despite its gains it was not without some loss.

On the other hand, existential study of literature and the acceptance of the absolute status of immanent interpretation were linked to a state of mind of the advancing twentieth century that became particularly noticeable in Germany after World War II. For many reasons (which I shall not go into here), this state of mind entailed the demolition—

the negation, even—of historical thought, and a deep-seated skepticism
toward history. The search for the existential signified the inward-
concentrating "I"-experience of the solitary individual who, banished
from the protective niches of history, a victim of its blandishments and
destructions, saw himself brought defenceless before the powers of existence and obliged to assert or vindicate himself to them. Works of
literature were interpreted as the response to this existential experience.
There was no denying, of course, that the historical period influenced
the form and presentation of such works; but the substance and inner
compulsion of "I" and work were made to stand emphatically alone
and apart from any absorption into the flow of history. In its most
radical form this observation method could not but entail a negation
of existence in terms of history—which is false, since the existential aspects of human life must always include existence in terms of history.

So it is only partially correct to say that the focusing of a work on
personal style or period style results from the particular problem as
reflected in the title of this essay; for above and beyond this there exist
between the two styles profound interrelationships that have in turn
undergone an evolution of their own. It has been of particular benefit
to the historical approach, and the methods of literary research spring-
ing from it, that the question of the relationship between individual
existence and the historicity of existence, between personality and period, has once again been raised and considerably expanded by the emphatically existential presentation of the question. Seen thus, it would
appear necessary to return to biographical research which, because of
its one-sided positivist orientation, was long held in low esteem: to return, that is, to research which must now be able to penetrate purely
factual, statistically historical material in order to grasp the substantial
and essential elements of individual existence with an acuteness of perception that must not balk at discomforting exposures. This implies a
restatement of the problem of the context and dialectic of period style
as rooted in and conditioned by history, and of personality style as an
existential phenomenon. What complicates the matter still further is
the addition of two questions as third and fourth components: first,
what are the conditions affecting the generic style of a work; and second, what are the conditions affecting the sociological group style with
a view to historical understanding? It is not hard to see, therefore, that,
looked at in this light, almost all our biographies of poets and writers
are in need of a thoroughgoing revision.

The fact that the basic question of immanent interpretation—what
is literature (in the sense of *Dichtung*), how should it be read, felt, under-

stood, defined—was raised with such urgency indicates the extent to which the understanding of literary art per se had become a problem. Since then, critical reflection on the scope of poetic language has found no rest, let alone definitive answers. On the contrary, it has acquired additional dimensions: to aesthetic questions on the nature of a literary work as such, and how far the latter's attributes are to be distinguished from colloquial and common speech forms, is now added the urgent sociological question of its function, which must of necessity redetermine its aesthetic structure. Today's concept of "literature" goes— with many good reasons—far beyond what was formerly distinguished and known as *Dichtung*. But at the same time it entails a degree of uncertainty toward *Dichtung*—not only toward its convention. This uncertainty extends to contemporary production as well as to works of the past. Creative production now seems possible only when submitted at the same time, with critical reflection, to an intensive self-questioning. Caution must be exercised in making perspective historical generalizations, but until well into the past century there were times when *Dichtung* was allotted an accepted place and a generally acknowledged validity in the cultural consciousness, times when it was included in this consciousness as a creation of authority and value. As a result, every genre had its standards of thematic and formal structure; these varied, of course, with era and period style, but the basic attitude toward the "higher" levels of literature remained constant. The literature of modern times, initiated with the Romantic era and acquiring self-awareness with Friedrich Nietzsche, presents a picture—insofar as it does not stagnate in dubious safe harbors of tradition—of constant critical questioning as to the meaning, authority, and legitimacy, the scope and function, of this art. This literature is fighting for survival against its own skepticism; its value rises in proportion to its increasing awareness of this skepticism and the degree to which it incorporates it in the work.

In these inquiries into the nature of artistic literary creation and literature in general, we have left behind those former disputes over the validity or permanence of this or that genre, form, or style; we are no longer observing a fluctuating and developing process within a recognized system of literary art. Now the question is: What *is* literary art, what are its functions, how can it be created? What were formerly valid, established value-concepts and articles of faith regarding the poetic, the beautiful, the tragic, the harmonious, the noble, the transfiguring—all these and others which, however relativized, were in common use until the first revolution in literature toward the end of the nineteenth century—have now become invalid, a process that has been enhanced along with our growing knowledge that poetic or literary utterance has a specific historicity, that it belongs to and is committed to a specific period. The very fact of this radically altered contemporary awareness demands an altered attitude toward the works of the past and engenders the search for a language of its own. This questioning naturally affected literary research, which is aware—perhaps more than formerly—of its common interests with the creative artist, while, by the same token, the latter is now directing greater, albeit critical, attention toward literary research. The awareness of the historicity of one's own time, of one's obligations to it, with which self-critical and creative unrest inform contemporary literature in a multitude of voices, must affect literary scholarship and not only its attitude toward history: it must also intensify its concern with historical phenomena. This has released literary scholarship from the spell of exclusiveness cast by immanent interpretation.

It is no longer necessary, as it was some fifteen years ago, to speak of its limitations and to plead that interpretation be opened up to the concrete historicity of a work. This need diminishes the more this historicity is implied by the increasing influence of the sociological perspective in literary research, although, as is already becoming perceptible, with a propensity on its part to regard a literary work as no more than a sociological document, to let it be swallowed up by sociological typologies and systematizations. Only where interpretation of a work *qua* an autonomous work goes hand in hand with its historical and/or sociological interpretation can the legitimate path—in methodological and factual terms—be initiated.

It can be seen that, despite the relativization of the methodological processes applied to the existential interpretation and immanent interpretation embarked upon some fifteen years ago to answer the question put before us, the question itself has lost none of its scientific topicality. In fact, as a result of sociological methods, it has expanded in dimension and become more complex. What is the relationship between a work's highly individual, "autonomous" elements of personal style on the one hand, and the historicity of its content, genre, and form, of the handling of language (including rhythmizations) on the other: in short, between its period style and, sociologically speaking, its group style?

Obviously there can be no over-all answer to this question, no answer based on a systematic analysis of stylistics. It is a historical question.

At various periods of time, period style and individual style have entered upon all kinds of shifting associations. The only reliable answer is the one given for each individual and historical case. It can vary from example to example even in the work of the same author, and even more so in works of the same era. It would seem that the opportunities for research offered here have for some considerable time been sadly neglected.

However, merely to contrast personality or individual style with period style is to oversimplify the problem. There is no such thing as an individual style that does not simultaneously relate to the style of the genre in whose traditions or innate laws its literary product is rooted. There is no such thing as a period style unrelated to a group style, regardless of whether the former is a reflection of the latter, or whether it evolves and takes shape by contrast with, by nonconformity with, the group style. Under specific historical circumstances, the majority of genres find their equivalents in a majority of group styles within one era or one particular time-span. As a matter of fact, literary generic forms and methods of presentation display a widely varying relationship to the principles of form and effect implanted in them, principles that may be altered but never wholly eliminated. They are alterable as style traditions and even more so as style conventions; they are not alterable as innate laws of form. At the same time, they are limited in scope by objective functional laws existing outside the artistic generic immanence. Drama is closely linked to the form of theater by which it intends to be presented if it is to achieve its true vocation and reality. This dependence may be strict, as in Greek tragedy or classical drama, or it may be loose, allowing plenty of leeway, as in the theater of today with its extensions to the "happening," to what is known as "director's theater." Either way it remains a close link derived from generic form and the functions of generic form. The genre of song is dependent on the innate laws of music and singing—i.e., of presentation: and whether we are dealing with hymns or popular songs, with songs of personal experience or mood, or with topical night-club songs, we will find highly variable forms and degrees of intensity within these links. Or take narrative prose: despite relatively greater elasticity in its available choice of forms, it too is subject to certain innate laws of genre and effect, depending on the chosen genre of novel, novella, short story, etc., laws that derive from the fact of storytelling and determine the story's constructional forms.

In addition to the poetological historicity of generic associations there is the work's functional quality—varying according to period—

that is easily lost sight of when interpretation is limited to poetic sub-stance. This has led to an overlooking of the influential significance and hence the historical determination of, say, the political-rhetorical or the didactic literary specimen—in short, of all forms of "applied" lit-erature. If literature is not only to "move" us but—to use a term much in vogue today—to become "engaged," it must be removed from its isolated position in "aesthetics," incorporated in its own concrete socio-historical context, and measured by this context. It need hardly be pointed out that interpretation cannot be restricted to these sociological relationships, nor can these be the sole source of evaluating criteria.

However, the problem of personal and individual style on the one hand, and period style and group style on the other, is not merely a matter of analysis and differentiation of individual expression and of the expression of period type or group type. It is also concerned with the knotty questions of literary evaluation which in recent times have been the subject of much vigorous discussion. One answer—although not the only possible answer—presents itself immediately: the more a literary work corresponds to period style, the greater its dependence on a particular and limited historical situation, topical within it, tran-sient like it, and the more it becomes a document capable of consider-able value as a historical witness, but—and this is the point—confined to the purely historical. Seen from the aspect of critique, the weaker the imprint of individual expressivity, the greater will be an accommo-dation to traditions and conventions, to topically prevailing trends in taste and style, and the less likelihood will there be of the language and its forms being strong enough to endure.

But there can also be another answer. There are certain works in which individuality and period, existential elements and history, co-incide to such an extent that it is in this very reflection of period style that the power of creative personality achieves fulfilment, and thus those great works of art become possible in which an era learns to un-derstand itself, to contemplate and experience itself, and in which the identification of genius and epoch produces secular creations embracing an entire and unified world as their content and form. What happens here is that the power of the artist is fully released through its encounter with a particular period, with the essential topics, interests, and assump-tions of form inherent in this period, whereas in other historical situa-tions a nevertheless possibly strong potential fails to find these assump-tions and is thus frustrated in its development and achievement. We might recall a saying of Friedrich Hebbel's, who himself suffered as a dramatist from having arrived too late on the historical scene: that if a second Homer were to be born now, there would be merely one more unhappy creature in the world.

The relationship between personal and period style must not be considered—as it was under the influence of the prevailing concept of genius until after the start of the nineteenth century—a one-way channel in which the generative force of a great individual impregnates the period in which he is living. What actually takes place is a reverse process of inner dialectics in which the artist, in creating, becomes the one who conceives and responds; while the period—seen as historical conditions, as society, as state of mind, as the public—becomes the challenging and molding element. There is nothing here that can be grasped by a system, no antithetical Either/Or; the task of literary research is to attain a synoptic view of the creative link between the individual and the historical, difficult though it may be to distinguish and define each of these in each case. Formulas that attempt to distinguish between personal and period style tend to produce, methodologically speaking, overly artificial isolations. Individual style and period style: there are still enough open questions here which, at any given time, can be answered only in terms of the particular individual and historical situation and which require the aid of interpretation and an existential study of literature.

There is yet another aspect to which we must call attention. The regarding of period style as a common and supraindividual constant of all representative forms in any one period in which trends evolved more or less compulsorily according to sociohistorical development led to a certain evaluative point of view being adopted. This point of view was based on the assumption that style was equivalent to identity of content and form, to a uniformity and wholeness of form. Wherever this unity of style occurred in history, a higher artistic rating followed automatically; this rating sank wherever plurality and contradiction in styles were encountered in a given period. This evaluative skepticism was especially prevalent where the nineteenth-century plastic arts and literature were concerned, since it was difficult to attribute a uniform style to these. This skepticism was directed typically—in various ways according to the various arts—at the crossing and mixing of different types of traditional and progressive style trends—often, indeed, in a single author and a single work. However, as against what was actually a classicistic prejudice for placing a higher value on a historically and artistically uniform style, it may be said that this other historic and artistic situation need not *a priori* imply something negative. A unified period style can also be negative in effect. It may conventionalize the artistic element, it may reduce it to a mediocre level and allow it to lapse into rigidity. It may impede individual expression, it may even cripple and stifle it. For the more firmly the ideals and demands of style are determined by a period, a society—and also by the innate generic laws always closely associated with it—the smaller becomes the scope for diversity and subjectivity in individual forms of expression. This reverse process did not begin until the early nineteenth century. As a result, that period's relationship between period style and individual style is an especially complex one, but, in terms of literary research, perhaps an especially interesting one.

That century was determined—at least since Goethe and the Romantics, even if we prefer not to go as far back as subjectivism and the pre-Romantic trends that began to appear around the mid-eighteenth century—by the category of expressive art; consequently it saw artistic utterance and form primarily in terms of their expressivity. It interpreted style solely as the particular personal expression arising from the artist's subjectivity and spiritual resources. From then on, the mark of protocreativity, of personal thematics, form, and utterance, was essential to positive literary evaluation. Hegel interpreted the artist's situation as a twofold one: the artist is no longer seen as restricted to certain forms and attitudes; instead, he is now entitled, because of what he is, to move freely above Things, and he has ceased to feel bound to any "as it were sanctified conditions . . . of his creative activity." Yet at the same time his creative product acquires the character of a subjective affirmation inasmuch as he informs it, by drawing on his spiritual resources, with a higher content.

In Hegel we read: "Thus the artist finds his content within himself; he is the truly self-determining human spirit who contemplates, imagines, and expresses the infinity of his emotions and situations, to whom nothing that can spring to life in the human breast is foreign."

This relegating of artistic creativity to the status of subjectivity has been prevalent since the close of the eighteenth century; it ceased to acknowledge any suprapersonal formal traditions and innate laws and did away with generic conventions and their social context, seeming to find reflection in those frequently quoted words of Buffon, the French natural scientist: *"Le style c'est l'homme même."* But we must bear in mind that those words were directed primarily at psychological-physiognomic aspects and not at those of expression and affirmation; they cannot be translated indiscriminately into the language of nineteenth-century aesthetics, as has been done in disregard of their historical context.

These words seemed to prove that style, in order to achieve any artistic quality, must always be the style inherent in the subjective and productive personality. This attitude of aesthetics toward experience and affirmation continued to exert influence until well into the twentieth century, although there was no lack of arguments and trends against it. Poetic utterance is still seen primarily as a personal statement, as the expression of subjective consciousness. "The personal tone is everything. . . . A new and bold combination of words is the most wonderful gift to the soul," wrote the young Hugo von Hofmannsthal. Franz Kafka remarked in his diary: "To fill the word wholly with oneself."

Seen in this light, style would appear to have become the personal existential decision of each artist. This, if taken to its logical conclusion, means that the only thing to be expected and achieved in style is "my" truth as offered in each separate poetic utterance. Yet it is Gottfried Benn's existential voice which claims to represent the phenotype of the historical-topical situation and which, moreover, aims at the "absolute" in art, just as Self and Time and an objective Being of art claim to interpenetrate. It is true that the decline of experiential and confessional writing which is the mark of contemporary literature has caused us to reopen our eyes to social function, to social content and application, and has defined poetic utterance according to its social utility; yet since social commitment is seen simultaneously as opposition to a given contemporary society, personal utterance, as well as subjectivity of style, are still further enhanced in this social commitment.

This contemporary literature, however, evinces a new interest in the traditions of Greek and Roman rhetoric—i.e., in those forms of speech and style that are woven throughout Occidental literature in an unbroken continuity and have marked off with reasonable accuracy the range of whatever linguistic and stylistic formal movements were available to it. These forms of speech and style constitute type examples and type models of such diversity that they are open to individual usage in combinations and variations that virtually exceed enumeration. Each separate structuring of form and speech moves within this historically preformed typization of style figures—in greatly varying degrees, of course, both historically and individually. But just because it is an individual structuring, it also, in these self-same degrees, brings flexibility into this typization; it endows it with a highly differentiated expressive content and can manipulate it at will, so that the same style figure can yield expressive potential and meaning-referents of great variability according to the structure, *ductus*, and context of the utterance as a whole.

The systematization of stylistic forms on the one hand, and the individual expressive quality yielded by each on the other, are not so easy to harmonize. When a writer creates a style, the power behind this act is revealed by the manner in which he manipulates rhetorical examples and models in his own way and liberates this style from its normative requirements and validities. In other words, the fact that style forms were restricted to a prescribed set of canons governing linguistic range did not run counter to the experience that every utterance and structuring can express a personal artistic experience of the self and interpretation of the world.

As we have already indicated, the need for this has become accentuated since the end of the eighteenth century. It started off with a definable historical phase in which a common and unified period style was rejected as an intolerable convention and standardization, one reason being that it was regarded as the group style of hitherto ruling classes. The opposition to an objectivized manner of utterance, to literary composition in established and prescribed forms that could turn into rigid formulas, indicated an altered social climate, a situation that found its first full expression in European reactions to the French Revolution. Paul Böckmann has been able to show that each of the various stages of the history of form until the eighteenth century was marked by a firm, period-oriented style superimposed so forcefully over personal expressivity that in prose and poetry this personal expressivity was virtually swallowed up by the objectivizations and common elements of the period style. Even when we can differentiate group styles within a certain period of time, we find that they are still dominated by the elements of the period style. This also applies where—as in the differentiation of various style levels during the seventeenth century according to the traditions of ancient rhetoric—we believe we can distinguish sociologically definable group styles.

Admittedly, the "lower" style and its corresponding forms in drama, lyric poetry, and narrative prose are used to represent the lower social classes. But this style was chosen from the perspective of the upper class and, supported by generic traditions, its function lay in its contrast with upper-class style- and speech-forms, a contrast that buttressed rather than ruptured the authority of these forms.

In the seventeenth century, therefore, the "lower" style played a corroborative role in the period and group style exemplifying the socio-intellectual upper class. It extended this style to include possibilities of comedy and satire which it relegated—as representing a "lower" reality —to a lower level than the higher claims and validities of the period and group style. However, neither style was aiming at a depiction of reality as the expression of an individual reality. It has often been asked where the boundaries between typization, convention, social canon, and experiential or expressive truth are to be found in Middle High German minnesongs, in the lyric poetry of the Age of Humanism or Baroque, in the poetry of the Enlightenment or the Rococo era; where the boundaries are to be drawn between the depiction of prescribed content and form and personal expression in seventeenth-century trag-edy. Until the end of the eighteenth century, prose and poetry devel-oped to their fullest extent within the structure of a suprapersonal objectivity that determined their form, style, and language, an objec-tivity that restricts the individual but at the same time provides him with great security and skill in the use of language. This objectivity is determined by the canon of generic poetics, of rhetoric, and by the society that has accepted this canon and given it a mandate. The eighteenth century opens with the confrontation with this canon and attempts to detach itself from it, a process that varies according to governing traditional ties, to the vigor and progressiveness of literary reflection and creativity, and to the social prerequisites of these latter. Until about 1800, period styles can be shown to be groupings of category and made to relate to the course of over-all intellectual and social history. A common element is given by the supporting religious, philo-sophical, and social orders and commitments, from which the individual neither wishes to nor can withdraw since it is within them that, even on the personal level, he can find full expression. In its unity with period style, his writing acquires a representative character. In this style he expresses himself as an individual, but this "I" knows that it relates constantly to what is common to all, and in this common element it finds sufficient scope.

However, it is as well to bear in mind a certain illusion stemming from the perspective of the historian; the greater the gap between him-self and the times under observation, the greater the tendency for indivuality to merge with uniformity, and the easier it seems to perceive or construct a totality that spans the separate and the individual and

may be called period style. The closer the eye approaches the objects
under observation, the more distinct become the outlines and contours
of single entities and individual aberrations; the farther it moves away,
the more these are lost to view in the general panorama of the structure
of the epoch.

Nevertheless there can be no doubt that, until the end of the eighteenth century, the determining factor in each historical period was more
a representative voice oriented toward object, form, and society than
one which subjectively broke down object and form and sought emancipation from social involvement, a voice in which the "I" looked
inward and sought self-expression in its own way. Until the end of the
eighteenth century it was the convictions, conventions, and exemplars
valid during a writer's time that were the source of the outer and inner
reality, together with all its associations, to which he gave shape. He
transformed what he received into an artistic achievement of his own
which, whether as composition, as beautiful, elegant, or noble form, as
glory and clarity of speech, as pithy and ornamental metaphor, as
evocative figure of speech, or whatever, was essentially a complete
artistic entity verifiable and assessable according to established and
generally accepted rules. Thus a linguistic work was a creation spring-
ing from an objective cultural consciousness evidenced in objective
forms. It was evidence of the formative power of Man vis-a-vis the
given world. At the same time it was evidence of the extent to which
Man could utilize the cultural heritage with which history provided
him. From the traditions and laws of his chosen genres in lyric poetry,
drama, and the epic as understood and practiced during his time, he
received the forms of presentation which he had to fill according to
their rules. From the society in which he moved and on which he
depended he received the norms of choice of material and theme, the
norms of manners, outlook, and morals. He schooled himself on the
relevant model, trying to attain and surpass this model by a still
greater artistic perfection. He created literature within the acknowledged continuity of literature. He moved within the categories of what
was—intellectually speaking—the general and social period style and
of the poetological generic style, categories whose scope was large
enough for him to avoid conflict with them in his search for a personal
expression of his own. Period style and generic style were data of a
supraindividual kind. Exceptional situations could, of course, arise, but
precisely because they were isolated exceptions, they do not alter the
over-all historical situation.

Drama in its forms of tragedy and comedy; poetic forms such as the ode, the ballad, or even the folk song (as still conceived and treated, for instance, by the young Goethe); the forms of the novel; all these were more or less established form types, prescribed as to contents, motives, and language levels. They had their place within the period's general system of thought and evaluation and thus transcended literature and pointed to the over-all valid system of looking at and interpreting the world. At the same time they had their place in the life of society, and from this life they received a function that is reflected in Horace's famous postulate, *prodesse et delectare*, which until the end of the eighteenth century was taken for granted. Awareness of the world, poetological theory, the creative practice of literature and the society that produced and supported it, formed a close network of interrelationships. Nor did this network slacken when in the eighteenth century the prevailing social class became the bourgeoisie struggling toward a sense of self. This emancipation process did not become fully effective until the individual emerged from it with a subjective sense of self. For a long time, German literary scholars, nurtured on the spirit of the Romantics and particularly on Goethe, were looking for a personal statement of expression and mood in a literature that was concerned chiefly with the expression of objective content and conformity to objective forms within the confines of period (or social group) style and generic style. Personal expression could be injected into this utterance, but there was no attempt to manipulate it with subjective freedom.

The period covering *Sturm und Drang*, the Romantic era, and its repercussions on the first decades of the nineteenth century, signified a shift, a crisis; consequently, in the confrontation between tradition and new creativity, it became an extraordinarily productive period. The suprapersonal religious ties disintegrated in the various trends of the eighteenth century—Pietism, Enlightenment, Sentimentalism, and so on; the French Revolution swept aside the suprapersonal authorities in political and social life; the standardizations of literary forms in content and language fell apart in the intellectual and literary revolution which was initiated by European subjectivism and which in Germany first erupted in *Sturm und Drang* and then blossomed freely in the Romantic movement and all that flowed from it. The individual, now conscious of a productive autonomy of his essential self, dissociated himself from those standardizations just as much as from those of society.

Lessing's aesthetics and critique were still based on objective and normative canons of form; Herder's aesthetics and critique are based on empathy, the power to experience and the resultant subjectivity. Lessing, despite the critical perspective he maintained toward ruling society, lived within his century; Herder, aware of the separate and superior claims of genius, dissociates himself from his century. Thus began the great, creativity-releasing drama of spiritual detachment— away from forms and toward personal, individual expression—in drama, in poetry, and in narrative prose (Goethe's *Leiden des jungen Werthers*). While it is true that this represents a common epochal event, a common generational movement, it is difficult to speak here of a period style in the old sense. What is crucial and unprecedented about it is that the writer deliberately and provocatively adopts a hostile stance vis-a-vis the given circumstances of his time, that he becomes a nonconformist and feels himself to be a solitary figure who must and will express himself as a separate individual. He "opts out" of traditions and society. He takes up an entirely new position toward the public. He challenges it with himself and his work—a split occurs between the self-awareness of the poet and the general climate of the public, a split that has remained essentially unaltered.

As a result, the necessity of finding, in the throes of the creative force of imagination, a wholly personal, uniquely individual language capable of expressing this otherness acquires an unprecedented urgency. The poet flings down his person, with its convictions, its experiences, its own interpretation of the world and its own sense of self, before the conventions of his time, of society, and of literature. The element of commonality in epochal period style is now replaced by generation groups. In *Sturm und Drang*, in the Romantic movement, then in the "Jungdeutschland" movement, and again in naturalism and expressionism, like-minded groups formed, each short-lived, which are characterized by their vigorous antitraditionalism, by their critical attitude toward literature and society, and these groups assume the task of representing the progressive spirit of the age as against the established *Zeitgeist*.

But this commonality, always a loose association, never suffices for more than a few years; eventually, and all too often, it drives the individual into a still further subjectivized state of isolation, or to accommodations which, compared with the original impulses of youth, look like compromises. The psychological, sociological, and literary history of nonconformist groups as a type, and the inevitable disbandings, transformations, and reversions that quickly follow, has yet to be written. Again and again, ever since the *Sturm und Drang* and Early Romantic periods, esoteric alliances of kindred spirits have ended in swift rupture and separation.

The writer suffers the fate of loneliness, which also means creative personal loneliness of language. If, on the other hand, he manages to adapt to tradition and to society, an artistic achievement fails to materialize, as is shown by the *Formkunst* circle of Munich after 1850. In adapting to the climate and style of the period—i.e., to literary traditions and the standards set by a given contemporary society, creative production loses those impulses which only the nonconformist individual can give it. In Volume II of his *Salon*, Heine wrote:

> What typifies modern literature is the fact that individuality and scepticism now predominate. Authorities have collapsed; reason is man's only lamp, and his conscience is his only staff in the dark labyrinth of this life. Man now stands alone before his Creator and sings Him his song. . . . Poetry is no longer objective, epic, and naïve, but subjective, lyrical, and meditative.

Seen in this light, the turning of Goethe and Schiller toward a classical approach to art acquires historical significance as being an attempt to leave the path of subjectivization—which was also a disruptive subjectivization of forms and style—and rediscover that of the order and validity to be found in the objective and the suprapersonal.

On the one hand, this meant absorbing and adapting one's historical heritage as the yardsticks of—not standards for—one's own creativity; while on the other it required a communication between individual and society which Goethe sorely missed among his countrymen, and for which the solidarity of intellectual and social life in France, both before and after the Revolution, was a model often advanced by him. Goethe's and Schiller's discussions of the inherent laws of generic forms, especially in epic poetry and drama; their intensive preoccupation with the exemplary masterpieces of world literature; their objectivization of artistic expression above and beyond the purely material reality of experience and the purely personal and subjective art of communicating experience (e.g., Schiller's critique of Bürger): all these are documents of a tireless striving to objectivize art with an eye to what is enduring and essential. It found its supreme expression in the classical symbolic style, which achieved a balance between the specifically individual and the objectively universal.

Goethe's search for the essence of things, his yearning for a view that was whole and pure, for what was true and continuing in all living matter, for the ordered regularity of all that exists; his quest for the protophenomenon, for organic order, for an "understanding of the historical, artistic, and organic manifestations of life as being various basic forms of one and the same nature" (Günther Müller): all this is aimed at that fundamental concern of the classical concept of writing, a concept whose style has gone beyond any ties to the purely personal and the purely temporal-historical.

Goethe the classicist suppressed the lyrical and subjective element pervading the poetry of his youth and penetrating his dramatic and narrative works, in order to make himself wholly receptive to all things in their truth and their own forms and bring about a fusion of spiritual essence and concrete reality. From the discovery of the protoplant he draws the conclusion that embraces all other living matter: ". . . not picturesque or poetic shadows, but an indwelling truth and necessity." The artist in him is now bent on capturing the essential element in the autonomy of the manifestation of beauty—i.e., in the visible objectivization wrought by beauty, in that autonomy of aesthetic manifestation which, through the medium of art, reflects the laws inherent in all things. All this culminates in those great, much-quoted words of his: "All that is arbitrary, all that is imagined, collapses: here is necessity, here is God!"

This receptiveness to the true nature of being in all its manifestations and forms presupposes a creative spirit capable of transforming them, by depiction and reflection, into the autonomy of beauty present in a work of art—i.e., it ingests that personal element which stands in creative correlation to the macrocosm of the suprapersonal. Thus Goethe achieved the synthesis of objective truth—which in the organic sphere is called Nature and in the artistic sphere the inherent laws of being—with the personal immediacy of seeing and experiencing. Goethe the artist achieved that fusion of nature and spirituality, of universality and individuality, in which the essential elements of classicism found fulfilment and in the face of which the divisive search for period style, personal style, and generic style was doomed to failure. For their separations become invalid where this unity has been achieved, where the truth of continuing being in the poetic word absorbs and yet, as it were, devours both historical moment and personal expression.

How this is exemplified in the aesthetic thought and individual works of Goethe and Schiller cannot be discussed here, limited as we are to a few summarized perspectives. Nevertheless it must not be forgotten that the classical concept of art and the classical art of literature were the work of two individuals who made a pact dissociating and isolating them from their intellectual contemporaries. They sought a renewal of the objective literary tradition and the formative influence of art on society. But at the same time they went beyond this tradition in individual creative achievements, and their aesthetic precepts did not succeed in bridging the gulf between themselves and contemporary society. Where the classical style did become the period style, it hardened into a formal classicism. It immured itself in the backward-glancing language of historicism. Classical style foundered on its own nature, on that which justified the sacrifices it demanded in its uncompromising hostility toward the purely individual, the capricious and arbitrary subjectivism and eclecticism of forms, and the pragmatism of the merely material and tangible. It could not hold up the process which was advancing during the nineteenth century in the opposite direction—regardless of the sanctification bestowed by that century on the works of both Goethe and Schiller.

When we look at the question of personal style and period style—always implying generic style too—in the context of nineteenth-century literature (taken to include, in general and simplified terms, the literature and art of the Romantic era), we find ourselves in a situation so complicated that the whole matter becomes equivocal in its range and interpretive capacity.

Beginning with the Romantics, generic forms blended and blurred, and the rhetorical tradition of the various style categories suffered a steady process of attrition. It was replaced by a plurality of style possibilities each depending on individual choice, on individual desire for expression. The subjectivism of poetic language and the antisocial emancipation of this language from contemporary standards and conventions continued to become more marked. The writer took his stand outside society (this did not change until after the abortive revolution of 1848/49). Although it is true to say that this society was shaped in a relatively uniform manner by the bourgeoisie, this bourgeoisie was divided within itself, split up into progressive and conservative groups, and, moreover, confronted by new sociological groupings (although these did not begin to show signs of a literary style of their own until the closing years of the century). The Romantic era saw that profoundly activating change in the concept of the poetic and of the artist's vocation, a change documented by the words of Hegel already quoted. *Dichtung* becomes the revelation of the "inwardness" of the spirit, the immediate and primordial unlocking of the self. Now it offers in its own right an interpretive view of the world; now man the poet no longer faces a given reality as a recipient and shaper: he has himself become the center, the creative point of reference. According to Hegel, a work of art is determined to create the identity of nature and spirit, of the tangible and intangible, through and out of its own self in the composition of the beautiful, and thus restore to man that unity of truth above and beyond reality which he can no longer find either in faith or in thought or in the concrete circumstances of life, but only in art.

The theological and idealistic premises upon which Hegel based his aesthetics continued during the nineteenth century to exert their influence on all thought concerning the nature and vocation of art. They are still clearly perceptible in the lectures given late in life by F. T. Vischer on "Beauty and Art." Here we find the following:

"Beauty restores wholeness to the divided man; it allows him to enjoy the complete harmony of his essential nature with itself and with the world. There is a cleavage running throughout real life between the material and the spiritual, between sensuous happiness and spiritual joy, between form and content, nature and reason, self-love and love for mankind, freedom and order. Beauty brings peace. In this sense the creation of beauty is a joining and a building together. . . ." It conveys "the feeling and the image of a perfect, a harmonious world." Beauty in art should restore from its own self a unity of being that no longer exists outside itself. Thus beauty is both medium and content of man's release from the cleavages of reality. The poet "focuses all the single lights on one point and tells us with conviction: yes, there is a higher law, the eternal, just, cleansing order. . . . The ordering of the world, which we would like to believe in and cannot see, is made visible in a single instance."

Art becomes oriented toward a "semblance of perfection," but now this semblance must be generated by the individuality of the creative gift, by "imagination," which has power to convey, in beauty, the "illusion" of truth. The poet no longer "receives" the objective laws governing art and dictated to him by the prevailing climate of opinion, generic tradition, and society; instead he produces in this semblance a world of his own, born of his creatively endowed personality which claims truth for his utterance, while acceptance of this truth is in turn a matter of individual emotional response to the work.

And so writing was subjectivized in such a way that it came to be viewed solely as the statement of a personality, as wholly dependent on the originality of that personality, down to linguistic techniques and concretizations.

Ever since the Romantics, individuality and uniqueness of style have remained values demanded of art, related not merely to each creative personality but, increasingly, to what is "new"—changing ever more swiftly and bewilderingly in our day—in succeeding period and generation or group styles.

Associated with this subjectivizing process has been, since the Romantic era, a concept for which Schlegel laid the groundwork and which was strengthened and finally established by Nietzsche: that of an aesthetic objectivization in artistry. Subjectivism and artistry are correlates within the same situation. Since the Romantics, a universalizing process of the potential of language and style has been associated with the subjectivization of language and its style forms, and this potential, now liberated as it were, can take root anywhere and has meanwhile expanded to an apparently limitless capacity for receiving and adapting. It dissociates itself from prescribed and established ties and enters upon the fluctuating phases of the "experiment," the toying with possibilities, now that forms no longer correspond to an authoritative objective reality and stand instead for whatever medium the artist's individuality happens to speak through—in short, for the moment in time grasped subjectively by the artist. In fragments by Novalis, written a century and a half ago, we read:

> The poet must be able to imagine other thoughts, to put down thoughts in every kind of sequence and the most disparate kinds of expression. Just as a musician hears different sounds and instruments in his mind, can mentally manipulate them and variously combine them so that he becomes as it were the living spirit of these sounds and melodies; and just as the painter, as master and creator of colored forms, can alter these forms according to his fancy, place them face to face or side by side, and multiply them, and has the ability to conceive an infinite variety of them and produce them individually: so must the poet have the ability to give form to the spiritual voice of all things and all actions in its various guises, and to produce every genre of linguistic enterprise and inform it with a specific meaning and soul of its own.

It would be a worthwhile project to follow the trend of the simultaneous diversification and individualization of poetic language since the Romantic era as a result of this subjectivizing and universalizing process; to trace the manner in which on the one hand it coined the unmistakable personal style—e.g., Jean Paul, Hölderlin, Kleist, Novalis —and on the other cultivated flexibilities of style change to the point of virtuosity and linguistic masquerade—e.g., Tieck, Brentano, or E. T. A. Hoffmann.

Side by side with this process there has been another phenomenon still evident today: that of the rapid obsolescence of language as a form of artistic expression. Signs of this were already beginning to appear during the Romantic era. For if language is restricted to a particular creative individuality and acquires its content from that individuality, it can obviously no longer be adopted and adapted as a common objective means of expression without forfeiting its power of expression and authority of substance. The personal molding of style and language depends on the personality that creates them; in imitation, it loses in substance and "genuineness," it deteriorates into formulas and finally winds up in triviality. A further phenomenon in the wake of the Romantics is the trivialization of Romantic language extending throughout the whole nineteenth century and even into the twentieth. This language was drained of its vocabulary, its fund of metaphor, its rhythm and melody, as soon as it ceased to grow out of the creative power of the individual and the resulting tensions and, reduced to an all-purpose "versifying" tool, became detached from the contemporary intellectual and social situation whose voice it had become. This was bound to happen, since to all intents and purposes it was no longer credited with any objective content.

At the same time, because of this process of subjective and universal emancipation, the literary art of the Romantics comprised yet another important phenomenon: the historicization of forms. This was a parallel but different outcome of the same process.

The tradition of established, "timeless" generic forms continued until well into the German classical period. It was maintained chiefly in drama and, in drama, chiefly in tragedy, up to and including Grillparzer and Hebbel. But with Herder this concept began to be questioned. He saw genres as forms determined by a given historical situation and thus established a new relationship to them. Forms could be dismissed as historically obsolete; they could also be retrieved from history and reintroduced into the present with a view to their renewal and rejuvenation. In a dialectical countermove, the subjectivization of Romantic literature sought a reorientation toward a historical objectivity of style forms. It drew these forms—fairy tale, folk song, saga, legend, chronicle, and many others—from a historical and grass-roots tradition which now, despite the paradox of being historical as opposed to period style, acquired its own set of values. This was the attempt to escape the grip of the subjective, and to speak with the voice of a suprapersonal totality of the historical and grass-roots spirit, a totality that appeared to be of loftier and broader authority.

However, it turned out that this subjectivization was obviously stronger, and that it could not continue creatively to maintain this style from another age, another way of life, other intellectual and social associations, but was bound to dissolve or disrupt it wherever the genuine poetic element sought and achieved self-expression. The combination of the subjective and personal on the one hand, and the historical and grass-roots aspects on the other, was able to succeed where certain prerequisites in generic form were present, as, for instance, in Eichendorff's or Mörike's adaptation of the folk song. The more extensive the generic form and the more material, content, and objectivized presentation forms it demanded from the contemporary situation—e.g., in epic poetry, drama, narrative prose—the more problematical and less satisfactory became the transposition of one's own language into the old forms that had meanwhile become historical.

Throughout the whole of the nineteenth century up to and including Storm and Raabe, we can trace the correlation between subjectivized language and historicizing language. The historicizing style is incorporated in the fundamental subjectivization of forms, since it appears more and more interchangeable and has become capable of ensconcing itself imitatively in any of widely differing periods and linguistic dimensions. Its principal area of penetration is the dominant literary forms of the nineteenth century: the ballad and the novella. The historicizing process is also manifest in Stifter's *Nachsommer*, *Witiko*, and the final text of *Die Mappe meines Urgrossvaters*. Here Stifter attempted to restore to the novel, after the great turning-point of 1848/49 in the countermovement against subjectivization and pragmatization of narrative forms, the suprapersonal and timeless-objective aspects of the classical style, albeit not without some forced stylizations. Nevertheless, although he tried to run counter to the style of the period, he was still unable to escape its exigencies.

In pointing out the subjectivizing and historicizing processes of the nineteenth century we still have not exhausted that century's highly stratified trends in form and style. Through and after Hegel, the general trend was to think of oneself more and more as part of the historical process, and one's own time was thought of as a fluctuating, waxing and waning temporality; hence literary awareness became beholden to the progressive dynamism and actuality of the climate of the day. This climate was seen as a supraindividual collective reality, and it was up to literature to reflect this climate. The *Zeitgeist* became the subjective spirit of the generation groups of the first decades of the nineteenth century; the style of the period became *their* style marked by a strong social commitment and subjective sense of self. We have already quoted Heine on this. A literature that has decided to speak in terms of the contemporary situation and its trends and transformations, and to activate the *Zeitgeist* as a continuing process of intellectual and social progress, sees itself called upon to develop this spirit, serve it, and adapt to it. In the choice of its forms, such a literature adopts, both in style and language, a period style, a "modern" stance, such as was demanded and formulated by the aesthetic program of the "Jungdeutsche."

This topicalized concept of literature and style, oriented as it is toward effect and dissemination, toward the concrete historical moment and its trends, represents a new and unique phenomenon of nineteenth-century German literature. In its program it produced the first instance of the concept of period style we are now discussing. Here, it said, was the possibility of a common period style of epochal validity, one that could acquire objective authority from the historical and social situation and its exigencies. The fact that this possibility never progressed beyond theoretical stipulations and aesthetic programs was due to the fragmentation among the "Jungdeutsche" writers attributable to the strong personal and subjective elements always present among them. Heine, an acknowledged master in the creation of new forms and a new language, was too subjectively individual to give rise to more than imitation, albeit with momentous repercussions.

The attempt to balance the subjectivized content of the poetic word by choosing themes, material, and forms that corresponded to the sociotopical as well as the public and general *Zeitgeist* could not gloss over the inescapable situation that writers were becoming increasingly dependent on the solitary personal voice, on its refusal to conform to society, on its withdrawal from society. Detachment and isolation also occur as themes where ties with home and grass-roots traditions, with middle-class society, with history, with accepted values of various kinds, are striven for and established, as, for example, in the "realism" that prevailed after the revolution of 1848/49 in opposition to the subjectivizing trends of preceding decades. The manner in which this is exemplified in Stifter, Keller, Storm, Raabe, Fontane, and others cannot be gone into here. Their choice of style, aiming at a balance between the subjective and the objective, between poetic utterance and contemporary parlance, corresponded to the over-all awareness of such writers of an obligation to the reality of their time, in their case the reality of bourgeois society: this was the society from which they sprang and which they exhorted with the values they imposed upon it.

Moreover, the consolidation of forms discernible in narrative realism was a further stimulus to this balance between reality and art. Indeed, the synthesis of personal and social, of artistic and "real" elements approached a fusion of individual style and social group style, as an expression of contemporary bourgeois mentality. But it amounted to no more than an approach. For in narrative realism there were soon signs of a drift into the purely provincial and individual on the one hand and, on the other, toward adjustments to the bellelettristic conventions of bourgeois period style (in Storm, Raabe, and even Fontane) which restricted the range of artistic content. This range increased, as the late works of Raabe and Fontane show, the more deliberately an author adopted a critical stance toward bourgeois society and the more he refused to conform to its period style and literary conventions by using his own form and language. Realism's original idea was to challenge the dominance of the subjectivized aspects of the literature immediately preceding the 1848/49 revolution with a greater commitment to the truth of reality. This, so it seemed, could yield a criterion for the artistic truth of narrative. But things turned out otherwise: the few truly artistic narrators dissociated themselves from the commonplaces of bourgeois period style, more and more of them becoming nonconformists to bourgeois society. They accentuated the artistic character of their work of narration vis-à-vis the empirical experience which they made part of this work; and in their productive individuality, in their own nature, and in their own "Self's" outlook on the world, they found the yardstick of the social, ethical-human, and artistic truth of their writing. For the sake of this truth they were compelled to abandon period-style schemata, together with the schemata of a literary realism such as had been theoretically and programmatically formulated more than once since the middle of the century.

But even when, in the continuing logical development of realism, the objective of literary naturalism was to attach oneself to the sublime truth of objective empirical reality, it was impossible to hide the fact that this inevitably turned into a subjective truth. For the more intent a writer was on grasping the reality of his time in literary form, the more he found himself dependent on his own specific segment of experience. We can only speak of a period style after the end of the nineteenth century in the sense of a generation or group literary style that was constantly and ever more rapidly changing, and that embraced this subjectivization as an expression of the generation or the group. In general terms, this thesis may well be maintained for the entire literary evolution that followed on the nineteenth century, an evolution that in its abrupt and headlong thrusts in development and change makes such concepts as period style and generation style problematical. Doubt is cast on the concept of period style by the plurality of various co-existing style strata, while in its time-span and social structure the concept of generation has likewise undergone considerable change in recent decades.

Among the significant new historical phenomena of the nineteenth century is the fact that a polarization has developed between personality style and period style that has turned this contrast or combination into an aesthetic and literary question of values. In our own day this polarization has been even more radical. Since the end of the nineteenth century and right up to the present time, it has been virtually impossible to characterize a period style as a collective, authoritative style in terms of epoch. But perhaps it also brings home to us how questionable it is to approach this development in the history of literature with an oversimplified antithesis of personality style and period style. For it breaks down wherever an artist of creative individuality has succeeded in absorbing and reproducing in his work the essential elements of the contemporary climate and historical situation, thus marking these elements with the style of his time. Historical research will be guided by this style and recognize the style of the period in it, and what we can call the average collective "period style" will lose historical relevance—unless it becomes the object of one specific interest of literary sociology that in turn acquires importance for the proper assessment of personal style. For it is helpful to recognize the extent to which personal style participates in the collective aspects of period style and the means it employs to stand out against, to emancipate itself from, this period style. Gutzkow certainly wrote more topically in terms of *Zeitgeist*, but it is in Keller's language that we recognize the essential style and spirit of the times, just because they bear the imprint of his own individual style.

The question of the relationship between personality or individual style, and period or social group style, is of greater relevance to literary scholars than ever. Both the existential view of literature and immanent interpretation have refined our capacity for recognizing the specific qualities of an author and a work—i.e., the personal or individual style. The aspects of historical and sociological methods now being brought to bear once again on this type of research point up the fact that every literary work requires the inclusion of the historical period, within whose framework belong both the author of the work and the society molding him and his readers. What is individual and autochthonous can only be grasped in terms of the over-all historical and social scene and in their degrees of dissociation from that scene. For the author, like any other human being, lives as a person and, in creating, within the collective space of the historicity of existence. His work lives in and from the history of representational forms and the historicity of language.

[Translated from the German by Leila Vennewitz]

George E. McSpadden

PHONETICS, INTONATION, METRICS, AND STYLISTICS

SOME TIME AGO, THIS WRITER NOTED THAT: "IT IS NOW POSSIBLE TO marry the study of phonetics and intonation with metrics and stylistics."[1] He was speaking in reference to results of the use of contemporary scientific equipment and the possibilities that such tools offer for exact linguistic analysis and synthesis. It is the purpose of the present article to demonstrate something of that assertion.

PHONETICS

We have but recently reached lofty attainment in the realm of phonetics, which has not been equalled before. Masterful workers in this field, Navarro Tomás, Amado Alonso, Pierre Fouché, Pierre Delattre (the last two of whom have died but recently—Fouché, Aug. 11, 1967, and Delattre, July 11, 1969—Alonso earlier), and others have accomplished much. They have erected an imposing structure of knowledge of aural-oral aspects of language, thoroughly scientific, which all workers in linguistics should know. Some time ago Navarro Tomás had given a model of the scientific description of the articulatory phonetics of a language—Spanish;[2] Amado Alonso and Pierre Fouché had excelled in historical phonetics;[3] and Pierre Delattre has more recently blazed a sure trail in acoustical phonetics, and in the welding of the latter with articulatory phonetics—which he has done by brilliant use of advanced electronic equipment, the sound spectrograph, low-power motion picture X-rays,[4] and the pattern playback, combined with his important perceptive generalizations on the pronunciation of the language in question (usually French or Spanish).[5]

Another great accomplishment of Delattre was his perceptive characterization of the main aspects of French articulation, and his energies directed toward characterization of the accents of our modern languages, of what we might call the basic phonetic attitudes of each of the modern languages.[6]

It was perhaps Pierre Delattre who first emphasized that pronunciation, when measured by modern electronic spectrographic equipment, is so accurate in recording all of the aspects of pitch, timbre, timing, intensity, and rhythm that we can confidently assert that no one ever repeats any sound or inflection completely identically in his whole lifetime, not to speak of the differences of one family, when compared with another, or of a given town, or of a whole country. Yet the unmistakable identity of the individual as revealed in the sounds of his speech are so sure that they are now used with probably greater exactness to identify an individual than fingerprinting. Dr. Kersta of the Bell Telephone Laboratories has shown how five clever imitators of the voice of the late President Kennedy were each fully identified by the electronic patterning of their voices, although the human ear was less exact.[7]

To students of Spanish and the modern languages generally, T. Navarro Tomás's brilliant, precise, *Manual de Pronunciación Española* (1918), with subsequent editions, especially the fifth (New York, 1957), became well known since its definitive form in 1932 (?) as the most exact phonetic description of a modern language.

The work of Pierre Fouché, Director of the Institute de Phonétique in Paris, who died Aug. 11, 1967, was powerful and varied. His phonetic studies of French, Catalan, and Spanish, as well as Latin and pre-Roman, and his general phonetic studies show how wide his interests were. His historical works on French phonetics, in 1952, 1958, and 1961, must be unique, and should be thought of along with his treatise on *French Pronunciation: the Words* (Paris, 1956, 604 pp).[8]

The one who has perhaps gone furthest in the application of phonetic law in Romance studies is Juan Corominas. In his great *Diccionario Crítico Etimológico de la Lengua Castellana* he has used it constantly to distinguish dialectal developments.[9] He has found that phonetic laws are very reliable for doing this, and reveal the course of etymologies across the centuries. He has carried foward this work in his *Breve Diccionario Etimológico*,[10] in which he reaches decisions about which he was formerly diffident and sets forth new information.

The work of these masters in phonetics should be recognized for its tremendous practical potential. With language laboratories we are in a period of great emphasis on practice in languages, which should always hold a very important place. However, at a time when there has been great scientific progress, practice has often been more drill (not to say dogged drill) than it has been enlightened by new insights from the most advanced technology. The present writer would hazard the opinion that the average Spanish teacher today perhaps knows less about the exact pronunciation of the language than teachers of a preceding generation, who studied Navarro more diligently. He would further question whether the French teacher today does not have less precise knowledge of French phonetics than disciples of Professors Parmenter, Delattre, etc. Let us by all means have the practice, but let it be as enlightened as possible. Practice alone is not enough; nor will phonetic study of aspects of articulation alone suffice either; we must have practice *and* understanding. With such facilities as we have today it is possible to acquire idiomatic inflection and pronunciation to near perfection in the study of foreign languages. Actually, we should be producing the finest linguists the world has ever known.

INTONATION*

In his work on phonetics, *Manual de Pronunciación Española*, Navarro wrote a preliminary chapter on the "Intonation of Spanish."[2] At that time, he realized that it was indispensable to make an extensive analysis of the intonation of the language in relationship to its syntax, which he estimated would take about twenty years. He undertook that analysis, and in 1944 gave us the first, and essentially complete *Manual de Entonación Española*, which was corrected for errata in the second and third editions.[11] Again, this work is a model for its scientific foundation and thoroughness, for its sound new terms, with which he most competently establishes a whole new science. In this book, Navarro was perhaps the first to set forth in detail the relationships of the intonation of a language with its syntax. This he did in the introductory and general observations (pp. 5–59), as well as in the later exposition of the subject.

Amado Alonso rightly praised the *Manual de Entonación* by Navarro as a classic in Spanish philology. Among its virtues he points out its maturity of judgment, concision, clarity, and exactness, the correctness of material, discernment, and good order.[12] As he says, these make the book an indispensable instrument for the teacher and the investigator,

---

* The section on *Intonation* was prepared with the assistance of Mr. Norman Underwood, to whom my thanks are due.

and a model for regional studies of intonation—for which it has paved the way. He pointed out that Navarro had broken away from the concepts and nomenclature of traditional grammar and created a new well-systematized terminology which should be of immense service in future studies of syntax and stylistics.

Gili Gaya has observed that in this work Navarro often indicates problems yet to be solved and areas still to be explored.[13] In this manual Navarro has studied Spanish intonation, especially in the speech of cultured individuals, although he alludes from time to time to regional inflections in Spain and America. The principal subject is standard intonation. As he indicates, intonation is at the very heart of linguistic expression. It is perhaps the most deeply rooted element in one's native speech. As Gili Gaya has pointed out, intonation is the most basic factor in the organization of human speech.[14] On it are based all of expression, each sentence, each melodic group, the patterns of syntax. It is the last thing to be surrendered as one learns a new tongue, and one of the most difficult aspects of the new language to learn; at least apart from systematic study, based on an entirely accurate description.

Navarro has observed that improper intonation may change the meaning no less than improper choice of words or construction. Both speaker and scholar of a language must know its intonation in order to be able to express himself in it, or to analyze it with accuracy. Some master other aspects of language, its vocabulary, its syntax, its varied forms, etc., but they are unwilling or unable to surrender the intonation of their own language and to take upon themselves that of the new. For most learners, this is perhaps the most difficult step in language learning. Yet, to pronounce Spanish with an English accent or English with a Spanish inflection is just as great an error as faulty grammatical usage.

He observes that in this study it is important to relate grammar and syntax to intonation. Indeed, in all of these things there must be an adequate combination of form and meaning so that perfect unity results. To assemble inflectional patterns without regard to the sense of the things they express, without uniting them to syntactical and lexical elements, in other words, combining form and meaning, such study will be fruitless to a very large extent. Navarro's great contribution, among others, has been just that—to analyze the intonation of the language in a manner that enables us to join its form and meaning. As Palmer observed,[15] the essence of language learning is the joining of form and meaning. To catalog inflections alone, merely according to pattern and not according to the nature of the meaning, is superficial as far as the deeper purposes of language are concerned.

This is not to deny the personal aspect of intonation. Indeed each writer, as Navarro has demonstrated, creates the melodic groups, essentially plants the pauses and inflections in the text as he writes. Any reading or anyone's speech reveals the personal aspects of intonation as well as the idiomatic. We may thus conclude that a complete study of inflection would make room for factors all the way from the individual and personal to those of the community, province, and nation.

American linguistic scholars with roots largely in the linguistic school of the University of Michigan have, as far as the observation of this writer goes, described in detail with series of numbers and arrows broad patterns of intonation for different languages (and they have hoped by this means to describe the inflections). Their work has often been based on little-known languages which have been studied but little, in comparison to those which have been examined for decades, if not hundreds of years.

Navarro's work in intonation has pointed the way for further studies in the Castilian language, in literary works, in Spanish dialectology, and the various national manifestations of intonation in the Americas. As Gili Gaya has pointed out, investigators now have traced out for them the direction they must follow, the numerous voids which still remain to be filled, and a firm basis for comparison on which to found their work. He believes that Navarro's study in this regard is the best that we have for any modern language. Navarro has perceptively characterized the Castilian accent in his inaugural address to the Spanish Academy, which is notable and has become something of a classic on the language.[16]

He has indicated that the minimum unit of Spanish intonation is the melodic group, identical with the phonic group. In Spanish as in English, the typical melodic group is 7, 8, or 9 syllables in length, with some 25% of the whole being in the traditional ballad meter. He observes that French melodic groups are characteristically 3–5 syllables in length, whereas those of Spanish, English, and perhaps German, are of 7, 8, or 9 syllables in length, and those of Italian are more variable and frequently much longer. In comparison with French, then, Spanish intonation has more ample, more serene curves; at the same time it lacks the high variations in intensity of the English accent, and particularly, the German; and in contrast to Italian, the melodic movement is more sober.[17]

Until this work by Navarro, it was hardly possible for a non-native to acquire the inflections of Spanish unaided by accurate observation. He might wonder about the high-rise in pitch, at the main division of the sentence; he might even adopt it, but other important features would generally escape him.

A primary object of the study of phonetics and intonation is to so cultivate the ear that it can understand the foreign accent; hence its words, phrases, clauses, and sentences; and at the same time to enable the learner to so pronounce as to be readily understood by a native. In a word, the practical end of study of phonetics and intonation is to understand and to be understood. Of language study we deliberately say that we learn to hear with the tongue, and we learn to speak with the ear.

METRICS

Navarro's book *Métrica Española*[18] is an extensive catalogue of metric types down through the ages in Spanish. Moreover, his treatment in the preliminary pages of a reading of various poems of the early literature, and elsewhere, of a poem of Ruben Dario[19] foreshadowed what I was to discover about speech rhythms by means of the more powerful tool of the sound spectrograms, in place of the kymograph which he had to use. My experiments, reported in the *Hispanic Review*[1] and subsequently,[20] indicate that authentic human speech in every language examined, is everywhere infused with minute rhythms of great accuracy and intricate proportionality. Perhaps more than any other factor, they are responsible for the lilt of language which so many have observed. It is probably this factor more than many other that, being unrecognized and difficult to measure, has been the unknown point of contention between the "measurers," the "scanners," and those who have insisted that poetic and prose rhythms are "psychological" and cannot be measured.

Because my second report has not been published, it should perhaps be outlined here:

In the *Hispanic Review* report,[1] after prolonged and detailed study of the speech rhythms in Jorge Guillen's reading, I inquired whether the intricate rhythms, the remarkable proportionality would be found also in the speech of other Spanish readers of prose as well as poetry. In the second study, I recounted that we had found the same minute rhythms with symmetry, proportionality, and intertwining. For example, in

Professor Eugenio Florit's reading from the *Quijote*, we found that the phrase "Eran en aquella santa edad" ("there were in that holy age"), at the beginning of the passage on the Age of Gold, is pronounced with perfect symmetry with two equal divisions on either side of the highest instant of intensity of the *s* of *santa*; the whole having this pattern in hundredths of seconds:

$$25 - 30 - 35 \quad / \quad 35 - 30 - 25$$
(accentual rhythm)   eran en aquella santa edad

Another time division of the same passage yields:

(intensity groups) eran en aquella / santa / edad
                        80   60   40

Still another:

(basic beat) e–ran–ena–que–lla–san–tae–dad
$$15 - 15 - 15 - 15 - 30 - / 30 - 30 - 30$$

The sound spectrogram with our measurements below (see Fig. 1) shows syllables, the accentual rhythm which is symmetrical ((15)– 25–30–35/35–30–25), intensity groups of 80–100 and of 80–60–40, the basic beat (15–15–15–15–30/30–30–30), and the two equal halves divided by the element of greatest intensity (90–90).

In the reading of Amado Alonso, a little further along in the same passage from the *Quijote* we found this phrase, taken at random from his reading: "Fue recogido [don Quijote] de los cabreros con buen animo." Here again we have intricate rhythms in Spanish prose (Fig. 2). First a very minute pulsating rhythm in hundredths of a second:

Fue recognido de los cabreros con buen animo.

F   u   e – re –   cog   – i   d – o   d – el – o   s   c a
7–6 –7 –8 – 9 – 10–9–8 – 7 –6 – 7 –8 – 9 – 8 –7 –6 7
b r e r o s c o n   b u e n   á ni mo
8 9 8 7   7 8 9 10   9   8 7 6   78 9

Some other rhythms among several are:

Fue	recogido		de los	cabreros	con	buen	animo
25–42	–	74	–6–	74	–	42	–25
67	–	77	–	77	–	67	

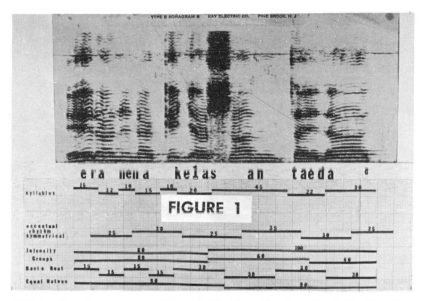

FIG. 1.   Sound spectrogram of Eugenio Florit's reading from *Don Quijote* (Spanish).

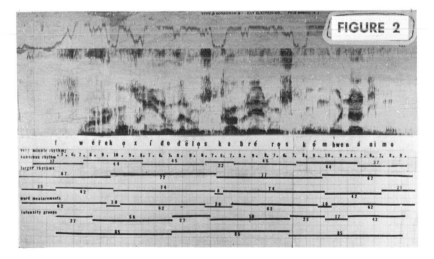

FIG. 2.   Sound spectrogram of Amado Alonso's reading from *Don Quijote* (Spanish).

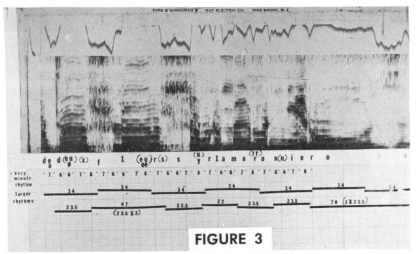

FIG. 3.   Sound spectrogram of reading by Colette (French).

Further speech rhythms present are:

Fue	recogido	de los	cabreros con buen animo(–o)
(10) 62	(10) 62	/20	62 /10 / 62 (whispered breath)

Fue	recogido	de los	cabreros con buen animo
/27/	58 /	10 17 /	58 / 25 /17 /44

27

85   85   85

Thus we see that other Spanish readers of prose have the same minute, intricate, exact rhythms as the poet Jorge Guillén did, except that Guillén did have a larger, regular poetic rhythm, in addition to the more minute rhythms seen above—common to prose readers.

We found that French readers likewise read with the same exact, intricate minute rhythms. For example, we cite Colette (see Fig. 3) in the phrase, "de deux fleurs sur le marronnier rose" with the very minute and the larger rhythms:

```
                   (s)                  (r)   (n)
      de  dø    f   l   ø   r    s y r lə m a r  o n    i er oz ə
      7 6–6–7 8–7–6 6 7–8 7    667 8 7 6 6 7 8  7 6   6 7 8 . . .
        34   /   34   /  34    /    34     /  34  / 34 / 34 /
```
And the larger rhythms:
```
      23.5   /    47      / 23.5   21/22  / 23.5 / 23.5 / 70
      (23.5 × 2)                                (23.5 × 3)
```

This writer and his graduate students have measured many analogous groups in English, others in German and Scandinavian languages; and Mieko Han earlier turned up evidence of similar exact proportionality in Japanese, which is even used with phonemic value, required for the right sense. Thus we see that these minute, intricate rhythms are evidently common to all authentic human speech—for we have not yet found a spectrogram where they do not appear. This underscores the importance of timing in speech, and the necessity for the learner to pay closest attention to rhythm in learning a foreign language. As we pointed out in our first study, not a small share of the charm of prose and poetry is due to these rhythms, and they account for some of the power of the orator to sway his hearers.

STYLISTICS

Literature is the highest expression of language, and a worthy object of study. A good teacher of literature should bring the student to the literary text and help him to understand it. The great Lanson pointed to the aim of helping the student to see everything that is in the text— and nothing that is not.[21] In other words he is not to read his own ideas into the text. An exercise of this nature which has become standard in the French and the Spanish schools, colleges, and universities is the *explication de textes*. The main objects in setting forth the text are to determine its background and theme and to perceive how it is presented by the author. In discovering the way in which the author presents his subject, step by step, we arrive at something of his art or style. This is the realm of *stylistics*. We have already seen oral aspects of the text; for example, the author is the one who plants the main pauses within it, in keeping with the nature of the language. He is the one who constitutes the words into the melodic groups, and if he is a consummate artist, he may even express his moods in the rhythms, as does Cervantes in his preface to the first part of *Don Quijote* (as well as in numerous other passages which might be cited). He begins by addressing the Reader as "Desocupado lector" ("Idling reader," as if to say, "if you had anything else to do, you would not be reading this"). He then says that it would be his desire that Don Quijote, as the offspring of his mind, should be the most discreet and charming son that could be imagined. All of these words are said in gay, flowing rhythms:

Desocupado Lector, sin juramento me podrás creer que quisiera que este libro, como hijo del entendimiento, fuera el más hermoso, el más gallardo y más discreto que pudiera imaginarse.

No. of syls. in melodic groups	Syntonemes (i.e., melodic groups or phonic sense groups)	Rhythmic pattern
7	Desocupado Lector	′__′__′
10	sin juramento me podrás creer	′__′___′_′
8	que quisiera que este libro	__′_′_′_
10	como hijo del entendimiento	′_′___′_′_
6	fuera el más hermoso	′_′_′_
10	el más gallardo y más discreto	_′_′_ _′_′_
8	que pudiera imaginarse	__′___′_

But, he continues (third sentence), as the law of nature is that like begets like, what could his sterile, poorly cultivated brain beget but a shriveled-up, whimsical son, never dreamt of before by anyone. This he does in the woeful, monotonous rhythm of the *verso de arte mayor*:

No. of syls. in melodic groups	Syntonemes	Rhythmic pattern
3 6	Y así, ¿qué podía engendrar	_′ ′_′__′
10 5	el estéril y mal cultivado ingenio mío	__′__′_ _′_′_
5 6	sino la historia de un hijo seco,	′__′_ __′_′_
5	avellanado,	_′_′_
5	antojadizo,	_′_′_
10	y lleno de pensamientos varios	_′__′_′_′_
8 5	y nunca imaginados de otro alguno,	_′____′_ _′_′_
11	bien como quien se engendró en una cárcel,	′__′__′__′_
9 5	donde toda incomodidad tiene su asiento	__′_′___′__′_
9	y donde todo triste ruido	_′_′_′_′_
6	hace su habitación?[22]	′_′__′

Note the prominence of the *verso de arte mayor*: ′__′ (8 times); the recurrence, especially in the series, of the pattern: _′_′_ (5 times); or an indefinite number of unstressed and stressed syllables: _′_′_′_′. It will be noted that the rhythm is monotonous, sad, and wooden.

Then he reverts to gay, flowing rhythms as he depicts a pastoral scene (fourth sentence):

No. of syls. in melodic groups	Syntonemes	Rhythmic pattern
4	El sosiego,	$--'-$ 3
7	el lugar apacible,	$--'--'-$ 3 6
8	la amenidad de los campos,	$---'--'-$ 4 7
9	la serenidad de los ciclos,	$-'--'--'-$ 2 5 8
8	el murmurar de las fuentes,	$---'--'-$ 4 7
8	la quietud del espíritu	$--'--'--$ 3 6
5	son grande parte	$'--'-$ 1 4
10	para que las musas más estériles	$--'-'---'--$ 3 5 9
6	se muestren fecundas	$-'--'-$ 2 5
8	y ofrezcan partos al mundo	$-'-'--'-$ 2 4 7
9	que le colmen de maravilla	$--'--'-'-$ 3 6 8
5	y de contento.[23]	$---'-$ 4

Note the increasing and decreasing of the length of the first seven lines, which is a remarkably soothing rhythm, similar to the movement of gentle breakers at the seaside. Note also the dominance of the foot of the *verso de arte mayor*; this perhaps connects it rhythmically with what precedes, but here $'--'$ (in 10 of the 12 lines) is incorporated into a pleasing flowing rhythm. Note the *versos llanos*, ending in: $'-$ (in 10 of the 12); the two other verses ending in *esdrújulas*: $'--$.

This is one of many possible illustrations of how *prose* metrics (not to speak of the potentiality of combining poetic rhythms) may be combined with stylistics. It will be noted that the phonic (melodic) groups are the unit here, and that in this way, phonetics and intonation as described by Navarro have been joined to metrics and stylistics.[24]

Navarro's studies in phonetics have received world-wide recognition and have long been held the model of clarity, precision, balance, and fruitfulness. Whole generations of Spanish teachers and professors pay him homage as their master in this field. His solid observations, based on careful and very extensive work in experimental phonetics, make his work classic, and it still stands decade after decade, in spite of the ephemeral nature of so much of the work in modern science. His sound unification of all aspects of the oral language give him an unequaled place among the scholars in this realm. His work at many points is germane to the study of stylistics.

Much of it is due to his teacher, don Ramón Menéndez Pidal, great master of these Spanish researchers and teachers, who should not be forgotten in a review of our progress and a desire to glimpse something of the path ahead. Don Ramón Menéndez Pidal died less than a year before this writing. It is difficult to estimate the vastness of his influence on so many disciples in every realm in the study of language and literature. We have mentioned the work of Navarro in phonetics; that of another of his disciples, Amado Alonso, master of stylistics, who demonstrated the power of an art-minded philology; and countless other scholars of second, third, or fourth generations. Perhaps none of the foregoing progress of the Spanish scholars whose contributions have been recounted here would have been realized without the great Menéndez Pidal.[25]

All of these varied aspects of phonetics, intonation, metrics, and stylistics are, of course, a part of the whole study of language and literature. In a day of so much analytical work we need the restoration of the idea and the ideal of philology as the science of all of language and literature and what it expresses.

Notes

---

1. George E. McSpadden, "New Light on Speech Rhythms from Jorge Guillén's Reading of His Poem *Gran Silencio* (Based on Measurements of Sound Spectrograms)," in *Hispanic Review*, Vol. 30, No. 3 (July, 1962), pp. 216–230, esp. p. 230.
2. T. Navarro-Tomás, *Manual de pronunciación española* (Madrid, 1932), fifth ed., 1957.
3. Amado Alonso, *De la pronunciación medieval a la moderna en español*, Vol. 1, Ed. by Rafael Lapesa, (Madrid, 1955), 452 pp..
4. Clarence E. Parmenter, Robert Moon, and Solomon Treviño pioneered the use of low-power motion picture X-rays for phonetic analysis at the University of Chicago after World War II.

5. See Pierre Delattre, "L'/R parisien et autres sons du pharynx," in *The French Review*, Vol. 43 (October 1969), pp. 5–22. This article was published posthumously.

6. Pierre Delattre, *Principes de phonétique française a l'usage des étudiants anglo-américains*, ed. 2, (Middlebury, Vt., 1951). Also: *Les difficultes phonétiques du français* (Middlebury, Vt., 1948).

7. L. G. Kersta, "Voice Print Identification," presented to Acoustical Society of America, May 24, 1962; "Voice Print Intelligibility," Acoustical Society of America, Nov. 7, 1962, Seattle, Wash.

8. For a summary bibliography of Pierre Fouché see *Annales de L'Université de Paris*, 38th year, No. 3, July–Sept., 1968, pp. 443–446.

9. Juan Corominas, *Diccionario Crítico Etimológico de la Lengua Castellana* (Berne, 1954–1957).

10. Juan Corominas, *Breve Diccionario Etimológico de la Lengua Castellana*, ed. 2 (Madrid, 1967).

11. T. Navarro-Tomás, *Manual de Entonación Española*, Hispanic Institute in the United States (New York, 1944), 306 pp. A second edition was published in 1948 and a third in Mexico, 1966.

12. Amado Alonso, In *Revista de filología hispánica*, Vol. 7 (1945), pp. 94–95, quoted in Homero Serís, *Bibliografía de la linguística española* (Bogotá, 1964), p. 64.

13. Samuel Gili Gaya, *Boletín de la Biblioteca Menéndez Pelayo*, Vol. 22 (1946), p. 280, quoted in Homero Serís, *Bibliografía de la linguística española* (Bogotá, 1964), p. 64.

14. Samuel Gili Gaya, *Curso Superior de Sintaxis d'española* (ed. 4). Chapters I, XIX, and ff.

15. Harold E. Palmer, *The Scientific Study and Teaching of Foreign Languages* (London, 1917); reprinted Oxford, 1968.

16. T. Navarro-Tomás, "El acento castellano," reprinted in *Estudios de fonología española* (Syracuse, N.Y., 1946).

17. T. Navarro-Tomás, "Grupos de entonación," in *Estudios de fonología española* (Syracuse, N.Y., 1946), pp. 77–101.

18. T. Navarro Tomás, *Métrica española, reseña histórica y descriptiva* (Syracuse, N.Y., 1956), 556 pp.

19. T. Navarro-Tomás, "La cantidad silábica en unos versos de Rubén Dario," In *Revista de filología española*, Vol. 9 (1922), pp. 1–29.

20. George E. McSpadden, "Further Light on Speech Rhythms," presented to the Experimental Phonetics Section of the Modern Language Association of America. New York, 1966.

21. Quoted in P. R. Vigneron, "Explication de textes," in *Modern Language Journal*, 1927, Vol. 12, pp. 19–35.

22. The first part of this sentence is paraphrased in the text. The meaning of the second part is: ". . . like one begotten in a jail where every inconvenience dwells, and where every sad sound makes its habitation."

23. One might paraphrase this sentence thus: "A quiet, peaceful place, amenity of the fields, serenity of the heavens, murmuring of fountains, quietness of the spirit, lend fertility to the most sterile muses so that they bring forth marvelous births that produce the greatest joy."

24. Studies of the relationship of rhythm and content—especially mood—are detailed in Helmut Hatzfeld's *A Critical Bibliography of the New Stylistics (1900–1952), applied to the Romance Literatures* (Chapel Hill, 1953). See the chapter on "Rhythmical and Musical Problems," pp. 136–142.

25. Don Ramón Menéndez Pidal died on November 14, 1968.

Marie Hochmuth Nichols

RHETORIC AND STYLE

UNDER A PLANE-TREE, BY THE BANKS OF THE ILISSUS, SOCRATES PUT A question to his friend Phaedrus, with whom he had been discussing rhetoric. "Do you know," said Socrates, "how you can speak or act about rhetoric in a manner which will be acceptable to God?" "No, indeed," said Phaedrus, and twenty-five hundred years later many of us would answer the question in the same way. We might also go on to say, as Socrates did, "If we had the truth ourselves, do you think we should care much about the opinions of men?"[1]

"The quest for certainty," Milton Konvitz, professor of law at Cornell University, has remarked, "ended some years ago. We live permanently in an encircling gloom, and the kindly light that we have is only a feeble candle of short-range vision.[2]

There have been, and still are, various "certainties" about rhetoric, just as there are calls for a "new rhetoric." Some of the early certainties grew out of philosophical differences. The Stoics, the Academic skeptics, the Peripatetics, each had his certainty, and each was, in fact, quarreling about fundamental philosophical assumptions. The Stoics cast their lot with contemplation and withdrawal from the marketplace and political arena to attain the good life. The search was for absolute truth as the foundation for the good life. The Academics were a little less certain, and the Peripatetics accepted the necessity of public life and a concern with the contingent nature of truth in a world of public affairs.

Such philosophic differences brought on differences in conception of the nature and role of rhetoric. From Plato they brought disdain; from Aristotle reluctant acceptance of the imperfections of men as they are in their moments of judgment.

In the ancient world, as genre, rhetoric was prose discourse, spoken or intended to be spoken, in order to influence judgment. Some of the efforts depended upon chance and the untrained mind; some depended upon such principles and rules as were taught by practicing orators or in the schools. Whether trained or poorly trained, in cases of urgency, one can wail and cry; he can couch his plea in strained language to win assent; he can speak in what he thinks to be a melodious way; he can try to ingratiate himself in a multitude of ways, and doubtless the early Greeks, as was charged against both teacher and practioner, used all of these affective devices in order to win decisions in the courts or to carry the day in the Assembly. That they did so Aristotle lamented in his *Rhetoric*.[3] It was his belief, however, that properly chosen enthymemes and examples were the legitimate means for bringing about rational judgment, although he recognized that enthymemes and examples had to be spoken by someone with certain physical and vocal endowments, in certain words in a certain order, and that all of these qualities modified the effect of the enthymemes and examples on the judges. The generator of rhetoric was a desire to make probable truth prevail in the minds of judges on questions of a contingent nature. Neither the laws nor constitutions could or did specify appropriate behavior in all particular cases,[4] and neither the laws nor constitutions could enjoin the populace to behave in such a way as to implement the workings of the state effectively, with justice and responsibility, a duty not only assumed by orators, but by poets, philosophers, and historians as well.[5] Rhetoric was a functional art, whose object was persuasion, and could never be thought of without reference to the audience for which it was intended—the free men of the Hellenic world, and later, of course, the free men of Rome, and elsewhere.

Frequently, with little basis in philosophy—a condition due partly to the posture of philosophy itself, bewitched for centuries, as Adler comments, by the "illusion of *epistēmē*"[6]—differences in conception of the nature of rhetoric have persisted. With almost no philosophic depth at all we contrast "truth" with rhetoric, rhetoric with "reality," "mere opinion" with truth; and we sometimes fling about such epithets as "body rhetoric," the "rhetoric of architecture," etc. At times, also, an ambiguous word is linked with one's particular competence and interest of the moment. Thus, according to Stephen Ullmann, "The disappearance of traditional rhetoric has created a gap in the humanities, and stylistics has already gone a long way to fill this gap. In fact, it would not be altogether wrong to describe stylistics as a 'new rhetoric' adapted to the standards and requirements of contemporary scholarship in the linguistic as well as the literary field."[7] Or, one may take such a position as that of I. A. Richards. "So low has Rhetoric sunk," he says, "that we would do better just to dismiss it to Limbo than to trouble ourselves with it—unless we can find reason for believing that it can become a study that will minister successfully to important needs"—the important needs at the time, for Richards, concerning himself with the nature of meaning, being that of "misunderstanding and its remedies."[8]

In 1966, the philosopher Henry W. Johnstone, Jr., wrote:

> . . . the need for a philosophical examination of rhetoric is most acute and the examination most welcome when the orderly processes through which people are normally able to persuade one another suddenly go awry and can no longer be counted on. Aristotle's examination of rhetoric was carried out in just such a period of reversal. Individuals claiming to be able for a fee to persuade anyone of anything were making a mockery of the art of persuading. In so doing, they unwittingly called attention to the need for a philosophical scrutiny of the foundations of rhetoric. Aristotle supplied such a scrutiny, disengaging persuasiveness from dialectical shenanigans and associating it firmly with virtue.[9]

There have been other major scrutinies of the nature of rhetoric throughout the ages; Augustine in the fourth century A. D., adapting to the needs of Christian theology; Peter Ramus in the sixteenth century, attempting educational reform to avoid duplication in the disciplines; Bacon in the seventeenth century, adapting to his own theory of the foundations of knowledge; George Cambell in the eighteenth century, adapting to current philosophical and psychological doctrine; Richard Whately in the nineteenth century, reacting against the excesses of elocution; James A. Winans in the early twentieth century, responding to the appeal of Jamesian psychology, and Charles W. Woolbert, responding to Watsonian behaviorism; as well as the most massive of all scrutinies, beginning in the third decade of the century, that of Kenneth Burke, witness to the breakdown of discussion during the years of the depression and reacting to Marxian dialectics and Freudian psychology, as well as to anthropological, sociological, and linguistic investigations.

We are again at a watershed moment in history, and "we seem to be in the midst of a revival of rhetoric unmatched in the twentieth century," says Wayne Booth, noting a variety of recent textbooks bearing in their titles the label of rhetoric. Possibly we need to raise the question, as Booth does, "What we are reviving?"[10]

No one can control the meaning of a word. Meanings reside in the interpreters of words, interpreters who bring with them varied learnings and experiences, needs and urgencies, and preferences. In our times, the word *rhetoric* is frequently used in a context of violence. Thus, we speak of the "rhetoric of the revolutionary," the "rhetoric of Black power," the "rhetoric of the New Left," or the "rhetoric of the radical." Even such an astute observer as Kingman Brewster, president of Yale University, is able to remark: "I see no basis for compromise on the basic proposition that forcible coercion and violent intimidation are unacceptable means of persuasion and unacceptable techniques of change in a university community, as long as channels of communication and the chance for reasoned argument are available."[11] Is not the prior question whether "forcible coercion and violent intimidation" are means of persuasion at all, acceptable or unacceptable, particularly when weapons and not words are involved? This is not to say, however, that persuasion does not result from other means, some of which are not verbal at all. It merely says that rhetoric is always verbal, and is directed to men only insofar as they are free; it also says that persuasion and coercion are to be distinguished.

Many of the calls for a "new rhetoric" and laments about the short-comings of traditional conceptions of rhetoric are not because of a quarrel with the fundamental principles of the art of rhetoric, although many critics do not recognize this, but concerned with the implementation of the fundamental principles, which is a function of changing understanding, cultural patterns, needs, institutions. Suzanne Langer has made what I think to be an important distinction accounting for many of the difficulties surrounding the conception of rhetoric and of the arts generally. Speaking of art, generally, she remarks: "To create perceivable expressive forms is a *principle of art*; but the use of any device, no matter how important, is a *principle of creation in art*. I think the belief that the concept of art changes from age to age rests on the fallacy of taking the most general principles of artistic technique operative in some particular period and culture as the principles of art itself."[12]

Traditionally, rhetoric, as theory, has been concerned with an art of persuasion. Aristotle defined this concern as "the faculty of observing in any given case the available means of persuasion. This is not a function of any other art," he continues. "Every other art can instruct or persuade about its own particular subject-matter; for instance, medicine about what is healthy and unhealthy, geometry about the properties of magnitudes, arithmetic about numbers, and the same is true about the other arts and sciences. But rhetoric we look upon as the power of observing the means of persuasion on almost any subject presented to us; and that is why we say that, in its technical character, it is not concerned with any special or definite class of subjects."[13]

Doubtless there is little need to recall that for Aristotle, implicitly, and for Cicero and Quintilian explicitly, rhetoric was concerned with discovering arguments and probable proofs that would contribute to persuasion, organizing these arguments and proofs according to a system conducive to persuasion, choosing language that would contribute to the most compelling presentation of the arguments, holding such arguments in the memory, and ultimately giving the most compellingly vivid oral presentation of the proofs to a populace that depended heavily upon the voice for articulating one's feelings or beliefs. It was language directed to a particular end, namely judgment. But the problems of integrating the contributions of the pagan writers with Christian theology altered the posture of "truth" and the character of judgments to be made; the growth of humanism in the Renaissance altered the posture of artistic expression; the change in psychological understanding in the eighteenth century altered various concepts pertaining to how language works on the human mind; the shift of attention to the poet and essayist in the nineteenth century altered the position of the audience; the demeaning of reason and authority in the mid-twentieth century has altered the posture of the witness to truth and of truth itself. None of these cultural changes, however, alters the basic assumption that rhetoric has as its concern the alteration of opinion, feeling, and judgment by effective verbal means. Whether persuasion lies in the articulation of revealed truth as it did for St. Augustine and much of the Medieval period, in excessive esthetics as it did in the Renaissance, particularly after Peter Ramus, in "associationism" related to the "faculties" of the mind as it did in the eighteenth century, in personal emotional expressiveness as it did in the nineteenth century, or in individual sense experience, and occasionally Oriental mysticism, as it seems to in the sixth decade of the twentieth century, is of little consequence so long as these changes are seen in relation to the fundamental nature and object of rhetoric. Quite possibly the resources of extra-sensory perception may be used as time goes on.

The evolution of rhetoric and of the theory of argumentation follows the fate of the epistemological status of *opinion* as opposed to *truth*. According as it is claimed that all truth presents itself as the most defensible opinion or that opinion is nothing but mock truth, the position allotted to rhetoric and argumentation will be more or less important. The controversies which opposed the sophists to the Eleatics, the Pythagoreans and the followers of Plato, provide us with the earliest writings on this subject. The question is whether truth is the outcome of dialogue, discussion and the confrontation of opinions, or whether there exist direct and immediate means of attaining truth, the employment of which would be preliminary to any rhetoric, this latter being transformed from a technique of discussion and discovery into a technique of presentation and persuasion concerned far more with the form than with the basic ground of discourse.[14]

In this judgment, P. Albert Duhamel and others have concurred.[15] If, for instance, the emperor makes the decision, as was the case during the Roman Empire, rhetoric could be expected to become a hypothetical exercise in investigation and decision-making at most; if the poet is, in fact, a "seer," effective presentation of his vision might be the starting point of his rhetoric; etc.

It is not strange that when effective use of argument and language to the end of persuasion is reduced to an art, by an especially acute thinker, that such use should be scrutinized and its relations examined by other users of words. If the philosopher argues—and he does—his philosophical argument must be a species of argument in general; consequently, doubtless he hopes that by the cogency of his argument, his view will prevail. If the historian concerns himself with presenting an interpretation of past events, their causes, and their consequences, he must also be concerned that the reader recognize the interpretation as being plausible. If the poet is concerned with presenting his perceptions, doubtless he hopes to present them compellingly. Nothing that man makes with words can be assumed to be self-evident; hence rhetoric as effective method of presentation is shared by most users of words. Wayne Booth has stated the problem cogently:

> In short, all of the clichés about the natural object being self-sufficient are at best half-truths. Though some characters and events may speak by themselves their artistic message to the reader, and thus carry in a weak form their own rhetoric, none will do so with proper clarity and force until the author brings all his powers to bear on the problem of making the reader see what they really are. The author cannot choose whether to use rhetorical heightening. His only choice is of the kind of rhetoric he will use.[16]

Booth is not saying, of course, that there are no differences between philosophy, history, poetry, and deliberative speaking, or any other art employing words as a medium. He is merely recognizing that users of words have many needs in common. That effective means of appealing to one's hearer for understanding and belief were presented in rhetoric books is not to say that such principles and rules are the property of rhetoric as genre.

Much energy has been wasted over the centuries, and much confusion brought about, by attempts to establish priorities—to establish the superiority of dialective over rhetoric, philosophy over history, poetry over rhetoric—when the possibilities of keeping such arts totally separate are negligible, if not nil. This is especially true in the light of contemporary theory regarding the nature of language. Language is not an objective tool; its symbols are not empty, but freighted with the experiences of men who are its makers, and interpreted by men who bring to it the feelings and experiences of their existential selves.

"Rhetoric proper starts with Aristotle,"[17] says the author of a recent work, revealing the unsupportable position that rhetoric refers merely to theory, or possibly genre. That Homer did not include compelling speeches in his epics would be difficult to sustain; that Isocrates in the *Antidosis*, selecting a mock-trial as a method to present and refute charges brought against him, was not using rhetoric cannot be sustained; that Plato did not choose the dialogue form and employ compelling arguments and figures throughout cannot be sustained, any more than could one support the notion that the daughter of Joseph Stalin in our time was not using rhetoric when she chose the form of the familiar letter to present her description of the Russia she knew. Clearly, the *practice* of rhetoric, "proper" or improper, did not start in fourth-century Greece, but in some remote time when men began so to manage language as to achieve their ends. The most that the author of such a statement as "Rhetoric proper starts with Aristotle" could mean is that Aristotle presented the most penetrating, systematic, and enduring account of the theory of rhetoric which has come down to us from ancient times.

Equally confusing is still another view of rhetoric contained in a statement of a contemporary literary critic, Murray Krieger, summarizing a point of view of Allen Tate and W. B. Yeats:

> So let me be frank. What can a theory do to help us toward relating rhetoric to poetic when it rests on the need to denigrate rhetoric in order to create the very possibility of poetry? One of the major documents in the formulating of this theory, Allen Tate's "Three Types of Poetry," offers not merely the commonplace that poetry is the work of imagination, but the extreme claim supported by the condescending question of W. B. Yeats, "What is rhetoric but the will trying to do the work of the imagination?" What, then, is inferior poetry or pseudo-poetry (as a work of the will) but rhetoric in disguise, poetry that has—to repeat the metaphor—fallen into rhetoric? In this supercilious strain, the hidden refrain, 'Alas, poor rhetoric!' . . . .
>
> Rhetoric, then, is related to decision and action; poetry, happily, is not. . . .[18]

And, thus, Krieger, accepting the superiority of the imagination over the "will," charges off with banner "happily" held high for poetry, with neither Tate nor Yeats nor Krieger having any particular yardstick by which the imagination may be elevated over the "will," or under what circumstances such elevation might be warranted, and little awareness, also, that rhetoric is method as well as genre, practice as well as theory. It is, as the classicist Roger Hornsby has observed,

> the means the author used to create his work and it is also the means whereby he wants us to understand it. . . . the ancient writers never made the peculiar modern assumption that a work exists in some sort of vacuum, that it does not have an audience. No poet, philosopher, or prose writer ever thought he worked solely for himself. They were concerned that others should know and understand, for they knew that to know was to be delighted.[19]

The critic Longinus unmistakably took his work to a court of appeal, imaginary or real, outside himself to determine its possible effectiveness:

> Therefore even we, when we are working out a theme which requires lofty speech and greatness of thought, do well to imagine within ourselves how, if need were, Homer would have said this same thing, how Plato or Demosthenes, or, in history, Thucydides would have made it sublime. The figures of these men will meet us on the way while we vie with them, they will stand out before our eyes, and lead our souls upwards towards the measure of the ideal which we have conjured up. Still more so if we add to our mental picture this: how would Homer, were he here, have listened to this phrase of mine? or Demosthenes? how would they have felt at this? Truly great is this competition, where we assume for our own words such a jury, such an audience, and pretended that before judges and witnesses of that heroic build we undergo a scrutiny of what we write. Yet more stimulating than all will it be if you add: "If I write this, in what spirit will all future ages hear me?" If any man fear this consequence, that he may say something which shall pass beyond his own day and his own life, then all which such a soul can grasp must needs be barren, blunted, dull; for it posthumous fame can bring no fulfilment. . . .[20]

To the extent that any poet is concerned that his perception be seen and understood for what it is, he has little choice but to use rhetorical method. Well used, it elevates; poorly used, it demotes. It is simply a mode of linking speaker and writer with his listener and reader. It is so putting arguments, ideas, and feelings as to make a difference to the reader or listener in his perceptions, his feelings, his judgment. There are, indeed, practical as well as aesthetic considerations in all the verbal arts, and separating these one from another is not as easy as one may suppose, just as it is not easy to separate conscious and subconscious aspects. The Aristotelian *Poetics* does not hesitate to send the tragedian back to the *Rhetoric* for an examination of the nature of Thought and a discussion of how emotions are to be aroused, and "things maximized and minimized."[21]

Perhaps no aspect of rhetoric has been more scrutinized over the centuries than has been the third of the traditional canons of rhetoric, style. In fully developed treatises the discussion was ordinarily organized around such virtues as correctness, clarity, propriety, and ornamentation.[22] Because of the meticulous identification and classification of figures of speech, and the attention given to this aspect of the management of language, frequently style has been considered to be the whole of rhetoric. This was particularly true during the Renaissance, after the Petrarchan acceptance of the Ciceronian ideal of the union of wisdom and eloquence.[23] Numerous handbooks on rhetoric, devoted chiefly to ornamentation, made their appearance, giving rise to an excessive aesthetics.[24] The emphasis on ornamentation was reinforced by the Ramean educational reform which separated the inventive and judgment phase of the ancient rhetoric from the stylistic and delivery phase, placing invention and judgment with dialectic, and reserving for rhetoric only style and delivery.[25] Bacon's distrust of the "sweet falling phrase" was undoubtedly due, in part, to the excesses of ornamentation, excesses which were to be cured by "the application of reason to the imagination for the better moving of the will."[26]

Aristotle was well aware that audiences have value systems pertaining to the management of language:

> The effect which lectures produce on a hearer depends on his habits; for we demand the language we are accustomed to, and that which is different from this seems not in keeping but somewhat unintelligible and foreign because of its unwontedness. . . . Thus some people do not listen to a speaker unless he speaks mathematically, others unless he gives instances, while others expect him to cite a poet as witness. And some want to have everything done accurately, while others are annoyed with accuracy, either because they cannot follow the connexion of thoughts or because they regard it as pettifoggery.[27]

It is "not enough to know *what* we ought to say," said Aristotle, "we must also say it *as* we ought; much help is thus afforded towards producing the right impression of a speech."[28] In our time one must credit some of the impression created by Churchill, De Gaulle, Adlai Stevenson, John F. Kennedy, Martin Luther King, and others to the uniqueness of their handling of language patterns.

When Demosthenes in his oration "On the Crown" spoke the following words, many of his listeners would have recognized the Gorgian antithesis, a persuasive way of presenting thought in fifth and fourth century Greece. Doubtless Aeschines knew the thought was compellingly advanced:

> You taught school, I attended school.
> You initiated people, I was an initiate.
> You were a minor clerk, I was a member of the Assembly.
> You were a minor actor, I was a spectator.
> You were hissed off the stage, I joined in the hissing.
> Your policies supported our enemy, mine, our country.[29]

That Demetrius found "the exact correspondence of parallel clauses" to be "poor art," and "more like a jest than an expression of anger,"[30] illustrates not only that the Greeks had an ear for uniqueness in the management of language, but also that such uniqueness had persuasive possibilities. So keenly aware was Demetrius of the persuasiveness of different language structures that he was able to identify language structures that could be "accusatory," merely "suggestive," or "high-mindedly exhortative." Thus, to him Aristippus was typically "accusatory": "Men leave property to their children, but they do not leave along with it the knowledge of how to use the legacy." Xenophon was typically "suggestive": "One should not leave only property to one's children, but also the knowledge of how to use it." Socrates, Plato, and Aeschines used the "question", a "vivid imitation of actual conversation and its high-minded exhortations": "Well, my boy, how much money did your father leave you? Quite a lot, more than you can easily account for?—Quite a lot, Socrates—Then surely he also left you the knowledge of how to use it?" Thus, "The boy is in difficulties before he realizes it; he is made aware of his ignorance, and set on the path of education."[31]

The ancients knew that, from the point of persuasion, it was one thing to say, "Your trees shall be cut down," and quite a different thing to say, "The grasshoppers will sing to you from the ground."[32] By such differences one identified his station in life; by them he was able to give thought appropriate public expression, exhibit feeling in himself and arouse it in others, ingratiate himself to his public or in some way reveal his relationship to it, or adjust himself to the purposes and occasions for which he talked; by such differences he could also display virtuosity for the sheer amazement and delight of the listener, as he combined semantic, syntactic, and phonetic features of language management. He habitually thought of language patterns in terms of their ability to teach, to please, and to move. For Cicero, the consummate manager of language was one "who can discuss trivial matters in a plain style, matters of moderate significance in the tempered style, and weighty affairs in the grand manner."[33] The talents of a Demosthenes were to be called into play "where the hearer is to be hard struck"; the talents of a Cicero when "the moment for diffusion" was at hand, where the hearer "is to be flooded with detail, as it is always appropriate in enlargement upon commonplaces, in perorations and digressions, and in all passages written for the style and for display, in scientific and physical exposition, and in several other branches of literature. . . ."[34]

If the testimony of the centuries to the importance of style needed support, we could find it in an unsuspected source—from one of the great atomic scientists of the twentieth century. Said J. Robert Oppenheimer:

> The problem of doing justice to the implicit, the imponderable and the unknown is, of course, not unique to politics. It is always with us in science, it is with us in the most trivial of personal affairs, and it is one of the great problems of writing and of all forms of art. The means by which it is solved is sometimes called style. It is style which complements affirmation with limitation and with humility; it is style which makes it possible to act effectively, but not absolutely; it is style which, in the domain of foreign policy, enables us to find a harmony between the pursuit of ends essential to us, and the regard for the views, the sensibilities, the aspirations of those to whom the problem may appear in another light; it is above all style through which power defers to reason.[35]

For Oppenheimer, as for the ancients, style was not only an aesthetic matter, but a practical one.

In its simplest manifestation, says Kenneth Burke, style is a mode of "ingratiation",[36] on the other hand, says A. N. Whitehead, it is an "aesthetic sense" which is "based on admiration for the direct attainment of a foreseen end, simply and without waste." It is an index of a preference for "good work," and in its most complex aspect the "ultimate morality of mind."[37]

The ideals of any age with reference to style may differ. The late John Livingston Lowes said of the King James Version of the Bible: "Its phraseology has become part and parcel of our common tongue— bone of its bone and flesh of its flesh. Its rhythms and cadences, its turns of speech, its familiar imagery, its very words, are woven into the texture of our literature, prose and poetry alike. . . . The English of the Bible . . . is characterized not merely by a homely vigour and pithiness of phrase, but also by a singular nobility of diction and by a rhythmic quality which is, I think, unrivalled in its beauty."[38] The twentieth-century revisers of the Bible were enjoined to "combine accuracy with the simplicity, directness, and spiritual power" of the King James Version, as well as to make it "more readable for the American public of today."[39] The rolling cadences of a Daniel Webster, feeling the expansiveness of patriotic fervor, have given way in the twentieth century to the irregular patterns of everyday speech, each of which styles has persuasive possibilities.

Over the years style has been considered the "shell of thought," the "choice between alternative expressions," a "set of individual characteristics," "deviations from a norm," a "set of collective characteristics," and as "those relations among entities that are statable in terms of wider spans of text than the sentence."[40] Style has been considered merely one part of rhetoric, and, on the other hand, the whole of it. P. Albert Duhamel has remarked: "The rhetorician's conception of the value of argument, the process of invention by which arguments are to be discovered, the extent to which the devices of elocution are to be employed, is the result of his evaluation of the reliability of the intellect, the nature and availability of truth, and the existence of certitude." And with rare insight, he has remarked of Cicero, as he might of other speakers and writers, "He sought to speak effectively, and his expression mirrors his conception of rhetoric."[41] From the point of view of rhetoric, style is one of the means for promoting attitudes of acceptance or rejection.

Notes

1. "Phædrus," in *The Works of Plato* (Vol. III), trans. by B. Jowett (New York), pp. 441–442.
2. Milton R. Konvitz, "Why One Professor Changed His Vote," *New York Times Magazine*, May 18, 1969, p. 61.
3. Aristotle, *Rhetorica* (I.1.1354a, trans. by W. Rhys Roberts, in *The Works of Aristotle*, Vol. 11 (Oxford, 1924).
4. *Ibid.*, I.1.1354b.
5. George Kennedy, *The Art of Persuasion in Greece* (Princeton, N. J., 1963), p. 7.
6. Mortimer J. Adler, *The Conditions of Philosophy: Its Checkered Past, Its Present Disorder, and Its Future Promise* (New York, 1965), p. 285.

7. Stephen Ullmann, *Language and Style* (New York, 1966), p. 3.
8. I. A. Richards, *The Philosophy of Rhetoric* (New York, 1936), p. 3.
9. Henry W. Johnstone, Jr., "The Relevance of Rhetoric to Philosophy and of Philosophy to Rhetoric," in *Quarterly Journal of Speech*, Vol. 52 (February 1966), p. 44.
10. Wayne C. Booth, "The Revival of Rhetoric," *PMLA*, Vol. 80 (May 1965), pp. 8–12.
11. *Higher Education and National Affairs*, Vol. 18, No. 20 (June 10, 1969), p. 4.
12. Suzanne K. Langer, *Problems of Art* (New York, 1957), p. 115.
13. Aristotle, *Rhetorica* (Vol. I), 2. 1355ᵇ.
14. C. Perelman, *The Idea of Justice and the Problem of Argument*, trans. by John Petrie (London, 1963), pp. 158–159.
15. P. Albert Duhamel, "The Function of Rhetoric as Effective Expression," in *Journal of the History of Ideas*, Vol. 10 (June 1949), reprinted in *The Province of Rhetoric*, Ed. by Joseph Schwartz and John A. Rycenga (New York, 1965), pp. 36–48.
16. Wayne C. Booth, *The Rhetoric of Fiction* (Chicago, 1961), p. 116.
17. W. Ross Winterowd, *Rhetoric: A Synthesis* (New York, 1968), p. 18.
18. Murray Krieger, "Contextualism and the Relegation of Rhetoric," in *Rhetoric and Poetic*, Ed. by Donald C. Bryant (Iowa City, 1965), pp. 46–47.
19. Roger A. Hornsby, "The Relevance of Ancient Literature: Recapitulation and Comment," in *Rhetoric and Poetic*, Ed. by Donald C. Bryant, p. 92.
20. Longinus, *On the Sublime*, trans. by A. O. Prickard, reprinted in *Readings in Classical Rhetoric*, Ed. by Thomas W. Benson and Michæl H. Prosser (Boston, 1969), p. 271.
21. Aristotle, *De Poetica* (19. 1456ᵇ), trans. by Ingram Bywater, in *The Works of Aristotle*.
22. George Kennedy, *The Art of Persuasion in Greece*, pp. 11–12.
23. Jerrold E. Siegel, *Rhetoric and Philosophy in Renaissance Humanism* (Princeton, 1968), pp. 31–62.
24. William G. Crane, "English Rhetorics of the 16th Century," in *The Province of Rhetoric*, pp. 212–226.
25. Walter J. Ong, "Ramist Rhetoric," in *The Province of Rhetoric*, pp. 226–255; see also Walter J. Ong, *Ramus—Method, and the Decay of Dialogue* (Cambridge, Mass., 1958); Wilbur Samuel Howell, *Logic and Rhetoric in England 1500–1700* (Princeton, 1956), pp. 116–172.
26. See Karl R. Wallace, *Francis Bacon on Communication and Rhetoric* (Chapel Hill, 1943), pp. 27, 183.
27. *Metaphysica* (a.2. 995ᵃ), trans. by W. D. Ross, in *The Works of Aristotle*.
28. *Rhetorica* (Vol. III), 1. 1403ᵃ.
29. *Demosthenes' On the Crown*, ed. by James J. Murphy, with a new translation by John J. Keaney (New York, 1967), p. 112; see also Galen O. Rowe, "Demosthenes' Use of Language," in the same book, p. 183.
30. *A Greek Critic: Demetrius on Style*, trans. by G. M. A. Grube, reprinted in *Readings in Classical Rhetoric*, ed. by Thomas W. Benson and Michæl H. Prosser (Boston, 1969), p. 258.
31. *Ibid.*, p. 264.
32. *Ibid.*, p. 267.

33. Cicero, *Orator*, trans. by H. M. Hubbell, reprinted in *Readings in Classical Rhetoric*, p. 239.
34. Longinus, "On the Sublime," in *Readings in Classical Rhetoric*, pp. 270–271.
35. J. Robert Oppenheimer, "The Open Mind," in *Bulletin of the Atomic Scientists*, Vol. 5, No. 1 (January 1949), 5.
36. Kenneth Burke, *Permanence and Change* (New York, 1935), p. 71.
37. A. N. Whitehead, *The Aims of Education and Other Essays* (New York, 1929), p. 19.
38. John Livingston Lowers, *Essays in Appreciation* (Boston, 1936), pp. 3–5, *passim*.
39. Dwight MacDonald, "The Bible in Modern Undress," in *The New Yorker* (Nov. 14, 1953), p. 175.
40. Nils Erik Enkvist, John Spencer, and Michael J. Gregory, *Linguistics and Style* (London, 1964), p. 12; see also, *Style in Language*, Ed. by Thomas A. Sebeok (Cambridge, Mass., 1960), p. vi.
41. P. Albert Duhamel, "The Function of Rhetoric as Effective Expression," p. 38.

Harry and Agathe Thornton

STYLE AND TIME

THOSE WHO ARE OCCUPIED WITH THE INTERPRETATION OF ORAL AND
written literature often encounter psychological aspects to those matters with which they have to deal. In this respect, they resemble a great
variety of many other researchers. There is almost no enquiry which
sooner or later does not pose the enquirer with questions of a psychological kind. In such circumstances it is natural to turn to the psychologists, but it is just as usual not to find what is sought, and then to do
it oneself as best as one may. Enough of this experience may lead to
distrusting and excluding psychology altogether. This solution is altogether too costly. Besides, the experience need not be wholly negative, if it produces the right sense that mere shrewd mother-wit is not
sufficient in matters of this kind. Psychology is indeed difficult enough
to leave a lot to be desired in simply becoming prejudiced about it, and
more discriminating investigators betray some uneasiness.

One large part, indeed the principal part of the psychological side
of our collaboration in *Time and Style*[1] is the use of a clear and detailed,
systematic body of psychology. It is important that this is understood
and respected so that the book may assist those for whom it was written
as much and as soon as possible. Our hope is that this will have at least
two results—viz., to make explicit much that is already implicit in
what is done by literary interpreters, anthropologists, and others when
they touch upon psychological issues; and further, to provide such with
a greater sense of orientation and security in dealing with them. It has
been suggested that in spite of its claims, *Time and Style* contains no
systematic psychology, or very little. Actually, it contains a very great
deal which is also well grounded in the development of psychology
historically, and well digested in the general acceptance of established
psychological fact. Any appearance to the contrary arises from the

necessity under which we found ourselves, in collaboration between psychology and interpretation, of subordinating the applied psychology to the purposes it is serving. It is because the psychology has been so thoroughly kneaded into the detail of the whole argument of the book that the appearance arises of there not being so much of it as we claim. This accounts for the illusion. Nothing is easier than making slap-down pronouncements in terms everyone obviously understands, and then passing on. Only this reminds us of what Kant said about that very good thing, innocence—it does not wear well—and in the sort of enquiries which arise in *Time and Style* such approaches lead us nowhere at all. Assuming that we are all psychologists, that we were born such and never required any advancement in it, is vulnerable innocence indeed. No, the familiar and obvious, far from being simple when we try to win insight and knowledge, is notoriously complicated. That is too old a truism in the history of scientific endeavor for us to labour here.

We propose, then, to put forward a fairly schematic, synoptic account of the relevant psychology. It will, we hope, do the right job well. The kind of help that is needed might be described as quasi-technical, affording ready assistance at definite places, even where it might in part be rejected. It might be compared to the way in which mathematical ideas are made available in a small handbook for the purposes of, say, a radio engineer. It would not be the purpose of such a book to go into questions about the philosophy of mathematics. No more is it our purpose here to broach corresponding questions about psychology. The blame for resorting to their own "psychologizing" cannot be fairly laid on a growing number of investigators in a variety of fields, if they have been unable to find suitable help from those who admittedly know more than they themselves do. What they need is something like a map, detailed enough for their purposes, and advantageous through its schematism.

Anything like a systematic expression of theoretical psychology works in a threefold way. It is descriptive, classificatory, and interpretative of psychology. As classificatory and descriptive, it fits the needs of those we have in mind too closely not to attract their attention strongly, if it is at all useful. However, the interpretative aspect of any schema ought never to be forgotten. The really important thing is to hold it firmly, but lightly, even if appreciatively. Even when one has an inside view of a psychological system, it is not easy to use it with such firmness and lightness, remaining aware of its elaborateness and tentativeness. Those who have not such an inside view should, without undue despairing, take warning that abuse of such a schema is easy, and begets distrust.

The substance of what is offered here derives from the psychological principles of James Ward of Cambridge, England. These, as Stout wrote nearly fifty years ago, constitute a central schema possessed of a remarkable unity and coherence. It is this which we should like to see made available for investigators who feel in need of something more than their own wits when they realize that their problems require in some aspects an alliance with a manageable general psychology. Stout also wrote that there were some present-day psychologists for whom such a central scheme proved a stumbling-block, cutting them off from understanding and appreciation of Ward's work as a whole. In the course of the last forty years the number of such psychologists has increased. Stout wrote in order to remove or to mitigate their difficulties, but he was wise enough to modify his expectations by the qualification that he was doing so "at least for those who are not dogmatically prepossessed with the view that psychology must be merely a special development or application of biology or physiology or any other physical science."

There are, of course, very great dangers inherent in accompanying such an account with diagrams like the schema we have provided. The hope is that it will facilitate the grasping of the matter, for much of it is notoriously difficult to put into words. Such schemata are limited, as being entirely subordinated, in what they can do, to the accounts given. They are meant, like illustrative materials to make hard going just a little bit easier for the reader. Certain minds will almost inevitably fasten on them and try to turn them into deductive systems, manipulating them in a manner wholly alien to anything for which they are of any use. To do this is to succumb to one's prejudices. We dislike being reminded that we have prejudices, but often we administer them like medicine to others under the description of our principles, which endears them to us very much. In this kind of fix, our rationalism misleads us into dogmatism, while our empiricism, forgetting the things it can see so plainly in the neighbor's eye, succumbs to the same vice—which in turn rejoices the neighbor, because he can then attack it so clearly and so confidently. Rationalism barks at relativism, while empiricism, fearing to become dogmatic, snarls at the source of its own dilemma. Deductivism bawls at induction, which in turn fingers its nose at the assailant, both forgetting that they could never be so exclusively opposed, if they did not still more belong to each other. In such quarters are the sources of our difficulties and misunderstandings.

If one demands a clear, concise definition, the answer is heaven knows what, which is why philosophers can weary both themselves and other men, as they have done in all ages. What after all is definition? Is there a clear, concise definition of definition? Probably not. So, if there is no lucid definition of definition, it may remain perfectly reasonable to say that illuminating definitions of definition are possible. This more limited achievement has to keep in view the matter to which the definition is related. We think that qualitative time as related to feeling and psychological attitude in the understanding of literature does its work well, which is allowed when a critic says that many of our observations are "relevant and helpful." That it is, or can be given "clear, concise definition," *simpliciter*, we do not hold to be either reasonable or possible, for we are talking about psychology, not philosophy, and in this sort of matter philosophy must observe its own limitations without exerting too much insistence on ordering other people's houses, when it can so easily be directed to the condition of its own.

There is also another influence which has emanated from certain circles in Oxford, and Professor Passmore pointed it out when he wrote: "In the last half-century, Oxford has won for itself the reputation of being the most notable adversary of the advance of psychology."

To realize this is to appreciate the achievement of psychology in being where it is in Oxford today. Neither Stout nor McDougall could stay there in their day. Professor Prichard put it about that at best psychology was "a hotch-potch of loosely related enquiries, not a proper science." Professor Ryle in his *Concept of Mind* has only continued this good cause. The source of it all within Oxford itself was Professor Cook-Wilson, when he wrote: "It is the business of the student of logic to determine the normal use of an idiom or a linguistic expression. Everything depends upon that." This has become a fashionable movement at mid-century, and Oxford's prestige has spread it widely about the world. There is nothing new about it and it need not detain us in seeking what it obstructs, the advance of the usefulness of psychology. As Professor Tennant pointed out thirty years ago, ". . . man's language and modes of thought, formed with a view to practical needs, may fall short of the precision and subtlety required for exact science and philosophy." It is futile to introduce a demand for precision and subtlety into ordinary idiom itself and then try to make out that this is still just ordinary usage. This is misleading and begets more obscurantism than the error it opposes, which is the abuse of terminology we term jargon.

To the tilting yards of these hoary ceremonial jousts we are not strangers, but we remain as alien as Simple Simon. Where the blessed nuptial ring that could symbolize the union between psychology and logic may be found, we have indeed little idea, unless it is somewhere in the quarter of that "abduction" mentioned by Aristotle himself, the originator of deduction and induction. However, it is more than probable (though, of course, not quite certain) that anything as imaginative as this would appeal to us in any case. Our regret is that we use expressions like "principle," "relation," "concept," even as much as we do, but in the very nature of the case there is much sheer force of circumstance which enters into these matters. If, of course, there is nothing with just that little bit more strength than circumstance, nothing, with just that sensation of Ariel to it, which can penetrate circumstance, then we are indeed lost. And now, having realized how deeply we must despair, let us begin again.

The argument of *Time and Style* establishes a relation between appositional form and qualitative time, the one a principle of literary style, the other indispensable in experience and, therefore, basic for all psychological principles. Figure 1 presents the content and structure of the argument. Appositional form is a specific sort of sequence obtaining in literary (including oral) utterances. Qualitative time is indispensable for understanding experience or any sequence of experienced happenings. It concerns them as lived through, with aspects of them in which interest and feeling, and the strength or intensity of these, are very much to the front. In an appositional utterance, the main item of a sentence or passage is stated first, seized on impetuously, and brought forward with an emphasis which expresses intense interest. Such an "initial statement" is then expanded and elaborated by descriptions, explanations of past events which illuminate and bring out the nuances of the "initial statement," and so on. Thus the onslaught of interest is calmed and deepened, its urgency satisfied. Then the speaker either returns to the "initial statement," which is now rich in perspectives and in feeling, ready to be rounded off, or he simply moves on to the next item of interest.

From Greek literature we have called in examples from Homer, Hesiod, Parmenides, Empedocles, Pindar, Herodotus and Thucydides (*Ch. 1*). From Latin, Naevius, Ennius, Cato, Lucretius, and Virgil are represented (*Ch. 2*). Sources other than Western Classical—viz., Sanskrit, Old Persian, Old English, and Hebrew, as well as the field of modern primitive peoples, are referred to (*Conclusion*) in order to suggest the more detailed extension and application of the basic relationship obtaining between appositional form and qualitative time. Thus

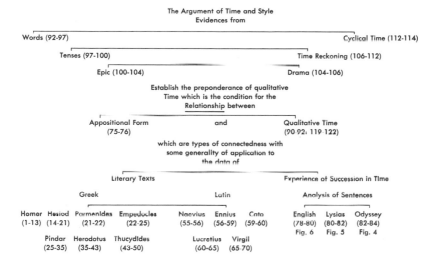

FIG. 1.   The argument of *Time and Style*.

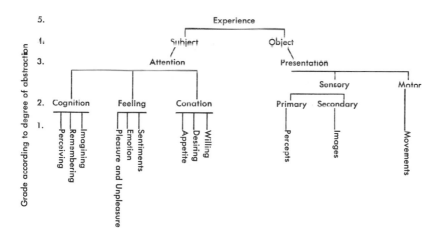

FIG. 2.   Concepts graduated according to their degree of abstraction from the psychological phenomena to which they pertain.

the bringing into connection of qualitative time and appositional form is the correlating of definite types of psychological connectedness and a definite type of literary, stylistic connectedness. It therefore represents an interdisciplinary adjustment, providing a powerful tool for literary interpretation through the help of psychology. For appositional form as a type of stylistic connectedness is as empirically derived from relevant experiences through observation and description as the types of psychological connectedness with which it is correlated. It finds its relevant phenomena in its texts. This line of argument, which is empirically based in the texts and formulates a general description of appositional style, converges with the other line of argument from the side of psychology (see Fig. 1). The principles and terms of a general psychology are described briefly in *Time and Style* (p. 77 ff.). It is this part which will be described more fully in this paper, with the help of a schema (Fig. 3). From an analysis of temporal succession, a qualita-

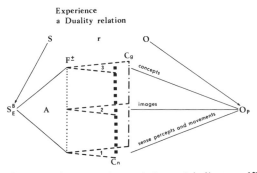

FIG. 3. Schema for general systematic psychology, S indicates selfhood, in psychological investigation a mere limiting concept; S_B, embodied self or living organism, the body-mind unity as an initial datum, not dualistic in any exclusive metaphysical sense; $S^E{}_B$, empirical embodied self, capable of investigation as experience and behavior on the basis of observation adducing direct and indirect evidence; $S^E{}_B$ r O, empirical embodied self as related to an Other, always standing in relation to selves or non-selves other than itself; A, Attention or selective interest; $F\pm$ (*dotted line*), feeling, positive or negative: interest with pleasure-pain tonality, a dimension permeating the attention of the empirical embodied self; Cn (*solid-box line*), conation, another dimension pervasive of the selective interest of the self; and Cg (*dot-dash line*), cognition, a third dimension of the self's experience. *1, 2,* and *3* (*broken line*) represent a functional unit at the appropriate levels (three of them, here) connecting the dimensions—viz., cognition and responsive conation through positive or negative state of feeling. Thus Level 1 is perception, a first-grade concept limited by the concept of sensing. Level 2 is (a) remembering (level 2 in relation to level 1), and (b) imagining (level 2 in relation to level 3). Level 3 is conceiving: a third-grade concept limited by the concept of intellection. Op represents the idea of "Otherpresented," that which as self or not-self is found in experience in relation to $S^E{}_B$ in accordance with the duality characteristic of experience. This idea covers all possible presentations in the experiential relationship.

tive aspect of time emerges as predominant. It is not amenable to precise measurement, although this does not necessarily mean that it is not measurable at all. The condition for the relationship between appositional form and qualitative time is a preponderance of a qualitative experience of time as found in the meaning of words expressing time-notions, the nature of Greek tenses, the ways in which action is presented in epic and in drama, the manner in which time is reckoned in chronologies and calendars, and the circularity of time in the ancient world. The arguments from these sources confirm the relationship between appositional form and qualitative time.

At the basis of *Time and Style* lies an analysis of time. It is an empirical, psychological analysis. It describes all experiences in which things follow one another successively with reference to present, past, and future.

The analysis of such experience in its qualitative aspect involves reference to types of connectedness which are all psychological. These have to do with the duality, the polar contrast of subject and presentation in experience, with its conservation or retention, with its strength and weakness, and so on. In fact, there come into play all the basic kinds of connectedness which contribute to the structure of a body of general psychology deriving through reflection from experience as constituting phenomena which interested, attentive subjects can perceive. This structure of psychology is more or less a constructed whole functioning as a governing, orienting, determinative totality in and through all the plastic activity of experiencing agents, yet so intimately and so mutually bound up with these agents as to be itself subject to modification.

Although we have articulated this analysis for ourselves, we do not think for a moment that it is original in the much overdone sense of that word, denoting "novel in an unqualified manner." From this idea we would discourage everybody with the tendency to suppose it. Aristotle, perhaps, had the root of this matter when he wrote that "Time is the number of movement in respect of before and after" (*Physics* IV.11.209.^{b}.1). Kant certainly spelled it out quite clearly, if he is given the attention he requires (cf. p. 15). Nor do we think that even Kant was any more original, in the sense mentioned, than we ourselves. Time as an experience of succession is too basic, too pervasive, too familiar, too elusive, and therefore too recurrently fascinating, for individual claims of such exclusiveness to be credible. We would hazard a guess, for instance, that Tetens was not unfamiliar with the idea and that, just as much as Kant, he was a transmitter, not a source *de novo*.

The literary "appositional form," when put in relation to an analysis of time such as this, sets one thing in high relief: how the attention of a listener or reader moves in response to what is said. As the movement of attention thus becomes clear through being connected with an intelligible account of temporal process, there emerge clear clues and definite indications of what the people were like with whose attention we are concerning ourselves. The interest of people as concentrated in the things they made and to which their listeners readily responded is thus made to yield up understanding of the mind, outlook, and preconceptions belonging to them. The forms, the traditions in terms of which they were what they were can be indicated in this way. But this is nothing less than to expose their "style," and "appostional form" is style in this more general sense. Among the Greeks, for instance, it is common to Homer, Hesiod, Parmenides, Empedocles, Pindar, Herodotus, and Thucydides. Within the style of these Greeks in this more general sense, each of these great names represents a highly articulated individual writer. To win any access to the style of any one of them in a more specific sense of style, knowing the man to whom the style belongs not merely as this or that sort of man, but as *this*, not *that* man, is an enterprise calling for yet greater refinements. There are, too, some fairly obvious limitations: the extant remains of the writers' work, for instance; and even more decisive, distance in time. Working with those more nearly contemporaneous with us, especially where there are rich bodies of work and supporting evidences to draw on, we naturally have the individual, specific and particular, foremost in our focus. On the more general side, we tend perhaps to neglect style, through taking too much for granted. Yet anyone who, for example, can select a passage from, say, Descartes, in which he refers to "the natural light of reason," and set it down on his title page as "the right of reason," and have this passed, printed, and published without alteration at the beginning of a big volume on psychosomatic medicine—well, such things show clearly that we are all prone to be unwittingly negligent about influential matters which we do not think about, because they have so much to do with our thinking about everything else. Nor does there appear to be any good reason for thinking that civilized men in any period are at all different. Historic sense seems to be the only guardian against such difficulties. It is quite a rare endowment.

One of our intentions in *Time and Style* is to provide a tool to be used in various fields by those concerned with interpretation, particularly when they seek to improve the handling of the psychological aspects of the issues with which they deal. It is quite true that this is not obvious in the book itself, which is first and foremost a sample of active collaboration, not an exposition of its psychology in an independent and probably disadvantageously abstracted fashion. The present contribution, while it is not a treatise on its subject matter, as time has excluded such an enterprise even if it were judged auspicious at present, does provide a somewhat more explicit account of the psychology worked into it from a consistently maintained view of a general psychology.

It is important to understand as clearly as possible what the relation between interpretation and psychology is, in order to forestall misunderstanding. Immanuel Kant, describing the core of *The Critique of Pure Reason*, wrote that there were two sides to the deep and laborious enquiry constituting his "Transcendental Deduction of the Categories." Kant wrote that one side of this investigation is essential. The other, he wrote, while not utterly indispensable, is still very important for his main purpose of answering the question: "What sort of concepts does the understanding use when it knows determinate objects?" The relation between interpretation and psychology is very like this. Interpretation is important, because it concerns the right understanding of that which is in question. Psychology cannot take its place. Interpretation has to appeal to criteria more numerous than merely psychological matters. It cannot be reduced to something simply psychological, explicable as a psychological effect. Psychology is, in this way, incidental and subordinate to interpretation. At the same time psychology pervades interpretation unremittingly. It has an importance which may not be put aside without substantial loss for interpretation. Interpretation, we may say, is concerned with making something intelligible. Psychology has to do with various aspects of the conditions required for this interpretative activity. Psychology is an *ancilla*, no more—but no less.

In experience, as James Ward wrote, all that we know and feel and do, all our facts and theories, all our emotions and ideals and ends may be included. The totality of the conscious events that make up an individual life, the discriminative reaction or the nonconscious response of an organism to happenings—within its environment—these make up what is thought in "experience." All this is observed in a direct way based upon sense-perception. The results are described and classified. The more general rules which seem to emerge are checked by means of experiment. In this way, the psychological concepts with a claim upon some degree of abstraction and upon definite generality emerge. These are conceptual ways of considering—reflecting upon—conscious, living organisms. Their use involves the employment of a schema of a general, systematic psychology. Such a schema shows some of the main concepts of psychology in coherent relationship with one another. In Fig. 3, this schema is exhibited, the part pertaining to the subjective aspect of the dual relationship, which is fundamental to all experience, being more fully presented. The limitation of our present attention to this has two reasons. Firstly, we need to illuminate the nature of that interest or selective attention which is so important in the argument of *Time and Style* in order to proceed with our present task. Secondly, the detail of the more objective, presentational aspect of the central experiential relationship is not so important for all that we are at present concerned with. Figure 3 offers a visible presentation of the main psychological ideas involved in the activities of any experiencing individual insofar as experience concerns process, not presentation. Its captions briefly summarize these leading ideas with reference to their content or their function.

In describing experience in a psychological way, it is necessary to take account of two matters: (1) the subjective side of experience, and (2) whatever interested individuals encounter in the environment with which they are concerned. To describe experience we must pay close attention to both these components. Their relation is at the bottom of experience and pervades all experience. Once the differences which arise from this relation are laid out plainly, we find ourselves in a network to which we have the key. We can take our bearings, and find our way, whenever we are faced by the need of giving a psychological account of anything. The key principle is this *duality of experience*. It puts into our hands a map of psychology, which can guide us through its territory, wherever it has to be crossed in penetrating any subject in which we are interested. This relation is important for understanding experience. It connects people with all that they encounter. At the same time, it distinguishes them from all they find.

Whatever an individual meets belongs to him. It cannot be separated from him. If it is, there is no possibility of talking about his psychology. In this sense all that belongs to him is the psychology of his experience, of his passing through everything that happens to him. In this, he acts; through this, he suffers. Agent or subject, he constitutes the subjective side of experience, which is part of what psychology studies through observing, describing, and classifying what it finds there.

What people encounter is not merely themselves. Nor, though it includes other people, is it limited by them. It also comprises things and animals. All this considered in unbreakable relation to individual people is what stands over against them and, as such, is presented to them in experience to be lived through and encountered.

We shall refer to it in what follows as the *presentational side* of experience. That which corresponds to it in the duality of experience on the side of the subject we shall call the *subjective side* of experience. Under this very considerable limitation the concept of Subject of experience describes an agent as either interested or not interested and, as such, singles him out as attending selectively to everything presented to him. The concept of the Subject of experience is both negative and positive. Negatively, it represents the self-limitation of psychology as a discipline. Psychology is not asserting or denying things about people which are outside her province. She has a definite subject matter of her own as well as a definite standpoint. In accordance with these, her procedure is observational, descriptive, classificatory, and, so far as may be, expperimental and predictive. From this ground she reaches out towards such general rules as can be supported by the ascertainable results upon it. Beyond this, the concept of Subject does not extend in the direction of elucidating or interpreting the complexity of selfhood. If it is so extended, then the concept is misused. In this sense it is negative. It is such a negative limiting concept with reference to the relation between psychology and other disciplines, especially philosophical disciplines, which are also interested in the nature and the value of selfhood. Within the science of psychology itself, it operates positively by determining the description of that side of selfhood which is amenable to investigation by psychology, so that in this connection it is descriptive of the individual experient as an embodied self or living organism. Whether the actual, living organism is viewed as being reducible materialistically, or whether reservations about this are made, does not much affect the psychological attitude to it. The individual, living organism is seen as the initial, central controlling datum in the investigation. Some psychologists hold that this is an embodied self. Others hold that it is an animal. None is without embarrassment when he comes to difficulties about these matters. All the same, central to the procedure of psychological investigation is the acceptance of its datum in a manner which tacitly denies any dualism in an exclusive sense among its constituent elements.

Psychology, then, tries to reflect clearly about the experience of individual people by means of agential concepts such as that of an "embodied-self" or its equivalent, a "living organism," manifesting interested attention to surroundings in which it encounters a continuing stream of presentations of all sorts which are possible objects for it. Thus the consideration of any living organism in its environment shows that there are things which it seeks and others which it avoids. Its bodily equipment, consisting of specific sense organs, gives it a range of things readily accessible to it. Equally, there are things this same equipment either excludes or renders very unlikely to be noticed. This means that on account of its bodily equipment for responding to its environment, it is selective in its responsiveness. This is still more noticeable when we consider human beings. Different sorts of human beings are much more markedly selective over much wider ranges of things which attract and occupy them, and to which they persistently return, than others. With them selectivity is not determined merely by bodily equipment. It is also driven by interest. Such interest and selectivity are attentiveness. Selective attention distinguishes the subject. It represents indeed all that in the Subject which can legitimately be investigated within the limits of a psychological, empirical method. It is, if you like, the Subject, positively handled with reference to the content of observable phenomena, not negatively handled as a "focus imaginarius" delimiting psycology's interest from the interest of other disciplines.

The Subject is attentive and, as such, is interested and selective. Six processes may be distinguished as coming under the selective attention of the Subject:

1. Sensing.
2. Perceiving.
3. Remembering.
4. Imagining as more or less passive fancy with an order mainly imposed upon it in accordance with associative rules.
5. Imagining as an active fancy possessing its own distinctive principle of order.
6. Abstract formal intellection.

Perceiving, remembering, both sorts of imagining—these are the most down-to-earth ways of ordering our experiences. Their contexts are directly concrete and their relationships vivid and practical. Through them all generality is most immediately connected with sensible phenomena. They represent the least abstracted of our concepts, which belong to the lowest grade of abstraction among our ideas. The plain reason why perceiving is like this lies in our bodies. Whether we think of ourselves as simply being bodies or consider that we are embodied makes no difference to this. It is the same with imagining, which also has this sort of sensory reference. It needs sensory, material media in which to work, and to which it must more or less directly refer. Thus perceiving, remembering, and imagining, through their immediacy of connection with sensory phenomena, are all ideas of one kind doing distinct jobs within their type and range. They are what we call empirical concepts or, with reference to putting forward a schema of general psychology, concepts of the first grade, or simply first-grade concepts.

The idea of grading concepts carries with it the notion of conceptual range, within which range concepts may be sorted out according to their uses and limits. Just as the ancient Hebrews said you need a pair of tongs to make a pair of tongs, so, when you are thinking, in order to deal with concepts about which you know something, you find you need concepts of another sort in order to do the job—and so on, to the limits of the abstraction to which you can attain and which you are able to control. Certainly, in this fascinating pursuit, most of us soon find we limp along far behind a Leibnitz, yet in general we can appreciate the idea that fleas have lesser fleas upon their backs to bite 'em and to keep their tweezers spry. Just so, then, within the limits of a general psychology based upon empirical methods directed to the investigation of phenomena there are second- and third-grade concepts, as well as auxiliary concepts. Such a second-grade concept is cognition, comprising those of the first grade such as perceiving, remembering, and imagining. So, also, conation and feeling are second-grade concepts.

Figure 2 will perhaps serve to illustrate the position, while also bringing out the way in which the third-grade concept of selective attention governs cognition, conation, and feeling. In this way, too, one may better understand the business of increasing abstraction in reflection, of constructing different grades of concepts in order to do different jobs at greater and greater removes of abstract thinking, which is only one disciplined and refined form of imagining. Looking at the matter in these perspectives, what we call abstract thought will proceed through a range or continuum, taking it increasingly away from elementary, first-grade concepts which have to do with sense-perception and everything derived from it in *ideation*—i.e., those elements belonging to remembering and imagining like images and "ideas" which derive from sense-perception. Concepts so rudimentary as these first-grade ones are in fact mainly "generic images," which are close enough to sense-experience, yet possessed of a schematic character giving them a foothold, so to speak, on ground from which generality and definition can more distinctively proceed and develop. At this end of the range, abstraction may be thought of as approaching asymptotically, so to speak, to zero, and here arises the question about sensing and sensa—i.e., about content of sense which is simply given as such. This idea is neither a nonconcept nor yet a first-grade concept or anything like it. It has to do with a characteristic of first-grade concepts such as sense-perception, viz., "sensiness." Being a concept concerned with this feature of the phenomena to which first-grade concepts themselves more directly relate, it does not refer to phenomena in the way these concepts do.

Actually, such concepts as "sensing," "sensum," "sensation," are of a high degree of abstraction. Far from being rudimentary empirical concepts, they are relatively highly sophisticated abstractions—e.g., pure redness. They, and concepts of their kind, crop up in the border-regions between diverse concepts along the range or continuum of abstraction, and we shall entitle them *limiting concepts*. Their main use is in delimiting the functioning of one set of ideas which may be more or less abstract than they themselves are. At the other end of the range of ideation, there is a similar story about limiting concepts. For imagining, as an active principle possessing its own inherent order, also reaches a border-territory. Here, abstraction reaches a great degree of remoteness from anything immediately sensible. Even its relations to sensible means of expression become very attenuated. It may, for instance, propose to deal with marks upon paper and with nothing else or with sounds which have no connections with verbal sounds at all. In such regions abstractive, ideational processes concerned only with manipulative rule-controlled signs are in order. This pitch of conceptual thinking we describe as "intellection," regarded as a limiting concept with reference to all ideational activities. Such conceiving, distinguished within ideation, is itself to be kept distinct from imagining of both kinds (higher and lower, as it were). It is associated with a claim to be completely independent of sensory phenomena, but with this we need scarcely here concern ourselves, as all the principles of connection, both psychological and literary, with the relationship of which we are concerned, are experiential and empirically derived from experience of phenomena. Thus such conceiving as we have described, like the sensing which we previously described, are limiting concepts for reflection about the psychological aspects of experienced phenomena. They are quite different concepts from the first-grade concepts like cognition, feeling, and conation. Into this it is not necessary to proceed here and, in relation to the schema of a general psychology, we shall rest content with viewing them as auxiliary concepts.

Let us now turn to second-grade psychological concepts, viz., feeling, conation, and cognition. Underlying them all as concerned with subjective experience is the idea of *process*. The circumstances needed for the appearance of living organisms and individual lives consist in unceasing, interdependent changes. By "process" we refer to these generally. Thus environment *is* process. It is made up of changes insofar as these can be observed and described throughout changes continuously succeeding each other. Individual living organisms are partly supported, partly thwarted, by such changes. They are stimulated, they respond; they are moulded, they select and shape. Considered as phenomena, they interact, from beginning to end of their duration, with environment. They are themselves process within environmental process, very specialized arenas of unceasing, interdependent changes. Now, consider such an individual living organism. Whether it is thought of at any particular time or through the course of its lifetime does not affect what is to be said about it as process. There are changes taking place within it. The organism can perceive these changes as internal changes. Consider these changes as constituting a class. Then, within it, there are species of change which are merely bodily changes. Within it, there are also other kinds of changes. These are not necessarily separable from bodily changes; they are distinguishable from them. Changes of this sort are feelings. To say that they are conscious is to say they are referred to the individual, living organism. With respect to them, the farthest one can go in defining them is to say the individual is inside them.

Feeling in the simplest sense is pleasantness and unpleasantness. Some prefer to express this as pleasure and unpleasure. This follows the German terms *Lust* and *Unlust*. It is important not to confuse the latter with pain, which is described and classified under the cognitional-limitative concept "sensation." Pleasure and "unpleasure" are polar opposites in a continuum of feeling. They come about as responses to sensations arising in a physical context of conditions under which the bodily organs are stimulated. They also appear when the bodily tensions accompanying instinctual needs or states of anticipation are relieved. Strong feelings like fear, anger, joy, grief, surprise, and many more, are important ingredients in the complex states of organisms called emotions. Psychology has no job for "feeling" in its popular use, as it is much too indefinite. One of its meanings, "touch sensations," has no relevance to the understanding of feeling. Feeling is a sort of dimension, so to speak, running right through the whole range of the attentive interest of an individual, with more or less strength. It pervades his experience like a variable atmosphere or climate. Conation and cognition are comparable dimensions of experience.

The phenomena of conation are bodily movements, appetite, desire, and volition. Bodily movements, incipient or overt, may be observed in behavior. They may also be remembered or imagined in conscious experience. Desire and volition are also observable in conscious experience. Conation is rooted in the body, where its phenomena can be observed as impulses arising from organic conditions or states of the body. William James said that man has all the impulses that the lower creatures have, as well as many others: also, that man excels all mammals, including monkeys, in this espect. Modern psychologists would generally support James in his view. These insistent impulses may be inherited. An animal, for instance, will eliminate its waste matter just where it finds itself, unless specially trained to do otherwise. So also will a human infant. Training to redirect the inherited impulse involves teaching through conditioning and implies learning. The result of such training is acquired impulses, but these do not concern us here. It is the inherited impulse, called by a variety of names such as instinct, urge, drive, and need, that matters. It is called conative in so far as it is a striving towards something and away from something else. In the instance cited, the striving is away from the discomfort of a full bladder, and towards the ease of an empty one. Such striving, arising directly from bodily conditions, is appetite. When it is inherited, and does not need to be learned, such appetitive impulse is instinctive. This is as close to a precise idea of instinct as psychology has yet attained. From this fundamental instinctual level all mental development begins. It is included under the general term *conation*, which embraces desire and volition.

In desiring, I think of something I should like to do or to happen to me. While I do so, my bodily impulses are aroused. Even if this takes place only incipiently, I feel moved towards actually doing it. I may have appetites and not know at all clearly that I do have them, but when I definitely think on something I should like, appetitive impulse is clearly directed towards some goal or other, and there is also a distinct drive to reach that goal. This kind of activity is distinct from, as well as related to, appetition. It, too, is conative, but its specific name is desire. We may sum this up by saying that desire represents an experience together with a tendency for the experience to be realized —i.e., with an appetitive impulse towards realizing it.

Suppose then, I desire to do something. I make up my mind I am going to do it. And, accordingly, I start trying to bring this about. Such trying is a sort of conation called volition or willing. Its characteristics are self-consciousness, attention to a clear definite end by way of selective choosing. Willing can only take place on the basis of impulse and desire. I may will negatively, of course, as well as positively —i.e., I may exert myself to see that I don't do something I have an impulse to do.

Cognition, to which we next turn attention, is contrasted with conation and feeling, yet like them it is a concept of similar generality. It covers perceiving, remembering, and imagining. As such, it denotes a function of conscious life just like conation and feeling. All three are diverse modes of knowing phenomena. In these studies we are not trying to pursue what is absolutely true for all intelligence. What we are after concerns what is true in a relative sense. All we have to do with belongs to human beings. Literature, oral and written, is produced by them. To study it in relation to the kind of minds which shape it is to bring it into relation to their psychology, again a matter which pertains wholly to them. About this there is nothing surprising, for all these things belong to human experience, and it is experience, and the relatedness at the core of it, from which all psychological study proper proceeds, by which they are governed and to which they return. This is to recognize that proper psychological study proceeds in accordance with the principle of the duality of experience.

We have already said a good deal about cognition as process in describing the first-grade concepts perceiving, remembering, and imagining. This is what principally concerns us in our present task, but we should also like to indicate that what else has to be said about cognition comes under the concept of presentation. Reflection upon the definite content of the cognitive aspect of selective attending requires reference to presentation, i.e., to the relating of the processes of attention to some sorts of presentations. This is in accordance with the principle of the duality of experience, viz., that all references to phenomena ineluctably involve relation to selectively attentive subjects of experience. Such presentations are classifiable as sensory (both primary and secondary) and motor. The primary ones are percepts: concepts pertaining to phenomena as encountered in sense-perception. The secondary presentations are images of a considerable diversity: concepts pertaining to phenomena as encountered in representational ways, as in remembering and imagining. The motor presentations are movements: concepts relating to movements as felt within the body, whether in perception, in remembering, or in imagining. The second-grade concept of motor presentation connects intimately with the body, for all the first-grade concepts of appetition, desire, and volition are closely related to felt bodily movement. As we have already pointed out (cf. p. 17) this presentational side of the dual relation in experience is not so demanding upon our attention in the matters with which *Time and Style* is concerned. The subjective side, which does chiefly matter, has been described with the help of a general schema (Fig. 3), and what is now needed is a psychological analysis of our experience of temporal passage. This is an analysis of time, limited to an empirical psychological analysis.

Experience is phenomenal, and in accordance with the principle of duality, is concerned with the connections between a subject and presentations. All phenomenal experience is basically connected with time, since even in its shortest items time has a certain extensity, "spread-out-ness," or duration in the midst of its flow. Such a temporal character always applies to phenomena, and apart from it there is no question of dealing with experience or phenomena. Now style, such as the appositional form with which we are concerned in the book *Time and Style*, is no exception. There are two salient features in style, the semantic and the syntactic. The semantic is concerned with meaning, with the way in which linguistic items such as words are chosen, for example. The syntactic is concerned with the ways in which they are connected or put together. It is, of course, this latter feature of style with which we are concerned. But, whatever is so put together is a sequence of some kind and, as experienced phenomena such as language uttered or listened to, it is ineluctably connected with temporal succession. So then appositional form as a sequence or connection of linguistic materials phenomenally experienced involves temporal succession. A correlation is therefore possible between an analysis of linguistic style and an analysis of our experience of temporal succession. We now proceed to an account of this analysis of time.

Any given presentation which is apprehended in sense perception at a given time is focused or marked, so to speak, in the selective attending of a particular subject. It is thus differentiated from all else in the presentational context at the time.

The statement of such differentiation may appear to be no more than a lot of cumbersome jargon, but it is nothing of the kind. It must be appreciated how much implicit reference there is to psychology even in a short statement of this kind.

To make this explicit:

> Any given presentation (1) which is apprehended (2) in sense perception (3) at a given time (4) is focused or marked, so to speak, in the selective attending (5) of a particular subject (6). It is thus differentiated from all else in the presentational context at the time.
>
> 1. A specific, definite presentation may be a variety of sensepercept, of image, or of some other concept or ideational construct. Any of these are first-grade concepts. Presentation in general as distinct from specific, determinate presentations, is a third-grade concept corresponding in the dual relation of Experience to the concept of process under which agential activities fall. (Cf. Fig. 1).

2. This apprehension is through the selective attending of the subject of experience. This involves reference to third-grade concepts.

3. Sense-perception is one way in which an experiencing Subject attends in his relations with phenomena. It is a first-grade concept.

4. This involves reference to the sequence basic to the relatedness of all phenomena, viz., temporal process.

5. This selective attending is referred to above (2).

6. The subject would be the empirical embodied subject of experience or living organism. This is that portion of selfhood which is psychologically proper for investigation as experienced phenomenon.

It will appear from this sample of drawing out more explicitly what is implicit in the statement about differentiation that the whole schema of a general psychology involving graduated concepts, with their meaning and source ultimately in the empirical observation of psychological phenomena, is operative all the time, and that much reference to such a definite system of general psychology is required. It is easy to miss the whole point here. It would be possible to go through *Time and Style* marking such words and to develop an extensive piece of writing which would explain and relate them so as to show the psychology explicitly. This, however, cannot be effectively or conveniently done at the same time that one is collaborating closely with literary interpreters who want to use the psychology for their own legitimate purposes. There are perhaps upwards of seventy such words involved. Interdisciplinary cooperation involves more than a make-do adjustment to one another of groups of creaking external matters. The vocabulary of psychology is not so very different from the words we are constantly using, so one can be easily deceived, but these same words are terms belonging to a whole body of systematic psychology on scientific lines which no more mean just what an educated reader is accustomed to read into them than "temperature" in the language of physics means merely "hot."

Let us return to our analysis of temporal succession. There is yet another distinguishable phase in the experience of this: retention. Any differentiated presentation occupying the focused field of selective attending is connected with accompanying presentations, which have been, but are no longer, conscious sense-percepts directly differentiated in apprehension—that is, are no longer primary presentations. These are sort of secondary presentations within the present as it passes, more or less diffuse ingredients in what is presented, but related to sense-percepts and to one another in an orderly way. They are not, strictly speaking, perceptual, although occurring in intimate proximity with sense-percepts. They are already representational in character. In terms of presentation they are rudimentary images, after-images or after-sensations. In terms of the selective attention of the Subject their detection in experience requires concentrated effort of introspective or retrospective observation, which may be assisted by suitable stimulations under contrived conditions.

Ordinarily, what we call facilitation, which is familiarity with sense-perception through practice, obscures them perfectly. During sense-perception, however, oblivescence is occurring, which is a dropping of more diffuse elements out of notice, a process which takes place by means of such after-images or after-sensations. Yet both the dropping-out of the more diffuse, and the holding-on to the less diffuse are subject to order, and the holding-on phase of such experience of temporal passage is called retention. It requires image elements of some kind unless the content of sense-perception is to degenerate into the occurrence of isolated units, whose connectedness must then remain obscure. It is retention that supports the basic psychological principle of the conservation of experience. It is retention that answers the question of how, in any present act of attending, everything that is required is actually available, and is so in the right order during present time. The retentive phase, then, which enters into the analysis of our experiencing temporal succession, implies the principle of the conservation of experience, as well as the principle of the duality of experience. It also points quite clearly to the requirement of some sort of hypothesis of subconsciousness, in terms of which the narrow focus of attention at any given time, and the wider, deeper, surrounding field of awareness within which such attention is active, are related to one another through a threshold or border region accounting for all that goes on by means of representational images more or less intense or diffuse. (However interesting it is to set the systematic ideas of an empirical psychology into relation to the ideas of Sigmund Freud, there is no necessity to embark on that here, for James Ward was independently at work on this long before Freud was anything other than another neuropath. And, let us add, in order to save ourselves from charges of idolatry, that he was not the only one at work.) Within selective attending, then, the differentiation of presented sense-percept in the course of a present-time interval involves the retention or perseverance of earlier elements of a representational kind. These have a definite order in depth corresponding to the recency with which they themselves were present as sense-percepts. They have a similar gradation in strength, derived from the original impact of the sense-percepts to which they belonged, and this relates them to cognitive process, within the selective attending of the experient subject. They have, too, a graduated vividness, derived from the intensity of feeling aroused in the subject under the impact of their original sense-percepts, and this connects them with the dimension of feeling in selective attending.

We come lastly in our analysis of the experience of temporal succession to a phase which we shall designate *assimilation*. It must be apparent from all that has been said that we have to deal with items of immediate experience which are both direct and reproduced, with primary and secondary presentations. Now these, as they unroll or evolve temporally, are recognized as succeeding one another—i.e., as being related in a definite order to one another. This also holds for the way in which they must be connected as occurring together in the course of any present time. So there is here a firm hold upon their combination both horizontally and vertically, so to speak. This phase of experienced temporal succession, this aspect of sense-perception which concerns such combination of presentations is *assimilation*. Such combining of direct and reproduced items into a whole introduces a phase in the context of the analysis, which is sense-perception, that is very similar to yet strikingly different from the other phases we have considered. For differentiation and retention, concerned with sense-percepts and after-images, or with sensations and after-sensations, are plainly deficient in generality, but assimilation brings into view something going beyond this lack. In this phase, even though still lowly and rudimentary, the imagery possesses more of the character of generality. It does so through its role in connection with grasping ordered succession. Still deeply involved in a sensational, bodily context, it brings a scheme of some sort into view, which neither of the other phases do. Humble enough, in relation to the full development of mental powers, it yet functions generically. Such generic imagery emerges into notice in this third phase, the phase of assimilation. The activity of ideation, which is the exercise of imagination in increasingly disciplined directions, working with such imagery, goes far farther in constructive refinement, and in degree of abstraction through the elaboration of ideas of great generality.

The way in which assimilation works appears very clearly in Goethe's poem "Jägers Abendlied," where the emotional quality of the word "still" changes strikingly. This word means either "tense strained quietness" or "stilled happy tranquillity," thus comprising two opposed states of emotion. For example, in the first two lines of Goethe's "An den Mond," the word is used for the stillness with which the moon fills bush and dale with shimmering mist, dissolving at last every tension in the poet's soul. Again, it is used in "Meeres Stille," for the deep still-

ness of the seas which harasses the sailor: "Keine Luft von keiner Seite!
Todes Stille fürchterlich! In der ungeheuren Weite reget keine Welle
sich." Here is the text of "Jägers Abendlied":

> Im Felde schleich' ich still und wild,
> Gespannt mein Feuerrohr,
> Da schwebt so licht dein liebes Bild,
> Dein süsses Bild mir vor.
>
> Du wandelst jetzt wohl still und mild
> Durch Feld und liebes Tal,
> Und, ach, mein schnell verrauschend Bild
> Stellt sich dir's nicht einmal?
>
> Des Menschen, der die Welt durchstreift
> Voll Unmut und Verdruss,
> Nach Osten und nach Westen schweift,
> Weil er dich lassen muss.
>
> Mir ist es, denk' ich nur an dich
> Als in den Mond zu sehn;
> Ein stiller Friede kommt auf mich,
> Weiss nicht, wie mir geschehn.

The structure of the hunter's song is elaborate and closely knit. The
two first lines of Verse 1 show the hunter in the field with his rifle, the
two first lines of Verse 2 the maiden going for a quiet walk. Lines 3 and
4 of Verse 1 represent the hunter picturing his love; those of Verse 2
refer to the image of the man that might arise before the soul of the
maiden. The third verse describes the restless discontent of the hunter's
mind and the last verse the peace which the thought of his beloved one
gives to him.

Within this perfectly balanced structure, thoughts and feelings move
easily and naturally. The hunter's heart goes out to his love. He imagines her walking quietly along the valley, and wishes that his own image might appear before her, this image of an unfortunate and unhappy
lover, who however finds quietness at last in the thought of his love.
Emotion fluctuates between the angry restlessness of the hunter and
the harmonious stillness of the girl, until the latter remains.

To return to the word "*still*": when we hear or read the words "im
Felde schleich' ich," we differentiate, retain, and assimilate the words,

one after the other—that is, their acoustic form (first as sense-percept, then as after-image and perhaps even as memory-image) together with their meanings. The word group "schleich ich" produces a feeling of tense stealthiness. When next, retaining what preceded, we differentiate the sound and meaning of "*still*," and then assimilate this word to the previous words which we have retained, the potential range of meaning of "*still*" is narrowed to the actual meaning, "tense restrained quietness." The other potential meaning of "*still*," as "stilled happy tranquillity," clashes with the tenseness of the retained words "schleich ich," and is therefore eliminated. We are not consciously aware of such elimination, because we are highly practiced in it. But if assimilation is made difficult by an out-of-the-way or even wrongly used word, we may feel brought to a halt, and have to think, and perhaps even reject the word as not making sense in the context. The poet then proceeds: "Im Felde schleich' ich still and wild." Here "*wild*" is readily assimilated to "*still*" and what precedes, and intensifies the tenseness, which is further increased in the next line: "gespannt mein Feuerrohr." A change is indicated at the beginning of the third line by "Da." The movement of "schwebt" is light and graceful; "licht," "lieb," and "süss" are expressions of warmth and affection. All these words with their meanings are assimilated into a whole of charm and delight. The second verse has the same structure as the first verse, except that the image of the girl precedes that of the unhappy lover. Here, "still" has the same position in the first line as in the first line of the first verse. But now it follows and is assimilated to the girl's sweet image of the previous two lines, and the words "du wandelst jetzt wohl. . . ." "Wandeln" expresses the gentle unhurried walk of the girl. When we apprehend and assimilate "still" to this context, we necessarily discard the potential meaning of "still" as "tensely silent"; here "still" denotes "peaceful tranquillity." The words that follow "und mild" strengthen this mood.

The poet's wonderfully precise use of his words makes the functioning of assimilation very plain here. The process of assimilation functions, of course, in a corresponding manner with regard to other sorts of contexts, as for instance among images or abstract concepts.

Let us now turn to the "appositional" mode of expression more specifically.

To give a fresh example of "appositional style" we shall analyze the appositional mode of narrative in a piece of Maori mythology. In *Time and Style* we have used sentences for our detailed analysis of temporary sequence, proceeding from word to word, so that the items of the temporary sequence investigated were single words. Here we intend to work with bigger items—sentences, clauses, or phrases. This means, of course, that each of our items is in itself already a temporal sequence, which could be analyzed word for word. We shall however here treat each sentence, clause, or phrase as *one* item in order to arrive at a detailed analysis of the passage as a whole.

As one of our rexiewers has suggested, the most important condition for the formation of the "appositional style" together with the "linear style" is probably the existence of an "oral literature." On the face of it, oral literature seems a contradiction in terms. Oral refers to the spoken word, and literature usually to the written or printed word. The phrase "oral literature" has, however, become a term for poetry or prose handed down by oral tradition. What the word "literature" suggests in this context is that there is not just the occasional poem or tale, but a full body of traditional material handed down orally. For the Homeric poems, this has been worked out very fully by Milman Parry and by A. B. Lord, and the work is proceeding further.

Our Maori passage belongs to a group of mythological tales which were first collected and published by Sir George Grey in 1854 under the title *Ko Nga Mahinga a Nga Tupuna Maori* (London: George Willis, 42, Charing Cross, and Great Piazza, Covent Garden). He says about these texts in his introduction: "These traditions were all either written down from the dictation of their [*scil.* the Maoris'] principal Chiefs and High Priests, or have been compiled from manuscripts written by Chiefs." This poses the question of when Maori Chiefs and Maoris in general learned to read and write. According to Eric Schwimmer (*The World of the Maori*, Wellington, A. H. and A. W. Reed, 1966, pp. 104–6) the first Christian missionary landed in New Zealand in 1814; by the late 1830's conversions to Christianity began to increase very rapidly, and the demand for Bibles rose steeply. This means that by the year 1854 Maoris might have been reading and writing for not more than twenty years. It is curious how similar the situation of these people is, in this respect, to the probable situation of Homer. We may then be reasonably certain that the style of these tales is directly derived from an "oral literature." (See also Te Rangi Hiroa, Sir Peter Buck, *The Coming of the Maori*, Wellington, 1958, pp. 360–1, on how young Maoris were trained in oratory.)

Maori Text

a. Kotahi ano te tupuna o te tangata maori, ko Rangi-nui e tu nei, ko Papa-tu-a-nuku e takoto nei

b. Ki nga tangata maori, na Rangi raua ko Papa take o mua,

c. ina hoki, i pouri tonu te Rangi me te whenua i mua,

d. ko Rangi raua ko Papa, e pipiri tonu ana,

e. kaore ano i wehea noatia.

f. A e rapu noa ana ana tamariki i te ahuatanga o te po o te ao,

g. e whakaaro ana ratou kua maha nga tangata, kua tini,

h. a kaore ano i marama noa,

i. e pouri tonu ana.

j. No reira enei kupu, i a Po, i te Po-tuatahi, tae noa ki te Po-tuangahuru, ki te rau, ki te mano,

k. koia tenei kaore ano hoki i whai ao noa,

l. e pouri ana ano ki te maori.

Translation

a. One only is the ancestral pair, the source of men, Heaven, the great, which stands up, Broad Earth, which lies flat.

b. According to men, Heaven and Earth are the origins at the first.

c. For, the heaven and the earth were always dark at the first.

d. Heaven and Earth were always clinging together,

e. they were not yet separated at all.

f. Now, their children were forever seeking for the likeness of night and day.

g. They were thinking that human beings had multiplied, that they had become a host.

h. Well, there was still not any light at all,

i. it was always dark.

j. From this stem the following sayings: From night, from the first night, right up to the tenth night, to the hundredth, to the thousandth night.

k. It is so, this night did not acquire any daylight at all,

l. it was still always dark for men.

Interpretation

a. The speaker states immediately and emphatically the substance of the first part of his tale—namely, that men originated from Heaven and Earth, their parents. Each partner of the pair is described in an expansion which is added or "apposited": Heaven as "great" and "standing upright," Broad Earth (the meaning of the three-word name is not clear) as "lying flat."

b. The "initial statement" of *a* is emphatically driven home by the next sentence: "According to men, Heaven and Earth are the origins at the first." This is an intensifying repetition of the first statement, apart from the phrase "according to men," which indicates that this account rests on what people say, in fact, on an oral tradition.

c. The phrase *ina hoki* means "for, since, inasmuch as." It introduces a reason or an explanation. Now, the fact that heaven and earth were always dark to begin with cannot be simply a reason or explanation for the origination of mankind from Heaven and Earth. *Ina hoki* does not merely introduce the sentence at the beginning of which it occurs; it introduces a full expansion explaining how mankind came to issue forth from Earth and Heaven. It is characteristic also that this expansion moves back into the past—that is, to a time prior to the birth of mankind.

d. The next sentence, "Heaven and Earth were always clinging together," explains in terms of myth—that is, in terms of the action of divine beings—why Heaven and Earth were dark. They were so, because the mighty bodies of Father Heaven and Mother Earth lay close together mating.

e. In the following sentence, "they were not yet separated at all," this is stated over again, but negatively. There is however a new element in what otherwise is an intensifying repetition: "not yet" points forward to the separation of the two mighty bodies.

f. The particle *a* indicates that the speaker is now making a pause, he is thinking for a moment, before he proceeds to take a step forward in his tale: "Their children were forever seeking for the likeness of night and day." Here, the all-pervasiveness of night is pierced for the first time by the search of Rangi's and Papa's children for a distinction between night and day. The children are, of course, thought of as being enclosed between the bodies of their parents.

g. The next sentence expands by way of explanation: "They were thinking that human beings had multiplied, that they had become a host." The great number of humans is expressed twice over for the sake of emphasis. It is, of course, the great number of men that causes the children of Rangi to search for day and night, that is, for a way out of the constricted space between their parents' bodies.

h. With the particle *a* the speaker tarries once again, and then returns to the beginning of this large expansion, namely to the darkness of Heaven and Earth; he says: "There was still not any light at all."

i. Then he states the same thing positively, "it was always dark," thus increasing its intensity.

j. This is further elaborated by reference to a traditional saying which makes it clear that there was not just one night, but many: from the first night to the tenth night, to a great number, to a tremendous host of nights. The number-words *rau* and *mano* are qualitative, that is, expressive of intensity and feeling, rather than quantitative, that is, a matter of counting or measurement. The point of this elaboration is to bring home to the listener the unceasing gloom of this primeval darkness.

k. The final, again double-barreled utterance is introduced by *kola*, expressing assent: "it is so." Then, the darkness is described again, first negatively: "This night did not acquire any daylight at all."

l. And this is repeated once more positively: "It was still always dark for men."

After this mighty expansion on the intense long darkness of the primeval night, the action moves on firmly. The children of Rangi and Papa thought: "Let us seek a method concerning Rangi and Papa, so that they may either be slain, or separated." In due course, Rangi and Papa were heaved apart by Tane, and the hosts of men which had been hidden between their parents' bodies became visible.

Analysis

As we read this story and apply our attention (selective as it is when, e.g., we choose to read, and to reject interruptions) to item after item, differentiation and retention function, of course, in the way described above, but the form which the process of assimilation takes is quite specific and characteristic for a description in the appositional style.

As *b* is assimilated to *a* there is little that is new, but *a* is reinforced by repetition of its content; *c*, being assimilated to what precedes, begins an explanation by the description of a primeval darkness. There is no indication of relative time; both *b* and *c* are placed in *mua*, that is, the time "in front." So, what is assimilated is a sense of darkness in earth and heaven in that early time. When assimilated, *d* gives more shape to this darkness by showing up Earth and Heaven in human form; *e*, when assimilated, reinforces the darkness by stating the completeness of their clinging together; "not yet," however, arouses expectation of a change; *f*, when assimilated, picks up this expectation and to some extent fulfills it; *g* elaborates on *f*, giving the reason for Rangi's children being concerned about night and day; it also refers back to *a* by mentioning the existence of human beings; in *g* the thought of the multitude of human beings is stated twice, that is, with great intensity. When *h* is assimilated, we return to the darkness with only a glimmer of expectation in "still." In *i* the darkness is reinforced and made complete; this refers back to *c*. Then *j*, when assimilated, intensifies the feel of this primeval darkness by adding the sense of an interminable duration to it. With *k* assimilated, this darkness is stated once more, in a final fashion. With *l* this is repeated, but with a slight arousal of expectancy by the word "still," which picks up *h*; the phrase "for men" also picks up what precedes in *g* and in the "initial statement" *a*, and arouses some expectation of change.

A modern English version of the tale would proceed rather differently. After the title, "Origin of Mankind from Heaven and Earth," it would start at the beginning, that is, with Rangi's and Papa's close embrace over a span of a thousand years or more, which meant complete darkness for those between their bodies—i.e., their own divine children and the growing host of men. In this situation their children began to seek for light; and then Tane proposed either to slay or to separate Rangi and Papa. He eventually separated them, and men appeared. Something like this would be our modern sequence of telling the story. The statements of events would be in a reasonably logical order, and they would not, except with explicit warning, diverge from the chronological order. There would be no repetitions, but the movement of thought would move steadily forward.

In our Maori text, which is characteristically appositional, other things are primary: first, the urgency with which the main subject-matter, the origination of mankind from Papa and Rangi, is immediately stated and repeated; and secondly, the intensity of feeling with which the primeval darkness is brought home to the listener by constant repetition and elaboration; the over-all movement of thought is one which again and again turns back to what was said before.

Here, of course, cognition plays a part, because no utterance could be either produced or understood without it. But conation, and, in particular, a desire to hear the tale, in fact an impetuous and impatient eagerness to hear or tell at once what it is all about, this is the driving force, which then leads to a carefully built-up intensity of feeling, in which speaker and listeners revel, and from the enjoyment of which they emerge satisfied in order to return to the starting point and to move on. Here, the underlying experience of temporal sequence (which it is bound to be, because the words of the tale form a sequence in time) is not that of an ordered progression, moving from the furthermost past into the more recent past which lies close to the present—namely, the emergence of mankind; but it is an experience of quality: darkness, immense in length, intense, perpetual. A style which proceeds either in a linear fashion, in which event follows straight on event in swift sequence, or in the manner described above, has its nose close to the trail. It is utterly involved and absorbed. The whole experience is one of feeling and intensity, and that is qualitative. Since it is at the same time an experience of temporal sequence, it is bound to be an experience of qualitative time.

Let us at this point consider the psychological concept of qualitative time.

One sort of minimal definition of qualitative time, or qualitative anything else perhaps, is nonquantitative what-have-you. It is obvious enough that the general distinction between qualitative and quantitative has been with us for a very long time. One ancient classical instance, for example, is its presence in Aristotle's table of categories. So it is also sufficiently evident that this manner of distinguishing experiences can claim a widespread importance for reflection on human experience, as well as a long history. Now the ideas of enumeration and measurement have also been around since, let us say, Pythagoras, but the development of applied mathematics, although long foreseen, is relatively speaking a short, if striking, story. The appreciation of these things makes it tolerably clear that the "century of genius," the seventeenth, marked a watershed in human life, society, and civilization. Until then, the distinction between the qualitative and the quantitative, while familiar, obtained in a context in which the claims of the quantitative were neither exorbitant nor so very remarkable. In fact, everything qualitative took up very much more room, so to speak, while the role of the quantitative was a humble one. Not so, subsequently. For several centuries the pace of achievement in the quantitative treatment of things has culminated in the technological know-how which commands so much prestige today; this bids fair to reverse the position. For the culmination is felt as such, yet it is apparent that the development is nowhere near its peak, and that in some quarters even the qualitative in experience is challenged and assaulted constantly, with a view to making it yield itself to calculation. The influence of so significant a thinker as Immanuel Kant moves with this in his dictum that whatever is not mathematical cannot be knowledge concerning phenomena. At least, such is the case to a marked degree, apart from very deep and searching interpretation of Kant's meaning and intention.

Against such a background, it becomes intelligible how in a general way we are all familiar with qualitative time, and how in some sense it is just as common in modern as in ancient society—this, too, in spite of any preponderance of quantitative aspects of experience in civilized life. For even in taking a holiday, if it is a successful and beneficial one, the dominant feeling of the experient about it so far as time is concerned is the curious one that it was all too short yet it seemed satisfyingly long. Accordingly, it may be expressed in some such way as: "It was only ten days, but it was one of the best holidays I ever had, and I feel a new man." In such familiar instances, the shortness refers to quantitative, measurable passage of time as recorded on clocks, calendars, and in the selective attention when, in its plastic, conative-feeling-cognitive unity, the cognitive is salient. And, contrary to this, the reference to length of time distributes the emphasis in the same milieu in an entirely different manner. Strength of responsive feeling and intensity of expressed emotion here stand out in high relief.

So, in *Time and Style* the matter is understood after an Anaxagorean fashion. There are elements of everything in anything, but not in such a way that all its ingredient elements are equally prominent or receive equal emphasis. That would make a thing hopelessly vague, unspecific, and indefinite. Some selection of ingredients must be more emphatically expressed in it for anything to be *this* thing and not *another* thing. In this sense, time is all pervasive (as change and duration), but that sort of time which is quantitative is more emphatically prominent in modern society than is qualitative time. The situation in ancient society was not different in the sense that time was all-pervasive, but qualitative or nonquantitative time was more in evidence. It is, of course, impossible to deny that there are more watches, clocks, and calendars in modern society than ever there were in ancient society. Indeed, these were developed gradually over a long period of human life and experience, and they are also the instruments of mastering and gaining facility in dealing with time as essentially quantitative. A great deal else also goes with them, and when all this is taken for granted in human society, there is a marked difference in the distribution of emphasis so far as the experience of time is concerned.

The distinction between qualitative and quantitative time is largely a matter of definition, for one could just as well say that one sort of minimal definition of quantitative time or quantitative anything is nonqualitative what-have-you. This is plain enough from the history of the development of mathematical thought, whether considered in its far past or in its modern phase. For there were times when the achievement of abstraction and generality was so little that there was not all that much which was quantitative about number itself, while today the sug-

gestion that number is a matter of sheer hard-headed precise calculation
would meet with derision as quite hopelessly inadequate by those highly
imaginative, if none the less strictly disciplined fellows, pure mathe-
maticians. In contexts like the discussion of *Time and Style* definition is
a good servant, but a bad master.

To return to our Maori text, the subjective attitude through which
temporal experience becomes qualitative—that is, of such a quality as
the subject feels it to be in experience—has, we hope, become clear
through our analysis of the above Maori passage.

There is clear evidence in addition for a predominantly qualitative
time experience among the ancient Maori. As in Greece, so among the
Maoris, it is apparent in the methods used for time-reckoning. To pinpoint events in past history the expression "generation" was used, as
much attached to concrete persons and as unprecise quantitatively as
in Greece (see Elsdon Best, *The Maori Division of Time*, Dominion Mu-
seum Monograph No. 4, Wellington, 1922, Reprint 1959, p. 10; see
also *Time and Style*, p. 108). The beginning of the year was marked by
the heliacal rising of the Pleiades or the rising of Rigel in Orion (Best,
pp. 11–12). It is probable that, like the very ancient Romans, the old
Maoris only had ten months in the year, which covered the round of
agricultural life, but omitted the two winter months, which were empty
of essential activities (Best, pp. 13–14; see also *Time and Style*, p. 108).
A striking account of ancient Maori time is quoted by Best (pp. 27–28)
from Dr. Thomson's *Story of New Zealand*: "Although time passes away
among them like a shadow, the unrecorded year is divided into 13
moons [Best believes this figure to be an error] and each moon is distinguished by the rising of the stars, the flowering plants, and the ar-
rival of two migratory birds. June is the first month of the year, and it
is recognised by the appearance of the Puanga star in the morning. July
is marked by the stars Kopu and Tautoru and the flowering of the
karaka tree. August is distinguished by the stars Mangere and Whakaau;
September by the rising of the Oetahi star and the flowering of the
kowhai, rangiora, and *kotukutuku* trees. It is in this month that *kumara* are
planted. . . . March is known by the ripening of the *kumara*, and in April
they are dug up. May, or the twelfth month, often passes unnoticed.
The thirteenth month is distinguished by the Puanga star, the har-
binger of the new year." Here, time has the quality of, or is "marked"
by, the sight of a particular star rising or a particular tree blooming. It
is not continuous or abstract. Again, the month was divided into thirty
days or rather "nights of the moon." But these, too, were not equal
items in a numerical series, but differed in quality, as in Hesiod's cal-

endar (see *Time and Style*, p. 94). The Maori planted his *kumara* crop only on certain days. Certain fish were caught only on certain days, and further, certain methods of catching fish, such as line fishing or fishing by torchlight, were restricted to definite days. Other days again were considered unlucky for fishing in general. The qualitative character of this time-experience could hardly be plainer.

In conclusion, let us come back to our Maori text as a product of an oral tradition of literature. We have deduced from the analysis of our text that the driving force in the appositional style is impetuous eagerness and strong emotional participation. The question may be raised whether there is any external evidence for this.

The very speed of performance in oral epic expresses strong conational drive. Odysseus is likened by the swineherd Eumaeus to a singer in the telling of his tale (Od.17.518 ff.); and according to Helen, he is peerless as a speaker "when he sends forth his great voice from his chest, and words, like snowflakes in winter" (Iliad 3.221 ff.). The snowfall with its density (see also Il.12.278 ff.) pictures the pauseless flow of his eloquence. Similarly, A. B. Lord in *The Singer of Tales* (Harvard, 1966, p. 17) remarks on the speed of performance of a Yugoslav singer: "It is not unusual for a Yugoslav bard to sing at the rate of from ten to twenty ten-syllable lines a minute."

The audience, on the other hand, is not always keen to listen, and the interest of the listeners has to be caught quickly. Telemachus has to admonish the Suitors not to "shout since this a fine thing to listen to a singer as good as Phemius, like unto the gods in voice" (Od. 1.370 f.). For modern Yugoslav villages A. B. Lord describes the singer's situation as follows (p. 14): "The singer has to contend with an audience that is coming and going, greeting newcomers, saying farewells to early leavers; a newcomer with special news or gossip may interrupt the singing for some time, perhaps even stopping it entirely."

The intensity of an audience's interest once caught is, in the Homeric epics, expressed by the word *kelethmos*, "spell" or "charm." Twice Odysseus's telling of his wanderings is rounded off with these verses: "Thus he spoke, and among them all there came a great silence [*aken* and *siope* mean the same; the repetition intensifies]; and they were held by a spell in the shadowed hall" (Od. 11.333–4; 13. 1–2). That *kelethmos* has much more strongly the force of a witch's spell than the English word "spell" is plain from Circe's bewildered remark that Odysseus's "mind is proof against sorcery" (*akeletos*, Od. 10.329) when he does not succumb to either her magic potion or her magic wand. The loyal swineherd describes the effect on himself of Odysseus's story-telling in this way: "Just as a man looks at a singer who has been taught by the gods and sings ravishing tales to men, and they desire incessantly to hear him whenever he sings, thus he charmed me [*ethelge*, which can also mean "bewitch"], sitting beside me in the house" (Od. 17.518 ff.) The "spell" of such singing is mythically expressed in the figures of the Sirens whose song covers "whatever happens on the much-nourishing earth" (Od. 12.191), and who are surrounded by a heap of bones of men who have died listening, unable to break the spell (Od. 12.44 ff.).

The intense absorption of the performer himself in his tale is graphically described by Plato. The rhapsode Ion is an expert in the recitation and explanation of the Homeric epics. When he tells a tale of pity, his eyes fill with tears; when he recounts something terrifying or dreadful, his hair stands on end with fear, and his heart leaps; when he tells a tale that is set in Ithaca or in Troy, his soul believes that it is actually in Ithaca or in Troy (Plato, *Ion* 535 C). Correspondingly, when the rhapsode is successful in his performance, his audience will weep, and he will reap a good income; but if they stay unaffected by his spell, if they laugh, he will weep afterwards, because they will not pay (535 E).

The fact that the ancient Greek bard considered as his aim the delight and enjoyment of his audience is made abundantly clear in the Homeric epics (see W. Schadewaldt, *Von Homers Welt und Werk*, Leipzig, 1944, p. 83 ff.). Surprisingly, this is also the aim for Hesiod in his *Theogony*. In this poem, the rise and development of the universe from elemental forces up to the just and civilized rule of Zeus is described in the form of genealogies and mythical events, the most important of which is a great battle between the Olympian gods and the Titans. We should expect that cognition would be primary here, and that this poem would be mainly intended for instruction. But Hesiod says about the gift of the Muses the following (p. 98 ff.): "For when a man, grieving even with a recently scared heart, dries up in sorrow, if the singer, the Muses' servant, praises the fame of men of old and the blessed gods, who live on Mount Olympus, then immediately the man forgets his misery and has no memory of his sorrows. But the gifts of the goddesses quickly divert him." Here, the poet states explicitly that, like heroic epic, so his theogonic poetry brings delight and happiness to his listeners, even when it has to overcome intense grief.

We have now completed, within the limits of the aims set us and of the time available to us, the task which we have been asked to undertake. We trust that the abstract offered, the further samples given, the explications of the psychological resources used, and the occasional animadversions which have been indulged in will all unite to stimulate interest in investigating further the connection between time and style in a diversity of fields.

Note

---

1. Here and in the following pages we are referring to our book *Time and Style* (Dunedin, New Zealand, 1962).

Eugene F. Timpe

THE SPATIAL DIMENSION:
A STYLISTIC TYPOLOGY

SOMEWHERE, PERHAPS, THERE IS AN OLD MAP, THE RESULT OF THE ACCU-
mulated efforts of a number of mapmakers widely separated in time
and place. In recent times it has been reworked by various cartogra-
phers, each of whom has augmented it or revised it in his own way. As
originally drawn and subsequently revised, it depicts certain formulations on the concept of space and its relationships to patterns of thought
and expression in literature. Like all maps, it is neither comprehensive
nor accurate on terms other than its own. So another version of the
old map, produced by a combination of projectional systems that has
not as yet been used, arranged in as coherent a way as possible, and
constructed in reference to those landmarks from previous renderings
which seem to have been most validly represented, constitutes the
justification for this study. If, in spite of the best of intentions, this edition turns out to be as quaintly inaccurate as those early maps of the
New World which are so widely used today for decorating lamps and
walls, it is to be hoped that it serves at least to invite others to explore
the region themselves and chart it in their own way.

Fundamental to any such attempt there is usually something axio-
matic. In this case there is an axiom and what might be called a the-
orem. The first states that spatial conceptualization is intrinsic in human thought and therefore commonly present in the literary expression
of that thought. Scarcely any mode of man's existence can be divorced
from the spatial dimension. His sensory perceptions, his quantitative
thinking, and even his temporal sense, are all basically related to his
spatial awareness. Without space, motion cannot exist; if motion is a
function of time, then time cannot exist either. Only some intellectual
and emotional abstractions seem exempt from a relationship with space;
yet even they must exist somewhere, and their expression is often dependent upon the use of spatial ideas. From a psychological point of
view it can be predicated that one of the directions in which man in-

stinctively moves is towards enclosure. Constantly he seeks to define and limit the space with which he surrounds himself. Then, secure within this personalized space, he ventures to generate, like Descartes, some of his most expansive thoughts. Psychoanalysts would go a step farther, to Whitman's cradle, endlessly rocking, and to such Joycean utterances as "mouth south: tomb womb."[1] Phenomenologically, Gaston Bachelard addressed himself, in his *La poétique de l'espace* (Paris, 1958), to the establishment of a topography for what might be called subliminal thinking. So many other examples are immediately apparent that to attempt to list them would be futile.

The outgrowth of this basic concept is that the spatial dimension is a necessary element in all forms of literature. Because of this its presence cannot logically provoke the question of so-called mixed forms, for to raise such a question makes about as much sense as to deplore the fact that water is a mixed form because it contains both hydrogen and oxygen. Literary expression, like a chemical combination, can exist only as the product of several forms.[2] And if this line of reasoning is logical, then it is not consistent with it that the spatial dimension be thought of as existing principally in the novel.[3] If it is inherent in human thought, it must be just as inherent in all the forms of literature which express that thought.

Not only is it more universal than is often acknowledged, but also it is less encompassing. It has been taken into ill-advised usage to describe one kind of nineteenth-century novel. Lines of skirmish need to be drawn about this system of designation, for not only does it imply the absence or subordination of the spatial dimension in novels of other periods, but also it suggests the domination of it in certain novels, a supposition which reason simply will not support.[4] Probably such terminology came from the same spirit of gratuitous categorization which, in the past century, has bequeathed to us an entire attic of stuffed trophies, e.g., the statement that Petrarch was "The Father of the Renaissance," the judgment that the eighteenth century was the beginning of the modern era, and the pronouncements which handed down to us Baroque, Romanticism, and other terms of like ephemeral and variable meaning. It could only have been in the tradition of such largesse that the term "Raumroman" was coined. And in such a tradition it makes a kind of sense, to be sure. One could quite legitimately speak of the epistolary novel, the picaresque novel, the Bildungsroman, the detective novel, the gothic novel, and the historical novel. Such terms had meaning enough when taken in context. So why not the novel of time, space, character, events, or drama?

The answer must be that distinctions based upon intrinsic elements do not, in the first place, produce valid differentiae; and in the second place, they can only serve to confuse by superimposing themselves on others, or superseding others, which have been created and accepted on the basis of content, emphasis of nonessential element, or compositional form. Those elements which are inherent within a work, since they are common to all works of that kind, cannot logically be used to distinguish one work from another within the same group. If an element not common to all forms of a genre, like stream of consciousness, is suddenly promoted to a conspicuous position in some work, then that new element quite logically designates that particular work and others like it. But to say that one type of novel is a novel of space makes as much sense as to say that it is written with words or contains thoughts or is about people or has pages. Certainly our reason should inform us that essential qualities, unless subjected to special usage, cannot be used to distinguish one form from another within the same genre. There can be no such thing as a novel of space just as there can be no such thing as a novel without space or, for that matter, any literary work which exists without any sort of reference to the spatial dimension.

More important than any commentary on how the term has been misused in the past, however, is some explanation of what it is and what it does. Space and its variable inner concentric, defining functionary (and synonym), place, are those formal elements which establish absolute and relative location and, by virtue of their multiplicity of existence, endow meaning of several sorts. Space is designated by an aggregation of explicit or implicit coordinate loci. Its identity is therefore a function of the basis or bases as well as the values of its defining loci. As the locational element of literary expression it can never be altogether devoid of meaning; on the other hand, in certain literary works its spectrum can extend to congruence with at least one of the total meanings of a work itself. Its definition, however, must remain incomplete until it has been discussed in terms of not only what it is but also what it means, what its characteristics are, how it functions, and what it actually does, insofar as these matters are, from the literary point of view, closely related or even coterminous.

Space denotes voluminousness. If place denotes the same thing, then place cannot be distinguished from space. The position that "Lokal" is a designated space in its empty reality while "Raum" is fraught with human connotations is untenable because such a distinction is both functional in nature and subjective in interpretation.[5] Does place, then, according to common understanding, mean that which is like but smaller than space? Taken to the extreme, dissimilarities based on quantification are also unworkable, for what if the infinitesimal point that in the extreme denotes place be enlarged even slightly? Is space formed then? Technically, of course, it is. But this begins to smack of scholasticism. So it seems that there is no usable distinction between space and place. "Place," as a matter of fact, exists only to create space, which it does through the establishment of loci in coordinate relationships. Space, then, becomes the function of lesser spaces or "places," all of which exist in respect to others. So every "place" is really a space and every one of these spaces exists relatively in reference to others of its kind and the total space which it partially defines.

Its perception may take place in several ways. To William James it is apprehended by a synthesis of singular empirical sensations which result in a total conception of voluminousness.[6] This conception is most commonly dependent upon the visual sense. The parts of the sensation of extent "must come to be perceived, through processes of association, in definite relations of mutual position and order" (XLVI, 183). While this implies that the existence of space is dependent upon hard empirical fact, it also suggests that the visual sense plays an important part in the recreation of the impression of space in a literary work.[7]

Somewhat more germane to literary studies might be the statement by Merleau-Ponty that space is "the indivisible system governing the acts of unification performed by a constituting mind."[8] Thus existence proceeds from an act of thought, and it becomes apparent that if the perception transmitted by the writer is singular, the rational conception achieved by the reader is plural. The next step, supplied by Robert Petsch, permits the separation of the perception from a tangible source. "Der geistige Raum, in dem sich z. B. das tragische Erlebnis in Kellers 'Romeo und Julia auf dem Dorfe' entfaltet, ist viel weiter, allgemeiner und bedeutender als die Summe der Stätten auf Seldwyler Gebiet, auf dem die Handlung abspielt," he says, (p. 181) and then continues to amplify his notion by assigning three dimensions to space—bestimmten, absoluten, and erfüllten. Each is less dependent than its predecessor upon the loci concretely established by the author or the character. "Absoluten" space is created imaginatively and extends beyond the confines of the author-created "bestimmten" space, while "erfüllten" space refers to another world, highly connotative, like that which Don Quixote created for himself. The last conceivable step is into Rilke's "Weltinnenraum," a region in which the loci themselves have a cosmic and mystic identity. For these, the word "implicit" seems scarcely adequate. Yet, like the explicit often visual loci which an author may conceive and place, they create the space of the work which is formulated as a whole in the "constituting mind."

The meaning of the whole is naturally a function of the bases and their valuations which comprise it, all of which achieve a meaning in the consciousness of the perceiver. It is not a function of the physical extent of the space involved. In *Candide* the bases were explicit geographical locales, extending over half the world; in *Ulysses* they were explicit locales in Dublin which corresponded to implicit locales from the *Odyssey*. Yet Voltaire, using much of the western hemisphere, produced for his reader a meaning which was closely circumscribed, while Joyce, using two dialectically interacting sets of loci, neither of which was as extensive as Voltaire's, suggested multiple meanings in varied contexts. Similar parallels might easily be drawn between a number of other writers, e.g., Cyrano de Bergerac and Marcel Proust, or Lazarillo de Tormes and Albert Camus.

If the meaning of a space is a function of the bases and valuations of its loci, then these loci themselves, or lesser spaces, must have values of sorts which extend beyond those of explicit and implicit, and which simply indicate the metaphysical basis and manner of placement. One dichotomy that may be useful is that which distinguishes between absoluteness and relativity. It is helpful to think of the loci as absolutes when they are themselves spaces within which a part of the work exists. For an example we may turn to Dante, whose Aristotelian-Scholastic concept of space (cf. Aristotle's *Physics*), in which our world was in a sphere which was in turn in a series of larger spheres until at last they were all surrounded by the fixed stars, lends itself most readily to such usage. Any of the circles of the *Inferno*, for example, may be considered absolute in the sense that it functions as total, self-sufficient space which represents one fixed human condition.

Each of these absolutes in turn, including the three cantiche themselves, have relative locations through which the "absolute" space of each larger division is created. It is these relative and coordinate relationships which not only confer meaning but also form the spaces of the work. Bachelard indicated this when he insisted on the polarity of cellar to attic in a house (pp. 24–27). The concept of relationships must depend, however, for its existence upon some notion of multiplicity; so the question arises, *between* what or *to* what are these "relative" loci related? Naturally, their locations and meanings are relative to each other, as in *La Commedia*. In addition, each must bear a relationship to the whole of which it is a part. Again, Dante's poem may be cited in support. Further, each has value or meaning in relation to its perceptor,

be it Dante or his reader. Finally, each of these perceptor's meanings
bears a relationship to another like it, so that an additional meaning
results from the two or more that have been derived by the perceptors.
To Virgil, Judecca signified one sort of treason; to Dante, it meant at
least one other in addition. The relationship between the two responses
places each in a sort of perspective and thereby modifies it. Another
single example of the several relative meanings may be found in *Ulysses*.
Bella Cohen's brothel stood in a relationship between the hospital which
occupied the position before it and the hut which was positioned after
it. It had meaning, not only in relation to the adjoining segments, but
also with respect to the total work. To Leopold Bloom it represented
one thing, to Stephen Dedalus another, and the relationship between
the two produced a subtle modification of each in turn. The relative
meanings of the spaces of a literary work, then, may be in relation to
each other, to the total, to a perceptor, or even to themselves when
seen from different points of view.

Two other characteristics which come from a different dichotomy
and which have to do with both the existence and the effect of space
are actual volume and potential volume, or extensiveness and extensionality. The first defines the actual sphere of action or existence. In a
sense it means "how big." In Poe's story, "The Premature Burial," it
was the size of a coffin; in Sartre's *Huis Clos* or Strindberg's *Miss Julie*
it was primarily one room; in *Madame Bovary* it was limited to the region
around Rouen; and in *Micromégas* it extended to the star, Sirius.

If the actual volume or total extensiveness can be thought of as a
static constant, like velocity, then the potential volume or extensionality may be regarded as a dynamic variable, like acceleration. It
denotes not how big a space is but how big it can become. Historical
clichés best exemplify this. Seen from such a viewpoint, the eighteenth-
century universe was limited but complete within the space permitted
it. Art was bounded by reason but not constrained by this reason or
rationalism because it did not seek to trespass beyond the boundaries
ascribed to it. In the preceding century, however, the human spirit had
refused to accept with complacency a space delimited by human reason.
The works of that age were fraught with evidence of the stresses imposed, internal pressures which betokened a dynamic, expansional
force. Light sources, apparently from outside the paintings, lured the
eye of the mind, phototropic like the eye of the body, beyond the
boundaries ostensibly set for the work. Windows, illuminating sculpture
from above, had much the same effect. Sunbursts signified an explo-
siveness in which parallel lines not only never met but grew ever

farther apart in a limitless universe. Borromini's church in Rome near the Quattro Fontana was apparently stretched out of shape as if subjected to mysterious and powerful pressures, and ceilings in numerous palazzi and churches were painted to create the illusion of an explosion to space beyond. The world of Segismundo, in Calderón's *La vida es sueño*, alternately contracted and expanded from prison to palace to prison to battlefield, creating in the process a sort of chiaroscuro, not only of darkness and light but of constriction and extension. Space, it seems, expanded to the heavens; conversely, it converged therefrom to a point of focus on earth. The location of the work of art implicitly undertook a dynamic migration. Something of the sort had taken place in more ancient times, in the *Odyssey* for instance, but there the extensional movement went essentially nowhere—the farther Odysseus was from Ithaca the less real life became—whereas the implicit meanings of the distant loci made the exact opposite true in Baroque works.

Up to this point our little map has suggested some salient features of its subject, but it has not located it precisely in reference to any constant system of coordinates. Nor can it do this. Where, really does space exist? In the empirical reality of Lucretius's universe? In the explicit locales of Chaucer or Erasmus? In an idealized concept of which we can perceive only the shadow? In a subjective, constituting mind? Does it have a collective existence, or may its existence only be posited by other notions, singly or in combination, as yet unexpressed? Its mode of existence is no more ascertainable, unfortunately, than that of a poem, an idea, or the sound of the proverbial tree crashing down in an uninhabited forest.

Since the intrinsic characteristics of something set limits and determine the kinds of functions of which that thing is capable, what space *is* cannot logically be considered apart from what it *does*. To a large extent the justification of such features as may be ascribed to the spatial dimension in literature must rest upon their function. As Petsch quite rightly stated, "Für sich selbst hat der Raum kein Daseinsrecht, sondern besteht nur in bezug auf den Vorgang und auf die Handlung" (p. 180). The subject of function or use can be approached in at least two ways. The first deals with the manner or way in which something functions, and the second deals with the effect which is produced. Although the word "function" itself seems to imply some activity on the part of the object, it may also be used in reference to a passive or static thing if that thing, like a painting, produces by its presence an effect or reaction. Actual or potential voluminousness, or extensiveness and extensionality, proceed from space which has been formed statically or dynamically. Whereas the static function may be either absolute or relative, the dynamic function operates in a framework of continually moving relationships which produce, among other things, perspective and character.

Space which functions in a static and absolute manner may be illustrated by reference to some of Unamuno's writings. His works evoke the impression that the space which they occupy is fragmented and of little significance. The emphasis, as every reader of Unamuno knows, is upon the revelation of the quintessential, daemon-possessed character. This character is essentially self-fashioning and certainly not subject to the forces exerted by an externally created sphere of existence. Scarcely any loci circumscribe the environment and locate the action in "Two Mothers," or "Nothing Less than a Man," or *Abel Sanchez*. The house in "The Marquis of Lumbria," typically, was described not according to its spatial location, but figuratively, so that its essence rather than the location of its existence was revealed: it was "like a chest of silent, mysterious memories."[9] True, the back of this house "overlooked the river," but this said little more about the house itself, and it did nothing to create a defined space in which the story might unfold, for this vague and mysterious river was never described as going anywhere or coming from anywhere or having another territory on its far side. Never, either, was anything significantly above or below anything else. Transferral of position within these spaces, whose existence seemed to register upon neither eye nor ear nor tactile sense, was accomplished in the vaguest of ways: "He returned to his wife" (p. 227), or "The children burst in . . ." (p. 58). Furnishings these were of the barest sort, certainly, and on no occasion were they ever rearranged. Nor do these static loci, so sparsely established and vaguely located, offer any hint that there might be any more distant space beyond that which they so sketchily outline. Perhaps the belief of nothingness beyond death explains the static spaciousnessless of such a theater of operations.[10]

Static space may also have relative meaning. As Heinz Werner explained, for primitive or childlike peoples, space "retains the property of termporal succession, that is, irreversibility,"[11] and "A child may be able to orient himself perfectly well so long as he can carry out a familiar sequence of movement, but be quite lost if he has to start from some new point of departure" (p. 176). From the psychological point of view, at least, there is evidently an essential relationship between static locales. This relationship comes into being through consecutive encounters. The field of action in which it exists is centered in the home territory. According to Werner, a small child returning from a long trip orients himself in the home only after he has first entered his own room, and a savage "knows" a river only if he can encounter its parts successively, from first to last (p. 176). There is, of course, an overwhelming literary tradition of the homecoming theme from the *Gilgamesh* on, but in few places is it more clearly illustrated than in Homer's the *Odyssey*. In his introduction to the Palmer translation, Howard Porter makes a nice case for the interpretation of the work as a poem of progression towards rebirth, home, concrete reality, and mortality.[12] Each episode in the epic is a step in this progression. "The journey of Odysseus is from abstract to concrete, from a world of witches and assorted monsters to the naturalistic world of Ithaca" (p. 7). The locales themselves—Ogygia, Scheria, and Ithaca—may be static, but their meanings, according to Porter, are specific, and these meanings come from their relationships to those which precede and those which follow.

The term "dynamic" implies movement and therefore a conflict of forces or at least a conflict between a force and that which resists it. Lessing seemed to recognize this: "Doch alle Körper existieren nicht allein in dem Raume, sondern auch in der Zeit. Sie dauern fort, und können in jedem Augenblicke ihrer Dauer anders erscheinen und in anderer Verbindung stehen. Jede dieser augenblicklichen Erscheinungen und Verbindungen ist die Wirkung einer vorhergehenden, und kann die Ursache einer folgenden, und sonach gleichsam das Centrum einer Handlung sein."[12] Extensionality, as exemplified in the age of the Baroque, is one kind of dynamic activity. Another may be seen in the conflict between two spaces, as in *Don Quixote*, wherein a tension is formed between the self-created space of action in which the Don mentally exists and the "real" space in which he physically exists. And in Sartre's *Huis Clos* the characters inhabit a world whose existence has meaning only through the repeated positing of a relationship between it and an outer or previous world. Also, in Hermann Hesse's *Siddhartha* there was a dynamic relationship between two spaces: as long as Siddhartha was figuratively in Kamala's "cage," he was in an inner space which was dialectically conflictive with an imagined outer space; after his "escape," she opened the golden cage symbolically, and released her captive bird, by which act she demonstrated that the conflict between the two spaces was resolved. In his brilliant study on Flaubert in *Les métamorphoses du cercle* (Paris, 1961), Georges Poulet, who presupposes the existence, meaning, and function of space and thereupon addresses himself to the task of the location and sanctification of its forms, closely analyzes a passage from *Madame Bovary* and remarks that when Flaubert wrote "toute l'amertume de l'existence lui semblait servie sur son assiette, et, à la fumée du bouilli, il montait du fond de son âme comme d'autres bouffées d'affadissement."

> Nouns assistons ici à une poussée concentrique de toutes les forces causales venant à la fois du milieu extérieur et des étendues intérieures de l'existence, pour aboutir à l'âme d'Emma, fixée dans la contemplation amère de l'assiette. Mais à peine Flaubert nous a-t-il rendu visible cette action qui va de la causalité périphérique à la conscience ponctuelle, qu'il nous décrit ensuite le mouvement inverse par lequel l'âme réagit excentriquement et projette à son tour, comme un objet, son sentiment dans les espaces. [pp. 374-375]

Further, he shows that the infinite contraction of the two spaces reflects a quite natural function of the human mind (p. 377). To Poulet, the essence of it all is the tension between the subjective consciousness and the objective things which are rendered in that consciousness. The essential metaphors are expansion and dilation, circularity and constriction. The essential means of perception is the visual. We have here an ordered and formal, yet dynamic, relationship which illustrates another of the active modes whereby space functions.

The effects produced by the functions of space have already been touched upon in relation to meaning, characteristics, and manner of functioning. Two, however, remain to be discussed. Relying, for lack of anything better, upon another dichotomy, we can distinguish those which are rather simple and objective from those which are more complex and subjective. If there is any historical demarcation line between the two—any such distinction would be arbitrary and not easily defensible—it would have to extend back at least as far as Dante.

Within the first or most traditional category there are three kinds of uses. The first of these promotes a change in scenes. When Boccaccio removed his ten principals from the church in Florence to the country estate nearby, he not only provided himself with an ideally tranquil and neutral location from which sallies might temporarily be made into more dynamic, external locales, but also he divorced his group and his readers from the unpleasant (but compelling) associations with Florence during the plague of 1348. Most other frame tales, and even Balzac's expansion upon the form, *La Comédie Humaine*, with its subdivisions of *Vie de Province*, *Vie Parisienne*, and *Vie de Campagne*, follow the basic pattern. Although frame tales usually contain internal divisions based on time or character, the basic metaphorical concept is obviously spatial. The *Canterbury Tales* inverts the basic arrangement, using the ancient quest format as a device for justifying the internal stories, yet the change of scene remains the common goal and basis, so to speak, for the entire work. Chaucer's work, as a matter of fact, is even more spatially oriented than most other frame tales in that each internal unit signifies a progression in space towards the goal locale. The same, of course, may be said of Dante—that he posits a spatial goal and that each new location which marks a change of scene, represents movement towards that goal.

For narratives wherein the setting is not regularly changed within the framework of one encompassing pattern but is instead a continuous progression within which the parts bear a coherent relationship to each other rather than just to some central design, the change of locale has the effect of indicating a change of circumstances; in this sense the effect is to further narration rather than to accumulate it. Place changes sometimes effect character changes, so it seems natural that, narrationally, as a character develops, each step in his development be marked, symbolically, by a change in locale. The apprenticeship novel is particularly resplendent with examples, from *Parzival* to *Wilhelm Meister* to *Jean Christophe* to *A Portrait of the Artist as a Young Man*.[14] The same is true in the novel of character disintegration. In *Tender is the Night*, for example, the successive stages of Dick Diver's decaying character are marked by a series of locales, the last of which is as vague and arbitrary as the nature of the person has become which it represents.

Narration may be advanced by change of scenes, and usually is, in which there is no occasion to symbolize either creation or disintegration of character. This is most apparent in those works in which character, although established, is not variable. There are abundant examples of works of this sort, but Vergil's *Aeneid* is one of the best. Aeneas's character, with its mixture of pietas, gravitas, simplicitas, and virtus, is not only central to the narrative, it is a clearly outlined, rock-hard constant. An externally supplied goal, Hesperia, is by no means incompatible with such a character. Given this character, then, and its goal, all that remains to be supplied is incident, to mark progress along the way. Not only does such incident have incremental effect in building the narrative, but also it moves the story forward chronologically, as well as geographically, because with each new episode there must be a comparable change of place. Had the attempt been made to confine the *Aeneid* to one area, say, just to Latium, the spectrum would have been diminished, the focus deepened, the temporal dimension restricted, the roles of the gods narrowed, and the character of Aeneas limited.

In a word, it would have been extremely difficult for Vergil to indicate progression in a nearly spaceless narration.

The third simple function or effect of the spatial element is essentially connotative. A location has a value, as did Hesperia to Aeneas or Cumae to Umbritius in Juvenal's third satire. In these cases it is positive, but it can also be negative as was the passage between Scylla and Charybdis in the *Odyssey* or the Slough of Despond in *Pilgrim's Progress* or the *Inferno* in *La Commedia* or Venice in Mann's *Der Tod in Venedig*. In simple cases of this sort, location is used to effect valuation.[15]

Of the uses which are more complex, one creates perspective and the other characterizes, either by association, delineation, or projection. Perspective comes from the contrast produced through the juxtaposition of two different angles or distances in viewing a subject. The sense of perspective is strongest when it is freshest; hence, the part played by time, even in most forms of spatial perspective, can be important. The two forms of perspective, of time and space, are somewhat analogous.[16] It is from the perspective of space, however, that the metaphorical term for the concept comes. Either can be reproduced in literature, and for an example of the latter the scene at the agricultural fair in *Madame Bovary* will do. In it, two modules of space were posited, one inside but off-center in relation to the other. The larger, that which circumscribed the county fair, represented that which was rural, overt, concrete, and socially approved; the smaller encompassed that which was urbane, clandestine, mistakenly idealized, and socially unacceptable. As Flaubert directed the reader's vision back and forth between the two scenes, he produced a perspective which threw each into a clearer, somewhat ironic light; this he did while ostensibly presenting the two sorts of worlds which were open to Emma and between which she was vacillating.

Perspective is often the foundation of a sane or reasonable judgment, so it is not surprising that some of the best examples of literature written to induce perspective come from the age which is traditionally associated with the appeal to human reason, the eighteenth century. One of the many examples that might be drawn from the writings of the time may be found in Swift's *Gulliver's Travels*. Because the tempo or rhythm is so much slower than that in *Madame Bovary*, the sense of perspective seems less immediate. Yet it exists in its spatial form, especially in the first two books. Each of these two books represents an explicitly defined space while Europe has a concrete location which is nevertheless implicit. There are three sets of contrasts between the several spaces—between Lilliput and Europe, between Brobdingnag and Europe, and between Lilliput and Brobdingnag. In Lilliput, Gulliver, witnessing everything through the eyes of the ostensibly impartial reader-observer, undergoes adventures in a place where in respect to its regular inhabitants he is a giant. The adventures are, as everyone knows, a burlesque of comparable situations in Europe. In Brobdingnag, he is, in comparison to the natives, a midget. There, he represents on occasion the European viewpoint, and his hosts one which is more enlightened. And since he and the reader have, by the end of the second book, compared both these regions to Europe and each region to the other, a multiple perspective, evolved from contrasting points of view which revealed the proportional importance of several matters is the inevitable result. Without such perspectives, the resultant judgments could not be so powerfully evoked.

One of the most useful devices for creating a sensation of perspective through the juxtaposition of spaces, contained and expanded, is the window. In Meyer's analysis of the *Chronik der Sperlingsgasse* he comments that "Nicht die Tür, sondern das Fenster stellt die Verbindung der vita contemplativa mit der Welt da draußen her; durch das Fenster geht der Blick zum schmalen Himmelsstreifen hinauf, in die Gasse hinab und besonders auch hinüber zum Fenster drüben" (p. 250), and that Raabe's ". . . zentrale Raummotiv, der gefühlvolle Blick vom umfriedeten Raum aus durchs Fenster, scheint mir einen Wesenzug darzustellen" (p. 251). Meyer noted also the presence of the same motif in the writings of E. T. A. Hoffmann, Mörike, and Stifter. Had he chosen to, he might easily have offered examples of its use in other national literatures besides the German. Emma Bovary, for example, stood constantly next to the window, that symbol of extensionality which, together with the explicit extensiveness of the room, formed a spatial perspective. Jean Rousset, in his *Forme et signification: essais sur les structures littéraires de Corneille à Claudel* (Paris, 1962), gave careful treatment to the subject in his chapter on *Madame Bovary*. "La fenêtre est un poste privilégié pour ces personnages flaubertiens à la fois immobiles et portés à la dérive, englués dans leur inertie et livrés au vagabondage de leur pensée; dans le lieu fermé où l'âme moisit, voilà une déchirure par où se diffuser dans l'espace sans avoir à quitter son point de fixation. La fenêtre unit la fermeture et l'ouverture, l'entrave et l'envol, la clôture dans la chambre et l'expansion au dehors, l'illimité dans le circonscrit," wrote Rousset (p. 123), and further: "Fenêtres et perspective splongeantes, ouvertures sur le lointain et rêveries dans l'espace, autant de points névralgiques du récit, de noeuds où le cours narratif s'arrête" (p. 127).

In a certain sense, the perspective of which Rousset writes does much to throw light on the character that experiences the perspective, and in this way it stands somewhere between perspective which produces judgments and characterization which is produced by less dynamic spatial systems. Two main methods of such characterization may be distinguished—the associative and the projective. In the first, the character's identity is derived from his association with a place. Naming conventions of most countries have, from antiquity, used this method, through the conferral of surnames which denote a place of origin. In a parallel way, characters which inhabit a literary composition may be given qualities which cause them to be associated in some way with a particular place. Babbitt, in Sinclair Lewis's work of the same name, has qualities which are comparable to those of the town of Zenith: both are conformity-conscious, bourgeois, status-seeking, financially ambitious, fraudulent, and so on. Dante's sinners, of course, have characters which correspond to those of the regions they inhabit in the *Inferno* and the *Purgatorio*; this correspondence is nearly exact in each case, the regions having been devised solely to represent the various categories of human sins. Hesse's Siddhartha, like Dante's sinners, revealed the state of his soul and the quality of his character by the place he occupied. When he was on one side of the river he was a seeker; on the other, he became the finder. This was not, as in Dante, a static situation: on his second crossing of the river he was plunged most deeply into himself, so the meaning of his first habitation of that region differed from that of his second. And Harry Haller, in *Der Steppenwolf*, sought a spatial and essential association with the bourgeois world, although it was denied him.

Topography is also useful for distinguishing between two characters or for delineating a subject in reference to the space which adjoins it. In Ibsen's *John Gabriel Borkman* the upper floor of the family estate is occupied by one whose ambition to advance the family fortunes has led to downfall and disgrace, while the lower floor is dominated by one whose neurotic ambition to redeem the fallen fortunes has converted a disgrace to a tragedy. In his pivotal essay on *Madame Bovary* in *Mimesis* (Berne, 1946), Erich Auerbach claims that Emma's character takes on its contour as it stands out against a background of spatially-located objects. And Georges Poulet, in his essay on Flaubert, asserts that space and its contents produce a dynamic and revealing relationship with both character and a subjective consciousness.[17] The spatial association system, then, may be used either to identify or to delineate character.

Characterization by association is a conscious or semiconscious act of authorship. It is not sufficient, however, to explain certain other kinds of characterization. What about those lost souls in Dante's or Sartre's writings who inhabit a hell of their own creation? And what about Faust? In his study he felt constrained; he had himself envisioned "die große Welt" of which Mephistopheles spoke, that expanded space of existence which, as the poem progressed, he came ever closer to inhabiting. Early in the work the Earth Spirit had announced to him, "Du gleichst dem Geist, den du begreifst." In a sense, the whole theme of the poem is Faust's compulsive attempt to expand his world through affirmative activity in opposition to the contracting forces exerted by the spirit of negation which very likely dwelt in his own breast. Through a kind of reflective duality, whereby the interior created the exterior and then inhabited the exterior, a circular pattern quite in keeping with Poulet's major thesis, Faust fashioned a new world for himself. The new world grew from an inner, imaginative world which transcended all tangible loci. Rilke, too, formed new worlds from his own subconscious. In a letter (Aug. 11, 1924) he wrote,

> Mir stellt es sich immer so dar, als ob unser gebräuchliches Bewußtsein die Spitze einer Pyramide bewohne, deren Basis in uns (und gewissermaßen unter uns) so völlig in die Breite geht, daß wir, je weiter wir in sie niederzulassen uns befähigt sehen, desto allgemeiner einbezogen erscheinen in die von Zeit und Raum unabhängigen Gegebenheiten des irdischen, des, im weitesten Begriffe, weltischen Daseins.[18]

This, Günther stated, ". . . ist Mittelpunkt und Ziel seines künstlerischen Erlebnisses überhaupt"; and ". . . seine Kunst immer mehr nur nach der immer genaueren Eingestaltung dieses Grundwesentlichen strebte" (p. 35). A classic example of this same basic process, founded upon a mental aberration rather than a mystical internalization, is to be found in Cervantes. The constant interraction between Quixote's mental world and the ostensible world, and the reactive and shaping influence of that world upon his mind, form not only a perspective but also a realm that owes its existence to a reflective formational process. Because the source of this effect is dynamic and internal rather than passive and external, and because it either converges or diverges, it may be considered projective.[19]

One of the best modern examples of this projective quality is Hesse's *Der Steppenwolf*. In it, inner spatial location is primary, and external space remains unimportant. Harry Haller is seeking self-realization. His early attempts to find it through the association and identification of one side of his nature with bourgeoisiedom are misdirected, insufficient, and satisfying only to certain facets of his personality. Ultimately, he is

able to discover the essential self that dwells within him. But to do this
he must begin again as a child—Hermine, of course, is his "mother"—
and advance through the *rite du passage* of the nuptial dance up to the
experience with the magic theater. There with the help of Pablo's drugs,
he explores the dark corners of his own mental existence. Temporarily,
he inhabits some of the multiple worlds which exist in his own subconscious.

One step farther, beyond the finite expansion of the inner self to
larger space, as in Hesse, takes us to the infinite expansion of the self
into exterior space or the parallel convergence of that space into an interior self, as in Rilke. This is not so much an intellectual projection
of a sphere of existence but rather a subliminal identification with, or
creation of, vast or infinitesimal space that is reminiscent of Hindu
mysticism. Günther discussed this in *Weltinnenraum*:

> In einem Blatt aus dem Spanischen Tagebuch—um die Jahreswende
> 1912—und in den Aufzeichnungen, betitelt "Erlebnis," hat Rilke in die
> Geheimnisse diesses Werdens blicken lassen. Er erzählt darin von jenen
> "Hingegebenheiten" an Unendlichkeitsempfindungen, wie sie sich bis in
> seine dumpfe Kindheit zurück bedenken ließen: Augenblicken, in denen
> die Grenze des Körpers wie aufgehoben schien und der Weltraum, "der
> Geschmack der Schöpfung" dermaßen in ihn überging, "daß er glauben
> durfte, das leichte Aufruhn der inzwischen eingetretenen Sterne in seiner
> Brust zu fühlen." In dieser "Leere" des nackten kosmischen Seins fühlt
> er sich gleichsam auf der andern Seite der Natur. An einem Baum
> lehnend . . . "eingeruht," . . . ist ihm als ob aus dem Innern des Baumes
> fast unmerkliche Schwingungen in ihn übergingen; sein Körper wird
> gewissermaßen wie eine Seele behandelt, es dünkt ihn, er stehe in seinem
> Körper "wie in der Tiefe eines verlassenen Fensters," "hinuntersehend."
> Aus "geistigerem Abstande," mit "unerschöpflicher Bedeutung" berührt
> ihn das Dasein von Pflanzen. [p. 36]

Where mysticism begins, the usefulness of maps ends. This one may
have served to suggest, from one point of view at least, some of the features of the terrain as it lies prior to that borderline. As seen by the
physical and mental eye, the territory is far greater than had been supposed. Its presence is established on several bases, and it manifests itself
through the varied forms of this presence, its meanings, and its effects.
These may be absolute or relative in different ways; they may denote
limitations or their transcendence; they may function statically or dynamically, simply or complexly; they may work through association or
representation; and they may create rational perspective or reveal subjective projections of the self. They comprise one significant dimension
of thought and its parallel expression in literature.

Notes

1. James Joyce, *Ulysses* (New York, 1946), p. 137. Miles Hanley's *Word Index to James Joyce's Ulysses* (Madison, 1951) lists a total of four references to "tomb" and fourteen to "womb."

2. Ida Fasel, in "Spatial Form and Spatial Time," *Western Humanities Review*, Vol. 16 (Summer 1962), pp. 223–224, quite rightly considered Irving Babbitt's consternation about the subject in *The New Laokoön: An Essay on the Confusion of the Arts* (Boston, 1910) as alarm over an artificially created problem.

3. In "The Possibility of a Theory of the Novel," from *The Disciplines of Criticism*, Ed. by Peter Demetz, Thomas Greene, and Lowry Nelson, Jr. (New Haven, 1968), Ralph Freedman states that "The metaphor for the novel, more than for any other genre, is spatial" (p. 72); further, after stating that the picaresque "may well serve as a *paradigm* of the novel as a whole" (p. 75), he concludes, in part, that "The suggestion that the picaresque, in its most general outline, may be symptomatic of the novel's basic form involves the following assumptions: First, the novel's world is a structure or 'space' . . ," (p. 77). Although he makes mention of the epic in a footnote, he appears to have imposed questionable restrictions on both the novel itself and all other literary genres from which, by implication, the element of space is wholly or partially excluded.

4. Edwin Muir, for example, in *The Structure of the Novel* (New York, 1929), divided novels into five categories, of which the most important two were character novels like *Vanity Fair* and dramatic novels like *Wuthering Heights*. According to Muir, ". . . the imaginative world of the dramatic novel is in Time, the imaginative world of the character novel in Space" (p. 62). Again, "The dramatic novel is limited in Space and free in Time, the character novel limited in Time and free in Space . . . it was the closed-in arena, we held, that gave the dramatic conflict intensity, and accelerated and emphasized the passage of time. It was the unchangeability of the characters, on the other hand, that made typical those relations between them which imaged the life of society" (p. 88).

   Wolfgang Kayser, in *Das sprachliche Kunstwerk* (Berne, 1948), went so far as to divide novels into three types: Geschehnisroman, Figurenroman, and Raumroman (pp. 362–367). Then in his *Entstehung und Krise des modernen Romans* (Stuttgart, 1955), he said, "Wir nennen Romane, in denen nicht eine bestimmte Handlung, sondern die Verschiedenheit und Fülle von Räumlichkeiten die strukturtragende Schicht bildet, Raumromane" (p. 24). In an excellent piece of work, "Raum und Zeit in Wilhelm Raabes Erzählkunst," first published in *Deutsche Vierteljahrsschrift für Literaturwissenschaft und Geistesgeschichte*, Vol. 27 (1953), pp. 236–267, and reprinted in *Zur Poetik des Romans*, Ed. by Volker Klotz (Darmstadt, 1965), pp. 239–279 (page numbers to be cited are from this edition), Herman Meyer commented on this: "So anregend diese Ausführungen auch sind, man kann sich mit ihnen doch nicht ganz zufriedengeben. So fragt es sich schon gleich, ob Geschehen, Figur und Raum—zu denen sich bei Kayser nicht die Zeit als vierte

Kategorie gesellt—gleichwertige Größen sind, oder ob nicht das Geschehen, das sich im Raume und in der Zeit abspielt, der übergeordnete Begriff ist" (p. 243).

5. This view is advanced in Robert Petsch's *Wesen und Formen der Erzahlkunst* (Halle, 1942), pp. 180–189.

6. William James, "The Perception of Space," in *Mind*, Vol. 45–48 (1887), pp. 1–30, 183–211, 321–353, 516–548.

7. Henri Bosco's *Malicroix* (p. 105 ff.) as quoted in Gaston Bachelard's *La poétique de l'espace* (Paris, 1958), p. 55. He presents an idea that is of great interest from the point of view of style when he says, "Rien ne suggère comme le silence le sentiment des espaces illimités. J'entrai dans ces espaces. Les bruits colorent l'étendue et lui donnent une sorte de corps sonore. Leur absence la laisse toute pure et c'est la sensation du vaste, du profound, de l'illimité qui nous saisit dans le silence. Elle m'envahit et je fus, pendant quelques minutes, confondu à cette grandeur de la paix nocturne."

8. Maurice Merleau-Ponty, *Phenomenology of Perception* (London, 1962), p. 244.

9. Miguel Unamuno, *Three Exemplary Novels*, trans. by Angel Flores (New York, 1956), p. 37.

10. An interesting example far back on the chronological continuum, the Greek tragedy, suggests a related question. Why, for example, was the space in which the drama existed so closely controlled? Aristotle cannot be held responsible: he was describing, not prescribing. Further, the only unity he considered essential was that of action. Possibly the centrality of man within his own segment of the universe could best be shown in a static and absolute realm. Or perhaps, by stabilizing and thereby neutralizing those elements exterior to the action, it was possible to sharpen the focus on the characters themselves.

11. Heinz Werner, *Comparative Psychology of Mental Development* (New York, 1957), p. 176.

12. Howard Porter, in introduction to the Palmer translation of *The Odyssey* (New York, 1962), pp. 1–20.

13. *Lessings Werke*, Ed. by Heinrich Kurz (Leipzig, n.d.), pp. 97–98. For a perceptive modern discussion of dynamicism, see Roman Ingarden, *Vom Erkennen des literarischen Kunstwerks* (Tübingen, 1968), pp. 113–115.

14. An apparent exception is, of course, *Der Zauberberg*. Although it appears to depict an entire education without reference to the spatial metaphor, it only does this in part because the first and last sections contain major spatial changes, ánd the central section is filled with small but implicitly significant spatial variations.

15. When the place or goal takes on a meaning like "home," then the matter becomes more complex. It leads, then, into a tantalyzing realm, especially when it embraces works like Kafka's *Das Schloß*, Stifter's *Bergkristall*, Apuleius's *The Golden Ass*, or *The Gilgamesh*, all of which may be examined from the archetypal point of view.

16. Roman Ingarden presents a carefully reasoned analysis of this analogous relationship in *Vom Erkennen des literarischen Kunstwerks*, pp. 109–111.

17. Georges Poulet, *Les métamorphoses du cercle*, pp. 374–375, and as amplified in the English version of the same article, in *Western Review*, Vol. 19 (Summer 1955), pp. 245–260. Thc essay, it should be noted, provides an interesting discussion of the dynamic convergence and expansion of space through the subjective metamorphosis of its loci.

18. Cited by Werner Günther, *Weltinnenraum* (Berlin, 1952), pp. 34–35. In a similar connection, there is a useful study on Rilke and others in Maurice Blanchot, *L'espace littéraire* (Paris, 1955).
19. The concept is suggested in Edward G. Ballard's "Renaissance Space and the Humean Development in Philosophical Psychology," *Tulane Studies in Philosophy*, Vol. 13 (1964), pp. 55–79.

Karl D. Uitti

LITERARY DISCOURSE: SOME DEFINITIONS AND APPROACHES

QUESTIONS OF STATUS AND ROLE ARE NOWADAYS AT THE FOREFRONT OF much thought concerning the language of literature (or poetry) and its analysis. Similarly, for many of us, truly profitable speculation on the nature and value of literary discourse must be worked out in terms of the set of problems one faces whenever one attempts to describe such discourse—even in conjunction with, or in contrast to, other kinds of utterance and texts. In my opinion this explains in part why so many contemporary scholars and critics have shown an astonishingly sustained interest in "reconciling" literary and general linguistic study—often despite somewhat slim practical results—or, for that matter, in incorporating such study into a more broadly conceived theory of signs. Reciprocally, concern for the nature of literature and its value necessarily implies interest in what makes up discourse *about* literature: the latter constitutes our only sure means of approaching the former. Literary theory, poetics, "style" studies, "practical criticisms," and so forth, all reflect this interest, in more or less formal ways. Finally, since neither literary nor—in the widest sense—critical activity takes place in a vacuum, but rather in a here-and-now, in a historical as well as in a cultural dimension, efforts have been made to deal cogently with matters of cultural value and historical scope. (Contemporary anti-historicisms and "structuralisms" have tended to undermine such efforts; the teachings of Edward Sapir provide a happy contrast to the deleterious effects of much modern structuralist theory, whereas, to cite but one striking example, the popular success of a Marshall McLuhan goes far to prove our need and taste for increased activity along these lines.)

By definition the philologist believes in the dignity of literary discourse, axiomatically, as it were. Consequently the status of such discourse—the poetic text, in any of its ramifications—depends in practice on the nature of the philological activity deployed about it. One's analysis influences the object upon which it is focused and, by the same token, the object certainly helps shape the contours of the analysis.[1] Practically speaking, what I have said has indeed been worked into the fabric of contemporary philology and even of much ostensibly non-philological criticism: a certain eclecticism dominates in fact such study nowadays. But theorists nonetheless continue to espouse monolithic doctrines; this tends unfortunately to cloud the issues. Before I go on to develop the questions raised above, a few words on this last problem would be very much to the point.

STYLE, POETICS, AND LINGUISTIC FACT

Here again linguistics turns out to be helpful. I am thinking especially of the masterful contribution by the late Uriel Weinreich (in collaboration with William Labov and Marvin I. Herzog) to *Directions for Historical Linguistics* (Texas, 1968)[2]: "Empirical Foundations for a Theory of Language Change." Attacking the notion of "all-encompassing" (i e , static) structure, Weinreich, Labov, and Herzog find that in order to describe and explain language change, the doctrines of coexisting systems and of variability (e.g., social, stylistic, etc.) of structures within the system permit far greater accuracy and analytic finesse than Saussurean structural theory and its more recent, equally monolithic, counterparts: "The present paper is based on the observation that structural theories of language, so fruitful in synchronic investigation, have saddled historical linguistics with a cluster of paradoxes which have not been fully overcome" (p. 98). The key word is, of course, "historical." Thus, the very notion of embedding must be reexamined in terms not only of linguistic structure but also of social context, unless one is willing to run the risk of downplaying certain specifically *linguistic* values. To put it in a nutshell, proper formal study requires the genuine incorporation of ostensibly extraformal features into the analysis. Our authors reach some seven conclusions that may be usefully summarized as follows: (1) linguistic change is more than a matter of chance; (2) far from being homogeneous, linguistic structure comprises a rather impressive variety of styles which, however, permit discrimination thanks to a gamut of rules; each speaker "possesses" the rules of his

mother tongue; (3) each linguistic change implies variability and het-
erogeneity; (4) generalization of a given change throughout the system
is neither uniform nor immediate; (5) only a grammar that records
naturally linguistic changes is worthy of being called the grammar of a
speech community; a grammar based on an idiolect will never be sufficient or "self-contained"; (6) changes are transmitted throughout the
entire speech community; they are not limited to the family; (7) linguistic factors and social factors are closely linked within the development of linguistic changes; many "regularities" will be missed by whoever neglects to take proper stock of both sets of factors.

These conclusions (and, indeed, the entire study leading up to them)
are very suggestive. Weinreich, Labov, and Herzog do not mean to
sacrifice the authentic achievements of modern linguistic science, that
is, its characteristic "way of stating," its stress upon the interpersonal
and the verifiable, or, above all, the high value placed by contemporary
linguistics upon formal analysis and experimentation. We are at a far
cry from the "antipositivism" of a Vossler or a Spitzer; for Vossler, one
recalls, the study of stylistic choice tended to preclude the pure analysis
of syntactic possibility. Nevertheless, our authors do not feel compelled
to wear the blinders so many post-Bloomfieldians (and Saussureans)
deem necessary in order to preserve the "way of stating" of contemporary linguistic research. Thus, in their view, "historical" and "diachronic" are by no means synonymous: the historical, as dimension, is
opposed to the very context of synchrony-diachrony. To put it another
way, the historical may be viewed, if one wishes, in a synchronic or
diachronic (or even panchronic) perspective. (One is reminded here
of Sapir's concept of "culture," an analytic dimension that offered a
means of relating, dialectically, poetic—or linguistic—creativity and
language form, in time and space, either diachronically or synchron-
ically.[3])

Going on to consider some of the broad implications of "Empirical
Foundations for a Theory of Language Change," we find that the authors' insistence upon the realities of speech leads to some highly re-
freshing viewpoints. A new lease on life is given to the Idealist proposition that linguistic choice exploits a multitude of expressive, cultural,
social, and grammatical conditions, and that creativity (as well as
eventual linguistic change) lies in the exercise of such choice. But, inasmuch as Weinreich and his collaborators have no intention of aban-
doning the study of linguistic system(s), they are inclined to interpret
the deployment of speech in terms of various registers of tone which,
in turn, are organized into stylistic sets that enlarge upon or otherwise

tend to reshape the more or less strictly coded and functional possibilities of expression. Our authors do not speak directly of dialogue, although, of course, they do examine the speaker's relationship to—and within—his "community." Thus, we learn, the child's peer group is usually more influential than his parents in the development of permanent speech habits. Dialogue—speaker and interlocutor within the speech situation—is clearly a matter of great import within the study's framework.

At this point the student of literature stands to benefit directly from what Weinreich, Labov, and Herzog have accomplished, namely, from their nonmonolithic approach to speech dynamics and from their stress —both implicit and explicit—upon the active collaboration of those who participate in the speech act. In a sense the interlocutor "creates" what he hears: without this "re-creation" the message goes nowhere. Analogously, in certain literary texts, a kind of Joycean difficulty principle may color a verbal exchange: the speaker demands of his listener that he make a greater, or more "creative," effort to understand. And this *difficulté vaincue* adds to—or detracts from—the value of the communication.

Yet, clearly, concentration upon historical factuality, the real speech situation in all its complex variety, should not be construed as grounds for free-wheeling impressionism. Weinreich's team hardly downplays either the need to know as much as possible or what we have called the "characteristic way of stating" of linguistic analysis. Formal descriptive statements encompassing and accounting for considerable bodies of data remain, obviously, the linguist's most cherished goal. Weinreich rejected earlier structuralist biases as unfruitful, as unable to attain this goal. One appreciates the term "empirical"—and its connotations— in the essay's title. If, then, in adapting to his own purposes aspects of Weinreich's approach to linguistic historicity, the philologist interprets "dialogue" in terms of some sort of active cooperation, in the text, of author and reader, he must not neglect to relate his findings to a more broadly viewed notion of language and speech. Indeed by studying in given texts the operations of such dialogue, the philologist may well go on to describe the degrees of stylistic sophistication present in a given language or, perhaps, in speech itself. This kind of *relation* constitutes a proper goal; it stands in lieu of a previous generation's "completeness" or "exhaustiveness."

One need only contrast this viewpoint with, say, the doctrines of Roman Jakobson in order to understand the important change of emphasis involved. In his fairly recent developments of Prague School

theory—see especially "Linguistics and Poetics," in *Style in Language,*
ed. by T. Sebeok (Cambridge, Mass., 1960)—Jakobson reminds us that
the poetic function of the message consists in its calling attention to its
own organization. Or, as the "Thèses," *TCLP,* I [1929], 18, put it:
"Le langage poétique tend à mettre en relief la valeur autonome du
signe." Jakobson does not mean to avoid complexities; the "poetic
function" is inserted into a whole set of functions, each of which enters
to some degree into the entire operation. Yet his bias remains formalist.
That is, he proxides grounds for distinguishing between ordinary colloquy and poetic language: the latter is in fact "marked" by its calling
attention primarily to its own order. The distinction allows him to in-
corporate poetics into linguistics, hierarchically as it were; analogously,
he attempts to integrate linguistics itself into general semiotic, the
theory of signs. Yet, as I have suggested, what poetry and colloquy hold
in common is at least as significant as what distinguishes between them.
I mean, very precisely, the historical and properly existential fact of
collaboration, of dialogue, underlying the poetic as well as the colloquial
experience. Of course this does not imply that one should dispense with
the analysis of the verbal structures that make up the text of the poem.
However, it is surely no less legitimate to examine the poem's rhetorical
dimension, the dialogue it initiates between poet and reader: the
mechanism of the operations that render its structures efficient and
meaningful. Briefly, reading is always *a* reading: this *situation* is far
"truer" than any theory of definitive interpretations.

An impressive case may be made for the proper incorporation of
"poetic documentation" into the study of language—that is, either in
general or, perhaps, specifically restricted to a given historical tongue.
(Indeed, it may be argued, any description of a great cultural language
like English, Spanish, or Latin that refuses to heed such documentation
must inevitably be considered truncated, even grossly deficient.) By
focusing the discussion upon dialogic operations, it seems to me, and
by attempting to determine the degree of stylistic sophistication reached
by a given text, the language historian will enrich very considerably
both the quantity and the quality of his information concerning linguistic phenomena. The word "style" implies variability, choice, freedom;
the term "poetic," conversely, suggests a precise goal, a limitation, or
perhaps the exploitation of certain clearcut possibilities to the exclusion
of others: constraints. Together the two concepts of "style" and
"poetic" provide a handy—indeed necessary—analytic antinomy or
polarity upon which the study may be adequately based.

Weinreich's historical linguistics thus not only suggests a kind of spiritual model, a point of departure for a new look at poetic and stylistic analysis, but in fact allows for an experimental widening of scope in connection with the study of linguistic workings. A certain theoretical purity is perhaps sacrificed, but to good effect. A kind of natural cross-fertilization of linguistic and literary studies might well result from such a "sacrifice." Nevertheless, an objection must be dealt with. Will not any analysis based on the "subjective collaboration" of the linguist-critic inevitably lack scientific rigor? How indeed are we to avoid the atomization of scholarly activity?

Yet, on the other hand, do studies in which the collaboration I have described is minimized or even left totally unexploited succeed in providing adequate descriptions? Is the *fact* of dialogue methodologically irrelevant? Common sense tells us that no self-styled "objective" analysis, say, of Rousseau's language has ever come close to informing us of the true linguistic innovations of that author. Rousseau did not merely invent a few words; he upset the very categories of Enlightenment usage, frequently employing ostensibly analytic categories in new, symbolic (and highly ambiguous) contexts. Unless one's active reading is coded purposefully into one's analysis, this kind of process is bound to slip through, and the study's worth is seriously undermined. I am given to understand that teams of scholars now working at Saint-Cloud on the vocabulary of given French writers of the eighteenth century have resolved not to register in any way their "response" to the texts—that their punched cards will contain only a kind of automatic context, e.g., an environmental sentence or two, for the items recorded. If this indeed is the case, we must deplore the guidelines chosen, for, particularly when computers are involved, operations and interpretations must be construed automatically as a function of data-collecting. Mere listing and sorting are trivial.

Conversely, if it can be shown that reading a text—i.e., actively submitting to its poetic order and collaborating in the creation of its value—does in fact deepen our understanding of linguistic process and can lead to a more pertinent grasp of linguistic history, then surely it must follow that similar scientific procedures would be at least as useful in the analysis of poetic style or the language of a given writer. (And, it seems to me, such an approach would constitute an important check upon the more abstract—"patterned"—accesses to verbal art just as, in their day, these techniques placed a brake on impressionism.) For the sake of illustration, let me paraphrase a section of study Yakov Malkiel and I recently devoted to the Old French suffix -*ois*.[4] We concentrated upon the facetious and playful uses of -*ois*—usage strikingly analogous to contemporary American -*ese*, as in *acadam-ese, journal-ese*, etc.; the suffix indicated types of language or jargon and behavior, and, as is the case with American -*ese*, the degree of detachability of -*ois* was quite high.

Examining the formal and semantic evolution of -*ois* as well as its extraordinary fortune in Old and Middle French, we found that the several uses of this suffix illustrate a process which, in turn, seems to clarify and to exemplify formally a fundamental aspect of suffixal derivation in French. We described this process by characterizing it essentially as a mutual "contamination" of semantic contents and grammatical formations—a contamination governed by metonymic tendencies in the history of the French vocabulary. By "metonymic tendencies" we understood semantic relations based on contiguity that seem to underlie the formal processes of suffixation in general; the latter "realize" functionally and economically these relations and, in so doing, receive a semantico-grammatical value that sets them apart from other types of forms.

So much, then, for background. We documented our study by careful perusal of dictionaries and previously established repertories, and by close examination of OF texts. Few of these were more helpful than the following thirteenth-century lines by Rutebeuf:

> Aillors covient lor penssers voise,
>> Quar dui *tornois*,
> Trois paresis, cinq *vienois*
> Ne pueent pas fere un *borgois*
> D'un nu despris.[5]

Rutebeuf not only exploits the possibilities contained in the -*ois* forms, his poem creates these possibilities. Thus the playfulness—and the detachability—of the suffix is worked into the construct, as is the fact that, in OF usage, -*ois* served to indicate (the provenience of) coins —e.g., *tornois*, 'money from Tours'; *vienois*, 'money from Vienne'; *borgois*, 'money from Bourges' (hence the pun on *bourgeois* and the irony of the *nu despris* never quite "adding up" to the proper sum).

The text is unusually dense. One must work to achieve the poetic process it sets up. It is the series itself—the principle of such a series— that is juxtaposed lexically and syntagmatically against the opposition *borgois:nu despris*. Also both rhyme and rhythm reinforce the series, extending to—and strengthening—the opposition:juxtaposition of *borgois:nu despris*; note the play of *Trois paresis* against *D'un nu despris* (four syllables apiece, the contrast of *trois* and *un*, the sound effects of *paresis:despris*).[6] The process unfolds itself and works. The sophistication of the poetic concept becomes apparent *in* or *through* our reading. (Similarly, as we noted in our study, the proliferation of semantic categories like *-ois* 'provenience→coin' alongside 'facetious language,' etc., will contribute to the inevitable fragmentation of this suffix, and to its final weakening: *-ois* ceases to be active with the advent of the Classical period in French literature.) Clearly, Rutebeuf's poem documents the true vitality and the complexity of an OF linguistic "fact," but, I repeat, the documentation depends on the reader's active understanding. One would get nowhere were one merely to record and classify *-ois* forms in Rutebeuf's work.

The kind of examination we have just hinted at is surely pertinent to the study of Rutebeuf's style and his poetics. One can find no better —nor more concrete—example of his playfully bitter irony or, for that matter, of his brilliant craftsmanship. And we could quite naturally go on to discuss the kind of ambivalence that seems to prevail in his highly intellectual lyric. Rutebeuf builds on oppositions—special kinds of antitheses—that retain their original terms at the same time these terms influence one another in quite provocative ways. In short, the stanza we glanced at offers a fine example of Rutebeuf's putting stylistic means (available within the rules and conventions of literary Old French as well as within the confines of lyric diction) to relevant poetic use. And yet, despite the nuanced sense of these means provided by our "reading" of Rutebeuf, we have not had to flounder about in sterile attempts at exhaustive catalogues of stylistic possibilities. It is possible to avoid the abstract: we need but to restrict our purview to relations involving relevant historical fact. By establishing these relations, the study itself gives them form and pertinence, and, in turn, they help deepen our understanding of literary Old French, of Rutebeuf's poetry, and to some extent, one hopes, of language and poetry in general.

Reliance on concrete readings does not necessarily block the path to higher generalizations. The style-poetic antinomy may be developed further. Thus, to continue very briefly the Rutebeuf commentary, our initial remarks could easily lead to a more thorough investigation of, e.g., suffixation as device in the OF lyric. Note the wordplay on *-oier* in these lines from "La Mort Rutebeuf" (Faral and Bastin, I, p. 575):

> Lessier m'estuet le *rimoier*,
> Quar je me doi moult esmaier
> Quant tenu l'ai si longuement.
> Bien me doit le cuer *lermoier*,
> C'onques ne me poi *amoier*

A Dieu servir parfetement,
Ainz ai mis mon entendement
En geu et en esbatement,
Qu'ainz ne daignai nés *saumoier*,
Se por moi n'est au Jugement
Cele ou Diex prist aombrement,
Mau marchié pris au *paumoier*.[7]

Forms in *-oi(i)er*—a highly creative verbal suffix in Old French—lent themselves to lyric invention, signifying, along with sheer inventiveness, a kind of personalized activity, and frequently straddling the limits of activity, appearance, and behavior. They often served to signal and thereby characterize the kind of discourse in which they were employed. Certain verbs in *-oi(i)er* came to be identified with poetic diction of a courtly, elegant type. The Chastelain de Couci uses *cointoier*, 'warble [like a nightingale]'; *foloier*, 'play the fool, behave foolishly'; *guerroier*, 'attack, torment [metaphorically]'; *maistroier*, 'rule, torment'; *raverdoier*, 'turn green [*reverdir*]' (*tens qui raverdoie* 'Spring'); these terms fit perfectly into the ambiance of the courtly love rhetoric and its sometimes stately, often precious, and sentimental diction. Rutebeuf's verses utilize the preciosity inherent in the *-oier* suffix—the verb *rimoier* starts the reader off on the right track. But irony once again wins out over courtly *tendresse* as *-oier* forms are played off deliberately against the heavy *-(e)ment* constructions. The contrast in the rhyme position is remarkable; it is based entirely on suffixal opposition—i.e., two quite separate categories of word-formation that nevertheless result in ambiguously similar verbal nouns and nominal verbs (*entendement; le rimoier* versus *lermoier*). The considerable pathos of Rutebeuf's text is a function, exactly, of this ambiguity and irony. One concludes that, even after so fleeting a look, it would be difficult to overrate the expressive capabilities of OF suffixal formation.

Despite the brevity of the above remarks and examples, it would seem that the successful revival of historical analysis—in literary as much as in pure language study—requires a certain theoretical loosening. And, as we have suggested, it may well be that the proper investigation of creativity in creation, in what has been "created"—which, to a considerable degree, is precisely what the study of poetic texts amounts to—depends on setting up the pertinent historical framework. It is in one's use of language—the texts themselves as well as in the ways they are composed and worked out in the reading—that the poetic process irreducibly occurs.

PHILOLOGY AND CRITICISM

Philological activity, we have said, assumes the inherent value and interest of literary, or poetic, discourse. Such activity is consequently and by definition critical; statements concerning the worth—pertinence, intensity, value—of texts are naturally built into even the most descriptive and "objective" of philological investigations. There can be no authentic divorce between, on the one hand, an "evaluative criticism" and, on the other, the body of informed literary *Wissenschaft*, though, it is true, ostensible evaluation, constant judgment at every turn, need not determine the tone of all work. Jakobson, in "Linguistics and Poetics," was right to inveigh against replacing "the description of the intrinsic values of a literary work by a subjective, censorious verdict," but his equating "literary critic" and "normative grammarian" (as opposed, respectively, to "investigator of literature" and "linguist") rather befuddles the issue, namely, the hows and whys of what I referred to above as the "ways of stating."

The question of literary value, that is, what is axiomatically assumed by philology, is a function of the kinds of discourse we willingly label literary. Since a poetic text is one that calls attention primarily to the principles of its own organization, to the ways certain "grammaticalizations" are achieved, its referential aspects are, in consequence, relatively less important than is the case with other kinds of discourse (syllogisms, scientific write-ups, reports). Perhaps paradoxically, but nevertheless quite authentically, the meanings of our cultural experience appear in their purest form in literary discourse; this is because such discourse is, by definition, linguistically symbolic. The fact of literariness, in this sense, is what is shared by texts otherwise so disparate as Rousseau's *Confessions* and *Nouvelle Héloïse*, alongside the poems of Coleridge and Cicero's speeches. Literary discourse tends to contain—insofar as such matters lend themselves to articulation—the aspirations, the myths, and the experiences that constitute the very stuff of culture.

Philological activity, therefore, implies criticism virtually at every stage, whether directly or indirectly; values and meanings are in fact what literary discourse is all about. Indeed a sense of these values is usually responsible for one's deciding to engage in such activity in the first place. One reads in order to broaden and deepen one's understanding. Thus, to illustrate the point briefly, nineteenth-century comparative philology stressed relations of a genetic sort whereas modern structural analysis has focused on other matters; each mode reflects, generally, the fashion or sense of values predominating at the time.

With this much said, then, and allowing for what has already been suggested concerning linguistic and literary fact—the question of true historical research and the role of "dialogue" in such research—we may turn to the "hows and whys" or critical of philological "ways of stating."

Quite typically, the mid-twentieth century prefers to view the poetic text as language; the reasons for this are implied in all that has been said here up to this point. Jakobson has advocated redefining poetics in terms of a general semiotic, or theory of signs, whereas René Wellek, pointing out the danger of abstraction present in Jakobson's doctrine (also in *Style in Language*), nevertheless freely admits that literary works are best seen as structures of linguistic signs.[8] However, himself no linguist, Wellek retains an aesthetic, "monumental" conception of the literary work of art. Both scholars share a taste for active interpretation, and in each case structuralist formulations bear the burden of such interpretation. More recently, the equation of language theory with that of mental creativity has prompted certain philosophers to identify "the theoretical constructions in a theory of language" as a source providing "the apparatus for constructing solutions to philosophical problems" (J. J. Katz, *The Philosophy of Language* [New York, 1966], pp. x f.). The elaboration of a "language theory," that is, the study of language, offers the paradigm for all formal inquiry into the nature and purposes of human creativity. Or, at some risk of oversimplification: What I say concerning "the principles that determine the necessary form and content of natural languages, etc." will furnish principles of order applicable in the analysis of instances and potentialities of human creativity. Structuralism here appears to be shifting gears; "subject matter" and "analytic technique," in a sense, fuse, but what I have called interpretation still predominates. Orders of various kinds, or "grammars," are actively created; the corpus—whether a natural language, a poem, or whatever lends itself to analytic reshuffling as sign-deployment—is in and by itself somewhat less primary.

Although, as was pointed out in earlier sections of this essay, much that is implied in these theories smacks of unhealthily monolithic attitudes (or arbitrary appeals to aesthetics, innate ideas, or other *a priori* concepts), there is considerable merit in today's sign-oriented fashions. To speak of "language" means nowadays to focus upon at least two distinct items.[9] On the one hand, linguistic usage, or discourse, as we observed, in literary forms may be seen as a kind of incarnation of cultural value and process. On the other hand, language or "linguistic form" is that which is grasped by formal analysis; such analysis, or "way of stating," as the structuralist tradition suggests, provides the necessary categories on which to base one's approach to texts. However, to repeat what I have said elsewhere, "the student must be thoroughly grounded in the techniques of formal analysis not . . . merely to 'apply' them, but rather in order to grasp fully the *possibilities* they contain" (*Linguistics and Literary Theory*). "Language" is thus at once a means and an end, technique and subject-matter. But two important and exemplary questions arise. First, may a poem lie dormant in an unresolved etymological crux or complex word family? And to what extent does a "linguistic" way of stating, especially when brought to bear on historically conceived problems, offer a properly cumulative analytic procedure, one to which others may easily contribute and to which, despite even substantial disagreement, they may feel they really belong?

The first question raises the issue of the status of literature as verbal art. I have suggested here and elsewhere that an aesthetic view of poetic texts does not always bring unmixed blessings, that, perhaps, differentiating in absolute terms between literary and nonliterary (e.g., Wellek and Warren's concept of "fictionality"), even for purely procedural reasons, tends to trivialize the value of such texts. Besides, aesthetic conventions themselves change from time to time and from place to place. Not everyone today will cheerfully subscribe to Croce's view of real and inauthentic poetry in the *Divine Comedy*. But is a "poem" then merely that which, in fact, lends itself to poetic analysis? And would not such a definition be uselessly tautological? An example of discourse that may fruitfully be subjected to such analysis, that is, within which certain "grammaticalizations" call one's attention to the ways in which they are worked out and how they function, is poetic to a greater degree than, say, a piece of discourse that does not in any significant fashion submit to this kind of analysis. (Of course, many texts demand at least outward recognition as poetry; they signal their claims through a panoply of devices: rhyme, typographical disposition, kinds of diction, etc. Others are perhaps more subtle, but this is a different matter altogether.) Does, however, the description and explanation of, e.g., an old Romance word family differ in any significant way from the analysis of poetic structures? Or will one's study of the word family lay bare the "poem" it contains? If what is poetic consists in mechanisms of intrinsically interesting verbal creation, surely the elaboration of a complex etymological problem fits the bill, since one's study imparts an intrinsic formal value to the patterns described as well as, frequently, cultural or historical relevance (cf. the *Wörter und Sachen* approach of a Schuchardt or the etymological investigations of certain aesthetically minded Idealists in Germany and Italy).

Common sense prompts one to differentiate in kind between poetic and nonpoetic linguistic objects. The beauty and economy of an etymological configuration—not to mention its ambiguities!—may well be quite analogous to the kinds of beauty and economy one willingly associates with poetic discourse, and, as I suggested above, the analogies seem to urge a common approach. Thus, to give one example, figurative process—metaphor, metonym—is as likely to play an important role in a poetic text as in the deployment of an etymological relationship. And the etymological scientist (or artist?) usually grants a special status to his material quite similar to that granted by the philologist-critic to the poetic text. Finally, as was argued earlier, the linguistic historian must exploit fully a truly poetic documentation if his investigation of the past is to bear authentic fruit. Nevertheless, despite all these similarities, the etymological "poem" is only metaphorically so. The etimological conjecture itself—i.e., the narrative describing the intricacies in even so hazardous an equation as TURBARE $>$ *trouver* or the Romance progeny of some common Latin roots, lays bare relationships that for the most part are no longer felt as such by speakers of the languages involved; these relationships are "re-created" by the etymologist who, in a sense, collaborates with linguistic history.[10] But in the re-creation of the poem the philologist-critic helps the poem accomplish what it was meant to do (or how it was mean to be): the poem's effective possibilities and values are clarified. The difference is fundamental. Yet equally important is the fact that the difference does permit—indeed encourages—so many significant similarities of approach and even tone in poetic and etymological research. On the levels of procedure and of ambiance few types of linguistic study resemble each other more closely.

The question of a "properly cumulative analytic procedure" and a "linguistic" way of stating has in recent years become harder to cope with; agreement on what constitutes the "linguistic way of stating" is no longer quite so easily come by. Some years ago Scholar A might have described the phonemic repertory of Language X and, presumably, Scholar B could have used his findings in the commonly agreed-upon "next step," a morphological sketch of the language. Linguists tried manfully to stay on common ground so that, e.g., the morphological sketch of X relied on terms and distinctions found in most other morphological sketches, even of the most varied languages. The question has become a good deal more problematic nowadays, but, quite significantly (and, at times, amusingly), the one-time common front in descriptive linguistic methodology has so impressed epigones in other fields that few structuralist literary critics (or anthropologist-sociologists), especially in France, judge they can dispense with at least several sentences of praise for the methodological advances made by a generalized "structural" linguistics, "discipline pilote des sciences humaines." (Thus, foreign *structuralistes* willingly consider generative grammar as an outgrowth of—or as complementary to—descriptive linguistics, in addition to its constituting a healthy reaction against certain abuses of the taxonomic approach. Conversely, in this country many scholars have surely exaggerated the differences between these two methodologies and doctrines.) In *Aspects of the Theory of Syntax* (Boston, 1965), N. Chomsky is careful to claim that by "generative grammar" he means "a system of rules that in some explicit and well-defined way assigns structural descriptions to sentences" (p. 8); unlike his taxonomic predecessors, however, he notes that "any interesting generative grammar will be dealing, for the most part, with mental processes." Thus, in fact, he defends the kind of "structural descriptions" provided by generative grammar on grounds of greater adequacy; he proposes to improve upon theories that, in his view, have reached a dead-end. Furthermore, Chomsky is quick to recapitulate "the position of the founders of modern general linguistics" to the effect that "linguistic theory is concerned primarily with an ideal speaker-listener, in a completely homogeneous speech-community, who knows its language perfectly and is unaffected by such grammatically irrelevant conditions as memory limitations [etc.] . . . in applying his knowledge of the language in actual performance" (p. 3). We have here an essentially traditionalist explanation and justification of a linguistic "objectivity" or "interpersonality" based on the *fact* of an idealized idiolect (Weinreich, Labov, and Herzog have already pointed out Chomsky's fidelity, in this respect, to the thought of Paul, Saussure, and others of the older schools).

"Objectivity" and "interpersonality," so defined, constitute a significant and long-lasting ingredient—virtually a constant—of the "linguistic way of stating." Indeed, Weinreich's criticism focuses on what, in his view, is Chomsky's inadequate understanding of the authentically interpersonal—on Chomsky's idealization of the individual speaker and on his unrealistic notion of "a completely homogeneous speech-community." Similarly, as we suggested, grounds of "adequacy" or "inadequacy" are called upon by most linguists to justify their work. Chomsky speaks of "explanatory" adequacy (p. 26) which he subsequently redefines in terms of "*external* grounds" (i.e., "of correspondence to linguistic fact") and "*internal* grounds" (i.e., "of its relation to a linguistic theory that constitutes an explanatory hypothesis about the

form of language as such"). Clearly, these categories go beyond the
step-by-step adumbration of purely descriptive layers that, by and
large, made up the dimension of "cumulation" in much previous work.
Generative grammar tends to preserve the tone of simultaneity present
in linguistic operations at the same time that it "solidifies" the discipline
it calls "generative grammar." It distinguishes between, on the one
hand, the "progress" of linguistic science as well as the degree of completeness of given "explanations" and, on the other hand, the elements
or "components" constituting what, precisely, is being analyzed: syntax
and phonology "coincide" in its statements. The corpus of operation
examined bears to "language" a relationship similar to the relationship
one notes between the corpus of grammatical statements and "linguistic science." "Language" and "linguistic science" exist in a kind of
dialectical rapport with one another.

Seen in this perspective, philology may profit from adopting a "linguistic way of stating" only by subverting this "way of stating" entirely. That is, philology, as we have spoken of it here, must treat the
linguistic way of stating as, in the past, literature has treated the more
logic-centered philosophy, namely, by making it over in its own image.
Such a remaking, however, will result in a clearer definition of what, in
fact, constitutes philology, methodologically and spiritually. There is
neither time nor space to elaborate in detail on this matter. However,
some general remarks on the problem will serve adequately to conclude
the present essay.

As has been suggested above, the philologist's concern is to relate in
various ways his analysis of given texts to what we called a broad view
of language and speech. This naturally requires him to be fully con-
versant with the techniques linguists bring to bear on the study of
speech. Literary discourse participates *in* and *of* language. We also
stated that the irreducible kernel of poetic discourse—as distinct from
other types—is found in one's experience of poetry, the dialogic situation or reconstruction of the relationships and values deployed by the
text. Consequently, we observe, the *ad hoc* linguistic situation assumes
a primacy in poetic analysis that is equal in, say, the hierarchy of
Chomsky's arrangement, only to "linguistic theory." Or, put another
way, what is being got at is not the competence-performance of the
"ideal speaker-listener," member of a "completely homogeneous
speech-community"—interpersonality incarnate—but rather the very
specific fourteen lines of mid-nineteenth-century French sounds, images, senses, allusions, and other forms strung out in a broken yet continuous line and constituting a sonnet by Baudelaire, as all these are

understood or made understandable. If, in a way, discourse exists in order to make possible a "language theory," since, to a degree, this "theory" duplicates what makes discourse possible, for the philologist-critic language theory exists in order to make poetic discourse comprehensible—at least on the methodological or procedural level. It is no more and no less than a question of putting explanatory hypotheses "about the form of language as such" (Chomsky, *op. cit.*, p. 27) to work.

Yet what is said about Baudelaire's sonnet, though judged ultimately in such terms as have just been mentioned, must also be evaluated with respect to general literary theory, or to "philology," if one prefers. And here again the linguistic "way of stating" offers a parallel. Chomsky points out that "gross coverage of a large mass of data can often be attained by conflicting theories," that, in fact, much has been learned even though the explanations do not function "on the basis of some empirical assumption about the form of language" (p. 26). A truly relevant linguistics relies on statements of the latter type, even though these may be—indeed *must* be at the present juncture—"small-scale studies." In short, though not the absolute represented in Chomsky's notion of "linguistic theory," the philological discipline does constitute a kind of body of activity and techniques which ought to benefit as such by the analyses accomplished in its name. The contribution to the understanding of Baudelaire's sonnet should be so conceived as to make of it, concomitantly, a contribution to philological theory—that is, a study of value to fellow or future workers concerned with other texts or with general problems. As a discipline, poetics is by definition hypothetical, a body of principles ceaselessly clamoring to be tested; it cannot be the kind of well-wrought discipline that logic or the several types of linguistics postulate as they deal with their diverse materials. But, like linguistics, poetics has much to gain from being a discipline, especially greater coherence and relevance.

If literary forms may be viewed, in specific poetic documents, as a kind of articulate distillation of cultural value, as the intimate expression of what the culture believes, fears, and holds dear, and if, as we have also affirmed, linguistic categories do indeed help us in very meaningful ways to grasp these forms, it follows that philological activity must eventually be of the widest significance to a general understanding of language.

I recognize the circularity that lies implicit in what I have just said. But, in effect, I do no more than repeat what was stated earlier, that documentation for linguistic history that has been derived from literary texts must, if it is to be properly exploited, take full cognizance of its poetic nature. (*Reading* Rutebeuf's poem was more valuable than merely listing the forms in *-ois* which it "contains"—even for a study of the *-ois* forms!) To take cognizance of the poetic nature of a text necessitates, as we observed, the subversion of the "linguistic way of stating." But we have not quite yet reached full circle. By according the poetic situation—the text as read and philologically re-created—the kind of absolute status described above, we "open" our interpretation in a fashion that encourages further experimentation with the categories still at our disposal (e.g., figurative possibilities, phonic values and symbolisms, types of expressive intensity, etc.). Whereas Chomsky denigrates the description of "data only by *ad hoc* means"—possibly quite rightly—the philologist concentrates on the *ad hoc* quality of the textual situation and on his slow construction of his discipline—might one say his tradition? This concentration, by providing the only justifiable means of dealing, as we said, with creativity in creation, might well even furnish a precious counterweight, within the broad purview of the study of language, to the very different kinds of grammar that inform modern linguistics. Has that not in fact been one of the principal functions of literary study, within at least the Western tradition? One has only to read *De vulgari Eloquentia* to see that Dante understood very clearly the opposite natures of literary and philosophical discourse, as, of course, did the Schoolmen themselves; *grammatica speculativa* may be usefully viewed as a forerunner of modern linguistics just as *De vulgari Eloquentia* belongs to the history of poetics and philology.

Readers patient enough to have accompanied me this far will note that I have not really spoken of "verbal art" nor, as some linguists will have observed, have I attempted to describe a universal human "poetic faculty" or "innate poetic ideas." An aesthetic viewpoint is not inevitably fruitful, and I have personally not found it very useful to shunt the jargon of one discipline on to the side track of another. Still, nothing in what has been said here may be construed as preventing critics from using aesthetic categories should they so desire: the special quality of the literary text has been fully acknowledged in the present study (albeit on other than aesthetic grounds). By the same token no attempt has been made to bar the application of terms borrowed from any other discipline. I recognize, for instance, the potential interest of R. Ohmann's recent experiments with the surface:deep-structure antinomy adapted from transformational grammar. Finally, I confess to having been perhaps inordinately cagey as regards problems of general semiotic. Although I do believe that the final interest of literary discourse depends on the chain of links involved in its manipulation of sign possibilities, that, in other words, the Jakobsonian hierarchy of poetics, linguistics, and semiotic is probably—or ultimately—valid, the state of each of these arts is still so rudimentary that flitting about the categories they include may be pyrotechnically fascinating but, in my view, of little scientific interest. The ostensible purposes—as opposed to many of the very valuable by-products—of much of Roland Barthes's work strike me as premature. Circular to the end, I think that the slow construction of a philology, the equally slow implementation of established linguistic theory, as well as more audacious experimentation in psychology, anthropology, and, of course, poetry, music, and the plastic arts, together constitute the best chance to deepen our sense of signs and their operations. After all, an authentic scientific understanding is also a matter of civilization.

Notes

1. The fact that fairly early in its development linguistics realized the truth of this statement has, I am convinced, done much for the popularity of this discipline among certain contemporary literary scholars. One recalls the well-known words of Saussure: "D'autres sciences opèrent sur des objets donnés d'avance et qu'on peut considérer à différents points de vue; dans notre domaine, rien de semblable. . . . Bien loin que l'objet précède le point de vue, on dirait que c'est le point de vue qui crée l'objet . . ." *Cours de linguistique générale* (Paris, 1949), p. 23.
2. I paraphrase here a number of statements from my "Remarques sur la linguistique historique," in *Romanische Forschungen* (1969), a review-article largely given over to *Directions* (ed. by W. P. Lehmann and Y. Malkiel).
3. Here, as at other times in the present study, I refer to and develop points raised in my *Linguistics and Literary Theory* (Englewood-Cliffs, N.J., 1969); See esp. p. 251.
4. *Revue de Linguistique romane*, Vol. 32 (Jan.–June 1968), pp. 126–174.
5. "La Griesche d'esté," from Rutebeuf, *Œuvres*, vol. I, ed. by Faral and Bastin (Paris, 1959).
   A rough translation is as follows:
   "Their thoughts must be directed elsewhere,
     For two Tours francs,
   Three Parisian francs, five coins from Vienne
   Cannot make a *borgois* [coin from Bourges, bourgeois]
     Out of a naked good-for-nothing."

6. Note here a relevant passage from the "Thèses" of the CLP (1929): "Tous les plans d'un système linguistique, qui n'ont dans le langage de communication qu'un rôle de service, prennent, dans le langage poétique, des valeurs autonomes plus ou moins considérables" (p. 18). Thus rhyme, which "est étroitement liée . . . avec la syntaxe (éléments de celle-ci qui sont mis en relief et posés en face l'un de l'autre dans la rime) ainsi qu'avec le lexique (importance des mots mis en relief par la rime, et leur degré de parenté sémantique)" (p. 19).

7. "I must give up rhyming,
For I must be much concerned,
So long have I kept at it.
My heart must weep,
Since never am I able to apply myself
To serve God perfectly,
But rather have I given over my intentions
To gaming and fun,
Without even condescending to write psalms.
If, on Judgment Day, on my behalf there does not appear
The Lady in whom God took shelter [was incarnate],
I shall get a raw deal when the bargain is struck [the palms are clapped]."

8. Thus Wellek criticizes Coleridge for distinguishing quite insufficiently "between psychic processes and capacities and the finished product, the work of art, which, in literature, is a structure of linguistic signs," *A History of Modern Criticism: 1750–1950* (Vol. II), *The Romantic Age* (New Haven, 1955), p. 165, quoted in *Linguistics and Literary Theory*, p. 97.

9. See *Linguistics and Literary Theory*, pp. 260 ff.

10. No better contemporary example of such a "collaboration" may be found than the numerous etymological essays of the Berkeley scholar, Y. Malkiel. For a handy collection of these, as well as for the text of three theoretical studies ("Etymology and General Linguistics," "A Tentative Typology of Etymological Studies," and "The Uniqueness and Complexity of Etymological Solutions"), see his *Essays on Linguistic Themes* (Berkeley and Los Angeles, 1968).

Stephen Ullmann

TWO APPROACHES TO STYLE

A QUARTER OF A CENTURY AGO, LEONARD BLOOMFIELD DECLARED: "IN
all study of language we must start from forms and not from meanings."[1] This statement is far too categorical. Whenever we have to do
with meaningful elements—morphemes, words, phrases, clauses, sentences, or even higher units of discourse—we may take either the form
or the meaning, either the *signifiant* or the *signifié* as our starting-point.
As one linguist has put it, "in the first case we take the sound (of a
word or of some other part of a linguistic expression) and then inquire
into the meaning attached to it; in the second case we start from the
signification and ask ourselves what formal expression it has found in
the particular language we are dealing with. If we denote the outward
form by the letter O, and the inner meaning by the letter I, we may
represent the two ways as O→I and I→O respectively."[2]

In lexical studies, the I→O approach, usually known as "onomasiol-
ogy," has been widely and successfully applied in dialectology and
linguistic geography; it also underlies Roget's *Thesaurus* and conceptual
dictionaries in general. More recently it has given rise to the theory of
"semantic fields," which is concerned with certain closely organized
sectors of vocabulary: colors, kinship terms, the sphere of knowledge
and intelligence, the system of aesthetic and moral values, religious
and mystical experiences, etc. In syntax, the I→O method is, for
obvious reasons, rather more difficult to apply, even though Ferdinand
Brunot demonstrated many years ago, in his monumental *La Pensée et
la langue*, that it can yield interesting results. In the preface to that
work, he gave a striking example of how such a change of perspective
could provide a more rational basis for linguistic description:

> Entre les formes les plus diverses de l'expression, entre les signes les plus
> disparates, il y a un lien, c'est l'idée commune que ces signes contribuent

à exprimer. Si on la prend pour centre, . . . tout s'ordonne autour d'elle; elle groupe des éléments linguistiques venus de toutes parts . . . De la sorte, QUELQUES *hommes* cesse d'être aux indéfinis, pendant que DES *hommes* est à l'article, UNE POIGNÉE D'*hommes* au nom, VINGT *hommes* aux noms de nombre; les expressions de quantité précises ou imprécises se cataloguent dans le langage, comme le font ailleurs les nombres et les mesures.[3]

In stylistics—one of whose founders, Charles Bally, was an advocate of the I→O method—there exists a similar choice between two alternative approaches; the terms of the problem are, however, rather different. Here we have to do, not with form and meaning, *signifiant* and *signifié*, expression and content, but with stylistic devices and the effects which they produce. Moreover, stylistic phenomena are usually polyvalent: the same device may give rise to several effects and, conversely, the same effect may be obtained from several different devices. To take a specific example, the mobility of the adjective in Modern French constitutes a valuable device of style which can be used for a wide variety of purposes. In some contexts, the anteposition of the adjective will generate powerful emotive overtones: "Les plus *lumineuses* et *éclatantes* et *réchauffantes* nouvelles" (Proust). Elsewhere, the same device will help to emphasize an inherent quality, as when the same writer speaks of "la *grise* vieillesse du portail," or Cocteau of "cette *française*, lourde et légère torpeur." The anteposed adjective may also form part of a chiasmus designed to produce a subtle contrast: "Passant difficilement du rang de *jeune* femme au rang de femme *jeune*" (Françoise Sagan); or it may become a vehicle for irony: "Les *rituelles* consultations de M. Vincent Auriol" (*Le Monde*); "Ce *superbe* et *grotesque* et *doux* prince" (Cocteau).[4]

This is the way stylistic analysis usually proceeds: It takes a particular device in a language or in a limited corpus and examines the different effects which emanate from it. But one could also reverse the process and investigate, for example, the various devices through which irony is expressed in the language or corpus in question. Leaving aside such obvious forms of irony as special intonations or clichés such as "a nice kettle of fish," or "a fat lot of good that will do you,"[5] irony can be conveyed, in Modern French, by a number of different devices, some syntactical, others lexical. One of the former is word-order: anteposition of the adjective, as already mentioned, or inversion of the subject: "*Ainsi arriva* à midi, un paon blanc grattant du bec sa queue, . . . *l'académicien Henri de Régnier . . . Ainsi vint*, le soir même du jour, . . . *l'académicien René Boylesve*" (Giraudoux).

Another syntactical device is the use of highly literary Past Historics and Imperfect Subjunctives in ordinary conversation: "Malheureux ami, pourquoi *commençâtes*-vous Paludes?" (Gide);[6] "Oh! par exemple! . . . on te pince avec mon concurrent . . .et il faudrait que je te *remerciasse*" (V. de Cottens-P. Veber).

To these and other syntactical devices must be added the whole gamut of lexical ones conducive to irony. Some of these—antiphrasis, oxymoron—are among the best-known figures of traditional rhetoric. Some neologisms owe their very existence to irony, such as three of Voltaire's coinages: the science of *métaphysico-théologo-cosmolo-nigologie*, professed by Pangloss in *Candide*; *folliculaire* ("hack writer"), which is one of Voltaire's permanent contributions to the French vocabulary;[7] and his description of Geneva as a "*parvulissime* république."[8] Foreign words can also be used ironically, as in this early specimen of "franglais" by Musset:

> Dans le *bol* où le *punch* rit sur son trépied d'or,
> Le *grog* est *fashionable*.

Elsewhere, irony is expressed obliquely, but all the more effectively, through the medium of imagery, as in Proust's devastating caricature of M. de Palancy "qui, avec sa grosse tête de carpe aux yeux ronds, se déplaçait lentement au milieu des fêtes en desserrant d'instant en instant ses mandibules comme pour chercher son orientation."

It is clear, then, that there are two alternative approaches to style. Bearing in mind the polyvalency of stylistic phenomena, the two methods may be represented as shown below.

The question now arises as to how the two methods work in practice and what their respective advantages are. The answer will depend on the nature and scope of any particular enquiry. If it is concerned with the stylistic resources of an entire language, then Method II will be clearly inappropriate. Effects of style *in vacuo*, divorced from the devices in which they are normally located, are too vague and general, and also too numerous and diverse, to provide an orderly framework for description and analysis. On the other hand, certain effects are sufficiently precise to be approached by Method II; in this way, monographs have been published on the various ways in which symmetry can be achieved in Modern French,[9] and on the devices available for emphasizing an idea in seventeenth-century French and in the contemporary idiom.[10] Other problems, such as, possibly, irony, could be attacked from the same angle. On the whole, however, this type of stylistic study lends itself better to Method I, firmly anchored in linguistic devices—phonological, lexical, or grammatical—around which the effects which they subserve can be grouped.

The position is radically different where the critic deals with a finite corpus, in particular with a single work or with the writings of an author as a whole, which are the two most popular forms of this kind of stylistic enquiry. Within the compass of a single work, which provides in many ways the ideal context for stylistic analysis,[11] major effects of style are easily identifiable and highly significant because they are closely bound up with the thematic structure of the book.[12] To take but one example, several critics[13] have shown how, in Camus's *L'Étranger*, a number of seemingly disparate devices concur to endow the narrator, Meursault, with a language of his own. Meursault is the embodiment of a peculiar human type, that of the "absurd" man, and the various features of his language have to be in keeping with his psychology and outlook. Short, *staccato* sentences, with a bare minimum of causal links; simple, concrete vocabulary; avoidance of images except in one crucial scene, the murder on the beach, where they reflect the narrator's confused and semihallucinatory state of mind; a peculiar choice of tense, replacing the traditional Past Historic by the more direct, inconclusive, and conversational Past Indefinite: these and other idiosyncrasies form a kind of linguistic syndrome of the absurd man; without them, the novel would not exist. Such an approach is certainly more interesting and more rewarding than the study of the various effects produced by tenses, sentence-structure, imagery, and other devices in *L'Étranger*.

Where the enquiry transcends the limits of single works and covers the writings of an author as a whole, it can still be profitably focused on major effects of style rather than on the devices which help to realize them. These effects will be identified and interpreted as expressions of some fundamental quality, general attitude, or abiding preoccupation of the writer. In a monograph published forty years ago on "classical restraint" in Racine's style,[14] Leo Spitzer gave a spectacular demonstration of this procedure. He brought together a multiplicity of linguistic elements which all have one feature in common: they all play their part in the vast process of "klassische Dämpfung," classical discipline, toning-down, and understatement, which Spitzer subsequently defined as "a continuous repression of the emotional by the intellectual," adding that, in his view, "the alternation between these two conflicting tendencies is the most distinctive characteristic of Racine's style."[15]

It is illuminating to discover that so many widely different devices have a common denominator, that time-honored rhetorical figures like periphrasis, chiasmus, and antithesis, as well as conventional metaphors and metonymies, have basically the same stylistic function as some delicate grammatical nuances such as the replacement of a first- or second-person pronoun by a less direct and intimate form[16] such as the indefinite article: "Voilà ce qu'*un* époux m'a commandé lui-même" (*Andromaque*, IV, 1), the indefinite third-person pronoun *on*: "Qu'entends-je? Quels conseils ose-t-*on* me donner?" (*Phèdre*, IV, 6); or even a proper name which a character uses when speaking of himself: "*Néron* impunément ne sera pas jaloux" (*Britannicus*, II, 2).

Works of this kind have amply demonstrated the advantages of an approach based on major stylistic effects when dealing with the style of a book or an author. Needless to say, there will be many cases where the converse method is equally legitimate or even more appropriate. Most students of literary style tend, in fact, to take the linguistic data as their starting-point, whether they concentrate on a single device, a group of devices, or the entire system of stylistic resources in a particular work or writer. Some may aim even higher and investigate the style of a group of authors, a school, movement, period, or literary genre; E. R. Curtius's study of the history of various key images in European literature is a classic example of this method.[17]

There is one highly important stylistic element which raises special problems as regards the two approaches discussed so far. Imagery—metaphor, simile, metonymy, and allied figures—may be regarded as a device of style which fits into the alternative models described above. Under Method I, it can, and often does, serve as a focal point around which various effects produced by images can be grouped: they may give symbolic expression to some major theme or motif; they may transcribe highly complex abstract experiences in concrete terms; they may, as we have seen, serve as a vehicle for irony, imply other value-judgments, play their part in the linguistic portrayal of a character, and have all kinds of other functions.[18] Conversely, imagery may take its place, in accordance with Method II, among the various devices designed to produce the same stylistic effect: in *L'Étranger*, for instance, it forms, as already noted, an integral part of the linguistic portrait of the "absurd" man. Apart from this fundamental duality in which all devices of style are involved, images also have a dual structure which is peculiar to them. In the words of Dr. Johnson, "as to metaphorical

expression, that is a great excellence in style, when it is used with propriety, for it gives you two ideas for one."[19] What we have here is not
a *signifiant* and a *signifié* but what French critics call a *comparant* and a
comparé or, in I. A. Richards's terminology, a "vehicle" and a "tenor."
The tenor is the subject we are talking about, and the vehicle is the
element to which the tenor is compared.[20] In the famous image in
Julius Caesar:

> There is a *tide* in the affairs of men,
> Which, taken at the *flood*, leads on to fortune,

tide and *flood* are the vehicles, whereas the tenor could be expressed,
more prosaically, as "great opportunities."

Since imagery has such a dual structure, it can be approached either
through the tenor or through the vehicle. The approach through vehicles, which analyzes and classifies the images of a work or writer according to the sources from which they are drawn, is very popular; in
some cases it has led to the discovery of "obsessive metaphors" and
other significant clusters of images which certain critics have interpreted
in psychological or psychoanalytical terms—the persistent recurrence
of crabs and lobsters in Sartre's imagery, on which so much has been
written,[21] is a striking example of such a pattern. The alternative
method, which approaches the imagery through the tenors, the great
themes which attract similes and metaphors from other spheres, can
also yield illuminating results: some recent studies have shown, for
example, what kinds of analogies Proust employs in his untiring efforts
to describe the complex and elusive phenomena of time and memory
with maximum precision,[22] or what images Sartre uses in his fiction
when talking about some of the fundamental concepts of existentialist
philosophy.[23] Both approaches are equally legitimate, and the critic
will have to weigh their relative advantages in each particular case. He
may even decide to combine them: in a recent monograph on Proust's
imagery, the two central sections, of about equal length, are devoted to
the themes and the sources of his images.[24]

One leading authority on metaphor has expressed strong doubts
about splitting images into their components. "Metaphor," he argues,
"is by definition the combination of a vehicle with a tenor; what will
remain of it if we methodically isolate the vehicles on the one hand and
the tenors on the other?"[25] The answer is that such separation is methodologically justified as a discovery procedure capable of revealing
significant patterns and tendencies which could not have been noticed
in any other way. At the same time, the critic will have to bear in mind

the fundamental unity of the two elements: he will have to pay attention to the "ground" of the image, the feature or features which tenor and vehicle have in common, and also to any characteristic relationships which may arise between sources and themes of imagery in a given literary work. To mention but one or two such relations, there exist cases of "correlative" images where one sphere of experience is consistently described in terms of another (e.g., love compared to illness in Proust);[26] "serial" images where, once a firm connection has been established between a tenor and a vehicle, changes in the former are paralleled by the development of the latter (e.g., the analogy between human life and the flight of a bird in *The Divine Comedy*);[27] "reciprocal" images where two different spheres are interrelated and provide metaphorical equivalents for each other: in the poetry of Donne, for example, "the interchange between the spheres of sex and religion recognizes that sex is a religion and religion is a love."[28]

What is true of the duality of tenor and vehicle is equally true of the wider dichotomies discussed in this article: the distinction between form and meaning in language, and that between device and effect in style. The linguist and the literary critic may have to separate the two components but must never lose sight of their essential unity and interpenetration. At one time it was customary to regard style as something external and ornamental: Lord Chesterfield defined it as "the dress of thoughts." Flaubert protested vigorously against this view: "Ces gaillards-là s'en tiennent à la vieille comparaison: La forme est un manteau. Mais non! la forme est la chair même de la pensée, comme la pensée est l'âme de la vie." Nor could this be otherwise if style is regarded as a unique and highly personal mode of vision. Flaubert himself described style as "une manière absolue de voir les choses," and Proust's narrator declared, when at long last he had discovered his vocation as a writer: "le style pour l'écrivain, aussi bien que la couleur pour le peintre, est une question non de technique mais de vision."[29]

Notes

1. Leonard Bloomfield, "Meaning", in *Monatshefte für deutschen Unterricht,* Vol. 35 (1943), pp. 101–106.
2. O. Jespersen, *The Philosophy of Grammar* (London-New York, repr. 1929), p. 33.

3. Ferdinand Brunot, *La Pensée et la langue*, ed. 2 (Paris, 1926), p. xviii. There is some similarity between this category and what the late Uriel Weinreich ["Explorations in Semantic Theory", in *Current Trends in Linguistics*, Vol. 3, Ed. by Thomas A. Sebeok (The Hague-Paris, 1966), pp. 426 ff.] calls "delimitation," although the latter is even wider.

4. The two Cocteau quotations are taken from F. Jones, *La Langue et le style dans la poésie de Jean Cocteau* (Ph. D. diss., University of Leeds, 1961).

5. Clichés, however, are by no means stylistically neutral; see M. Riffaterre, "Fonctions du cliché dans la prose littéraire," in *Cahiers de l'Association Internationale des Études Françaises*, Vol. 16 (1964), pp. 81–95.

6. This technique was already used by Voltaire in *Candide*: "le baiser innocent que vous me *donnâtes*, et les coups de pied que vous *reçûtes*"; "quand vous *eûtes* été bien fessé."

7. See O. Bloch and W. v. Wartburg, *Dictionnaire étymologique de la langue française*, ed. 5 (Paris, 1968).

8. Quoted by C. Bruneau in F. Brunot, *Histoire de la langue française*, Vol. XII (Paris, 1948), p. 214.

9. G. Schlocker, *Équilibre et symétrie dans la phrase française moderne* (Paris, 1957).

10. See M. Mangold, *Études sur la mise en relief dans le français de l'époque classique* (Mulhouse, 1950); M. L. Müller-Hauser, *La Mise en relief d'une idée en français moderne* (Geneva, 1943).

11. On this problem, see my book, *Language and Style* (Oxford, 1964), pp. 127 ff. On the question of context in style analysis, see M. Riffaterre, "Stylistic Context," in *Word*, Vol. 16 (1960), pp. 207–18 (repr. in S. Chatman and S. R. Levin, *Essays on the Language of Literature* (Boston, 1967). Closely related to the phenomena discussed here is that of "convergence," which has been defined as "the accumulation at a given point of several independent stylistic devices" all of which contribute to the same general effect. On convergence, see M. Riffaterre, "Criteria for Style Analysis," in *Word*, Vol. 15 (1959), pp. 154–74 (repr. in the same volume; pp. 428 ff. of repr.), and Y. Louria, *La Convergence stylistique chez Proust* (Geneva-Paris, 1957).

12. On this term, and on the main varieties of thematic structure, see recently Eugene H. Falk, *Types of Thematic Structure: The Nature and Function of Motifs in Gide, Camus, and Sartre* (Chicago, 1967).

13. See, for example, J. Cruickshank, *Albert Camus and the Literature of Revolt* (London, 1959), Ch. 7, and quite recently, W. M. Frohock, *Style and Temper. Studies in French Fiction, 1925–1960* (Oxford, 1967), pp. 103 ff.

14. Leo Spitzer, "Die klassische Dämpfung in Racines Stil," repr. in his *Romanische Stilund Literaturstudien* (Vol. I), (Marburg, 1931), pp. 135–268. See also P. France, *Racine's Rhetoric* (Oxford, 1965).

15. Leo Spitzer, *Linguistics and Literary History. Essays in Stylistics* (Princeton, 1948), p. 110.

16. See also R. Barthes, *Sur Racine* (Paris, 1963 ed.), pp. 45 ff.

17. E. R. Curtius, *European Literature and the Latin Middle Ages*, English transl. (London, 1953).

18. See *Language and Style*, pp. 193 ff.

19. Quoted by I. A. Richards, *The Philosophy of Rhetoric* (New York-London, 1936) p. 93.

20. This analysis is also applicable to metonymies and other nonmetaphorical figures;

the word *crown*, for example, is often used metonymically as a "vehicle" for the "tenor": "the rule, position, or empire of a monarch" (*Shorter OED*). The discussion which follows will, however, be confined to images based on similarity— i.e., to metaphors and similes.

21. See recently M. D. Boros, "La Métaphore du crabe dans l'oeuvre littéraire de Jean-Paul Sartre," in *PMLA*, Vol. 81 (1966), pp. 446–50.

22. See E. Gülich, "Die Metaphorik der Erinnerung in Proust's *À la recherche du temps perdu*," in *Zeitschrift für französische Sprache und Literatur*, Vol. 75 (1965), pp. 51–74; and my book, *The Image in the Modern French Novel* (Oxford, repr. 1963), pp. 208ff.; and my article, "Images of Time and Memory in *Jean Santeuil*," in *Currents of Thought in French Literature. Essays in Memory of G. T. Clapton* (Oxford, 1966), pp. 209–26.

23. See my *Style in the French Novel* ed. 2, (Oxford, 1964), pp. 242 ff.

24. V. E. Graham, *The Imagery of Proust* (Oxford, 1966).

25. H. Weinrich, in *Romanische Forschungen*, Vol. 73 (1961), p. 201.

26. See *The Image in the Modern French Novel*, pp. 133 ff.

27. See M. Hardt, *Das Bild in der Dichtung* (Munich, 1966), pp. 54 ff. The book also discusses other examples of such "serial" images in Dante himself, as well as in Aeschylus, Shakespeare, and Flaubert.

28. R. Wellek-A. Warren, *Theory of Literature* (London, repr. 1954), p. 214.

29. The quotation from Chesterfield is taken from the *Shorter OED*; those from Flaubert are cited by W. v. Wartburg, *Évolution et structure de la langue française* (ed. 5). (Berne, 1958). The quotation from Proust, which has sometimes been misquoted, occurs in *Le Temps retrouvé* (Pléiade ed., Vol. 3 p. 895).

Klaus Weissenberger

THE PROBLEM OF PERIOD STYLE IN THE THEORY OF RECENT LITERARY CRITICISM: A COMPARISON

IN TURNING ITS ATTENTION TO THE 20TH CENTURY, LITERARY CRITICISM in Europe and in the United States indicates a steadily increasing departure from the positivism of the last century. The manifold criticism of positivism takes its point of departure from a positivistic analytical discussion of literature, the greatest part of which amounts to little more than a linear arrangement of facts, and attacks subsequent continuing efforts to imbue the humanities with an aura of methodology and scientific credibility by applying laws which rightfully belong in the domain of the natural sciences. These antipositivistic efforts to arrive at a new understanding of literature lead, on the one hand, to the descriptive school of linguistics and, on the other, to a synthetically oriented literary criticism. Essentially it is only the latter which, through its supraindividual consideration of literature, provides the prerequisites that make it possible to consider the phenomenon of period style at all. To be sure, the diversity of synthetic attempts has had a confusing effect and hitherto has resulted in a noticeable lack of truly satisfactory clarifications concerning the problem of period style; nor is there, as yet, a methodically foolproof and exhaustive treatment of the style of an entire epoch.

The problem of period style is closely linked with that of periodization; for both the principle applied in periodization and the length of the time unit have a definite bearing on any analysis of period style. At this point it ought to be anticipated that, generally speaking, the style phases which cover a shorter span of time can be accurately determined by intrinsic investigation, while those phases covering a larger time span are considerably more difficult to establish—i.e., they are established only after many years' research and exclusively by intrinsic methods. The style of a considerably larger time span furthermore presupposes an additional consideration of results gained from related sciences outside the sphere of literature proper; for only thus could one retrace to a common background the multitude of stylistic characteristics in larger units of time—be that background conditioned, for instance, by the *Geistesgeschichte* of a certain epoch or by cultural-sociological factors. This implies that these results gained from related sciences, now to be applied deductively, be in turn the result of inductive analysis and find their confirmation in literature.

Work in the field of period-style analysis has been hitherto confined to initial attempts, because the criteria we have established are slow to be realized. This critical view of the various methodological orientations will make this fact apparent and simultaneously point the way to be taken if we are to do full justice to the phenomenon of period style. An objective evaluation will serve to call attention to possible sources of error which are inherent in certain methodological orientations or are based on the wrong application of a method. The discussion begins with contributions based on intrinsic investigations, then passes on to contributions more extrinsically oriented, and finally considers various attempts which have little or nothing in common with literature.

THE FORMAL-AESTHETIC CONTRIBUTION

Although descriptive linguistics, the beginning of which we may date with de Saussure, has since Bally also directed its attention to purely stylistic problems, its exponents generally avoid treating the problem of period style. The first concrete results that purely linguistic research has yielded amount to insights gained from statistics alone; as such they will be discussed in due course. However, descriptive linguistics, with its detailed analysis of elements of speech, has provided stimuli and established prerequisites for a formal-aesthetic period-style analysis which, in turn, has been of help in treating the problem of period style.

It was probably Leo Spitzer who first succeeded in actually bridging the gap between linguistics and the scholarly study of literature. Following the principle of the "hermeneutic circle," Spitzer's examination begins with a significant style element characteristic of the author in question and gradually relates it to larger units of style—i.e., the style of the same work, the personal style, and finally, period style; and althought Spitzer has only to a small degree concerned himself with period style, he has nevertheless pointed the way. His "Stilkosmen" of Charles Peguy, Jules Romains, and Marcel Proust, for instance, may be considered preliminary studies of French Expressionism.[1]

Gerhard Fricke's work, *Die Bildlichkeit in der Dichtung des Andreas Gryphius*,[2] is such a preliminary study for the period style of the German Baroque. With the inductive establishment of the metaphor inventory of poetry so representative of the Baroque period one can generally deduce that the Baroque metaphors are an essential element of that period style. In much the same way, with his *Die Klangmalerei bei Harsdoerffer*,[3] Wolfgang Kayser contributes to the formal-aesthetic analysis of one aspect of Baroque period style especially prominent with Harsdoerffer, by putting it into its historical sequence and by pointing to previous examples and guidelines. With few indications as to the acceptance and the diffusion of onomatopoeia, Harsdoerffer's reputation may be corroborated and endorsed both during and after his own time.

Fredi Chiapelli arrives at Tasso's stylistic idiosyncrasy through a detailed style analysis[4] which even goes so far as to include observations on the grammar. In combining and linking the various stylistic elements, Tasso occupies a place apart from the Renaissance-type separation of stylistic elements, on the one hand, and from the interweaving of stylistic elements in the Manneristic period, on the other. Thus the stylistic analysis of Tasso leads to a stylistic characterization of Renaissance, Baroque, and Mannerism, whereby Tasso is considered as belonging to the period of the Baroque. With his book *Torquato Tasso. Studien zur Vorgeschichte des Secentismo*,[5] Ulrich Leo contributes to Chiapelli's thesis on a much broader basis. His thorough stylistic analysis treats Tasso as a precursor of the Secentismo, because, above all, he has not yet transformed the "concetto" into the mannerism of the Secentismo. Historical categorization, however, does not take place until after a summary glance at Tasso's stylistic development. To the extent to which Tasso is representative of his own period, this investigation is also relevant to the problem of period style.

In Spain we find chiefly Dámaso Alonso and his pupil Carlos Busoño who, on the model of the Geneva school of linguistics and of Spitzer, consider literature from a formal-aesthetic point of view. Their concepts of period style, however, remain somewhat nebulous. Although Dámaso Alonso, in his *Poesía Española*[6] inductively arrives at the style of a work and the personal style of individual poets, he moves from these facts almost intuitively to a conclusion as to period style. From the formal opposition of a few verses of Garcilaso and Góngora on the same theme Alonso summarily deduces the stylistic and *"geistesgeschichtliche"* contrast between the Renaissance and the Baroque periods. Methodologically just as questionable is the declaration that Lope de Vega is symbolic of the Baroque.

Willi Flemming's attempt to reduce the style of the Baroque to "the fugue as the epochal principle of composition"[7] must be considered an unsuccessful German contribution to that period style. To be applicable in the sphere of literature, the stylistic phenomenon of the fugue must be amplified to such a degree that it loses all relevance as a valid point of departure for the period style of the Baroque. Herbert Read proceeds inversely in his *English Prose Style*,[8] in which he examines different prose styles which may be present independent of historical factors, but are relevant to period style by the frequency of their occurrence at certain times. Thus Read arrives at an "impressionistic" prose style which has as its first exponent Sterne, but which is most convincingly manifest in Proust and Virginia Woolf.

Probably the most exemplary piece of work in the field of formal-aesthetic period-style research has been presented by Karl-Ludwig Schneider.[9] With direct reference to Spitzer he begins by inductively identifying the metaphor inventory of Georg Heym, Georg Trakl, and Ernst Stadler, and he is able, in conclusion, to offer proof for the same deliberate style and literary thought in all three. Schneider has thus established the metaphoric period style for the limited style phase of early German Expressionist lyric poetry. To determine the larger period-style epoch of Expressionism he has produced other essays which will be discussed under *Formal-Historical Contributions* and *Aesthetic Contributions*.

Also under Spitzer's influence, Helmut Hatzfeld is another literary scholar to leave the field of purely formal-aesthetic investigation. With his essay, *"Der Barockstil in der religioesen klassischen Lyrik in Frankreich,"*[10] Hatzfeld refers to Spitzer's *"Die klassische Daempfung in Racines Stil"*[11] and relegates this religious lyric poetry to the period of European Baroque. He comes to this conclusion by considering the period as part of the Counter-Reformation—permissible for the religious lyric poetry of Catholic France—and by proving the relationship of that lyric poetry to contemporary poetry in Italy, Spain, and Germany on the basis of an investigation of isolated prosodic and structural features. He also relates his results gained by formal-aesthetic considerations to the graphic arts, to arrive thus at an exhaustive period-style analysis of the Baroque. In this respect he fully conforms to the criteria we have established for the period-style analysis of a larger epoch. Nevertheless it remains questionable to just what extent one can take the religious classical lyric poetry of France as a point of departure for such far-reaching conclusions. More convincing in this respect is his book *Estudios sobre el Barroco*,[12] in which—apart from *geistesgeschichtlichen* and art-historical discussions to be examined later on—he dedicates the main part to inductive analysis and formal comparison of passages extracted from the works of the principal exponents of Romance Baroque literature. The success of these investigations is directly based on the deliberate exclusion of their respective historical bases, whereby the comparison and the establishment of period-style characteristics of the Romance Baroque are made possible only under these circumstances.

THE FORMAL-HISTORICAL CONTRIBUTION

In the light of the formal-aesthetic approach, the formal-historical approach presents merely a shift in emphasis. The latter stresses to a greater degree the historicity of the respective stylistic elements, but without taking as its point of departure a superimposed *geistesgeschichtliche* unity which must necessarily forego verification by the individual literary features or, in our case, by the stylistic ones.

There are several American contributions which, in their limitation to one period-style aspect of prose, have come up with outstanding results. Morris W. Croll examines the syntax of 17th-century English and French prose[13] and concludes that the sentences found therein differ from the example of Ciceronian style of the Renaissance and present an alternation between, or mixture of, "curt period" and "loose period." In pointing out the stoic or open-minded attitude basic to these two types of syntax, and thoroughly in keeping with the outlook of that period, these period-style characteristics of Baroque prose are supported in terms of their *geistesgeschichtliche* background. George Williamson's book, *The Senecan Amble*,[14] may be regarded as a direct continuation of Croll's essay. Williamson limits the scope of his investigation to English prose of the 17th century and proceeds from an analysis of the prose stylists of classical antiquity who, in their capacity as models, achieve prime importance for the English language in the Humanistic period. The prose style of the 17th century is included under the label "Anti-Ciceronian" or "Senecan." Williamson offers proof of the differences from Renaissance prose and of the various examples of "Senecan style" by including predominant theories of poetics and an analysis of several prose excerpts. These excerpts in fact could have done with a more thorough treatment as representative of the manifestation of the deliberate style typical of the poetics of the period. Ian Gordon attempts to accomplish the task aimed at by Croll and Williamson for the whole of English prose.[15] Since the work is very much restricted in its physical dimensions, it is unable to furnish evidence of a legitimate inductive analysis. As a result, the almost cursory view cannot pass as a convincing treatment of the prose period styles of English literature.

Richard Alewyn's treatise on "Vorbarocker Klassizismus"[16] can also be classified under the category of formal-historical contributions. Alewyn starts out from the historical facts in Greek tragedy in Germany at the time of Opitz, and then proceeds to compare the original with Opitz's version. On the basis of that comparison he can, for Opitz's poetry and that of the "First Silesian School," point to a style of smoothness and clarity which he calls classicistic. Although Alewyn in his discussion does not pretend to go beyond the scope of a style phase, as he has limited himself to the analysis of Opitz's tragedy, his findings cannot lay claim to general validity for the remainder of the then-contemporary poetry. Hans Pyritz' book *Paul Flemings Liebeslyrik*[17] has a broader inductive basis and is consequently methodologically sounder. As a contribution to the history of Petrarchism, Pyritz emphasizes this stylistic phenomenon as a period-style-formative factor in the love poetry of the Early Baroque from Opitz to Fleming. Despite the high degree of individuality Fleming achieves in his late love poetry, he nevertheless depends on Opitz. As a complementary investigation, an additional work which should be mentioned is Joerg-Ulrich Fechner's contribution, which concerns itself with "anti-Petrarchism"[18] as an expression of Baroque love satire. Starting from an inductive analysis of the stylistic findings, Anti-Petrarchism is established historically and viewed against a social background. Fechner includes the representative poets of the Baroque, so that this work is of interest as a study of one element of period style, though not as a study of an entire period style.

To shed twentieth-century prejudice while considering English Renaissance poetry, Rosemund Tuve confronts Renaissance poetry with literary criticism of its own time.[19] The *geistesgeschichtliche* background of the scholar is thus eliminated; the metaphors are examined according to the laws of their contemporary poetics, and their logical function is demonstrated. Ruth Wallerstein also uses poetic prerequisites in her interpretation of various elegies and poems by Marvell as contributions to the period style of the seventeenth century.[20] Unfortunately the inductive basis is too narrow to afford results valid for the entire epoch. In contrast, Eric A. Blackall's style analysis of the "Sturm und Drang" period can lay a much more convincing claim to validity.[21] He explains the stylistic peculiarities of "Sturm und Drang" language by its exponents' antitraditional attitude, which is primarily directed against the previous rationalistic style. Karl-Ludwig Schneider has taken the same approach so as to broaden his basis sufficiently for a grasp of the entire period of Expressionism. His lecture "Themen und Tendenzen der expressionistischen Lyrik"[22] includes not only the inductive inventory, but the programmatic trends of the "New Club" as factors determining language and style. The antitraditional nature of these trends entails a more formal-historically-oriented approach, while his pointing to the solidarity-producing nature of the "New Club" would suggest that sociological studies ought not to be neglected in the attempt to more accurately define the period style of an epoch.

The grandiose scope of Paul Boeckmann's undertaking, *Formengeschichte der deutschen Dichtung*,[23]—the second volume of which is still to come—represents a comprehensive effort to establish the period styles of all epochs of German prose and poetry. There are two respects in which Boeckmann fails to do justice to our problem: on the one hand he neglects the inductive establishment of the formal-historical inventory—at least there is no guarantee that the few examples he presents are truly representative—and on the other, the cultural-sociological background previously formulated as a mandatory point of reference is entirely discarded. The merit of the work thus consists of the division of the work into subsectors wherein style phases are discussed, while the methodological prerequisites to establishing the period-style criteria of an entire epoch are conspicuously absent. Boeckmann's procedure is possibly justified for periods where normative poetic guidelines predominate; for the time span extending from the poetry of the "Sturm und Drang" to the Modern period (to be treated in the second volume) his method would inevitably forfeit any claim to validity. As it is, the method appears to contain thinly veiled *geistesgeschichtliche* tendencies, as when Boekmann superimposes the concept of stylistic phenomenon of wit as a label for the entire period of the Enlightenment.

Fritz Martini develops his discussion of "bourgeois realism" from a methodologically sounder basis.[24] He sets literature against an inductively gained *geistesgeschichtliche*, or better, cultural-sociological background, and examines drama, lyric poetry, and epic forms in the light of the history of the genres. The various genres are first broadly staked out poetologically and according to the then-contemporary concept of one's self. Subsequent analysis of the respective works then affords an opportunity to do justice to further individual developments. Martini thus comes to the conclusion that it is essentially in the epic forms in which " 'realism' was able to achieve most adequately its style-coining and language-coining effect and influence." (p. 849).

Martini's work has already shown that discussions of the history of the genres may be counted as formal-historical contributions towards establishing period style. Whenever the requirements of a genre are met in terms defined by its own time, a period style is obviously manifested. To be sure, investigations concerned with the history of genres —and here one ought to mention those investigations by the Germans Karl Viëtor[25] and Friedrich Beissner[26]—have hitherto only concerned themselves with first determining the traditional criteria which constitute a genre and then relating all other members of a genre to these criteria. With this historical-descriptive approach, however, a genre is summarily narrowed down to previously established norms, and historically limited. But even these criteria of genres, handed down to us by classical antiquity though they may have been, are subject to the changes of period style. A historical investigation of a genre must consequently recognize the limited validity inherent in these criteria, and isolate and emphasize *that* manner of speech basic to a genre, which, in accordance with the style of the period, has been realized in various forms. This principle permits that genres be traced right up to the poetry of the Modern period, which, incidentally, is by no means as amorphous as some researchers who espouse the historical-descriptive approach would have us believe. Furthermore, this principle would facilitate our coming to more tangible conclusions on a style of the Modern period.

THE *GEISTESGESCHICHTLICHE* CONTRIBUTION

In treating the subject from the *geistesgeschichtliche* point of view, we must, as in most of the contributions still to come, distinguish between two streams of thought. One has stipulated the Hegelian self-realization of the *Zeitgeist* as the over-all governing principle, and finds its most prominently developed manifestation in the German school of *Geistes-*

geschichte of the twenties and thirties. Religiously oriented literary criticism runs along similar lines. The other stream of thought establishes the character of an epoch determined by its *Geistesgeschichte* from an inductive analysis of contemporary *Weltanschauung*, philosophy, and concept of one's self as they become apparent, among other things, as period-style-normative factors in literature. German *Geistesgeschichte* of the twenties is so predominant as to have succeeded in additionally casting its spell on the exponents of the "reciprocal illumination of the arts." Oskar Walzel and Fritz Strich are indebted both to the categories of Woelfflin and to Neo-Hegelianism; for reasons of simplicity in perspective, the discussion of their contributions to our topic will be delayed until we turn our attention to aesthetics.

German *Geistesgeschichte* is especially indebted to Wilhelm Dilthey, who has established the humanities on a methodological basis of their very own, independent of the methods employed in the natural sciences. In his view, an understanding of poetry is to be gained solely from the homogeneous experience of the poet, a concept which, for the exponents of Neo-Hegalianism and Neoromanticism, leads to the axomatic view that the manifestation of *Zeitgeist* is basic to that homogeneity of experience. Dilthey, in setting up three types of *Weltanschauung*, has been a further source of inspiration for the German school of *Geistesgeschichte* to engage in synthetic discussions of literature and the classification of epochs.

Starting from the hypothesis that individual manifestations of intellectual activity are the "emanations of the overall climate" of an epoch —as, for instance, does Rudolf Unger—period style assumes the task of documenting this *Zeitgeist* or climate formally. All of these *geistesgeschichtliche* theories have the following feature in common: a preconceived philosophical idea is the point of departure for any and all individual considerations, including style, and this idea furthermore lacks any historical-sociological basis. The Baroque and the Romantic periods, especially, have been turned into the "playground" of theories centering on *Geistesgeschichte*. Arthur Huebscher reduces the intellectual attitude of the Baroque to an "antithetical sense of existential awareness"[27] which, in conformity with the precept of change, must alternate with a "harmonious existential awareness" and consequently entail an antithetical style. Emil Ermatinger similarly views Baroque style as determined by *Weltanschauung*—i.e., by the tension between "medieval-Christian transcendentalism and modern-natural realism,"[28] of which the latter passes through the optimism of the Enlightenment to the worldly and frivolous period of the Rococo.

Being mainly interested in the historical development of *Weltanschau-*

ungen, Rudolf Unger narrows the history of literature to a propaedeutic role and views period style as a valid mirror of the predominant *Weltanschauung*. In his view, "content of meaning and configurative form develop from the same root; from the poet's awareness of life, and furthermore from that of his period."[29] In his preoccupation with "perspectives on essence," Max Deutschbein no longer heeds the individual phenomena of Romanticism,[30] but regards this period, in terms of form and content, as a synthesis of diversity and contrast which eventually is to lead to both Romantic universalism and Romantic symbolism. With his major work, *Geist der Goethezeit*,[31] Hermann A. Korff, however, remains the only exponent of this school of thought whose contribution survived its own time. Korff retraces the literary diversity of that period to the fundamental concept that the classical period represents a synthesis of the irrationalism of the "Sturm und Drang" and the rationalism of the Enlightenment; the Romantic period as the subsequent organic response to the irrationalism of "Sturm und Drang" embodies a Hegelian synthesis. Viewed against the humanistic form of the Classical period, the romanticization of form corresponds to the "*ideengeschichtliche*" romanticization of content. Against this background of *Zeitgeist* and period style Korff turns once more to the individual work and succeeds in advancing to valid results, as the isolated case is not directly related to the over-all concept. The fact that his methodological approach is nevertheless questionable cannot be entirely discounted.

Willi Flemming's earlier discussion of the Baroque also runs along "*ideengeschichtliche*" lines.[32] To his thinking, the style of that period reflects the Baroque-expressive heightening of "ego-awareness" and achieves its purest realization in a fervor of creative energy. Although he limits himself to the relatively short style phase of the Biedermeier period, one must regard Paul Kluckhohn's *geistesgeschichtliche* period-style analysis[33] as erroneous. Above all, his results lack verification by literary, "*weltanschaulichen*," and historical-sociological factors, the combination of which alone can claim a proper assessment of period style. In his *Ideengut der deutschen Romantik*,[34] Kluckhohn distinguishes himself from Korff only by having his intellectual superstructure—and the concept of the Romantic period style resulting from it—degenerate into a meaningless blur; essential, to his thinking, is "a symbolic configuration allowing the idea, the yonder, and infinity to become transparent, a configuration which is consequently transparent or open towards infinity, reaching beyond reality, pointing beyond itself." (p. 182).

The German school of *Geistesgeschichte* based on extrinsic approaches to literature can, on the basis of its deliberate limitation, be compared only to religiously oriented literary criticism. Etienne Gilson, for instance, in *Les Idées et les Lettres*,[35] reduces the style of the 17th century solely to Scholastic tradition. José Camón Aznar declares the period from 1560 to 1610, a period of transition between Renaissance and Baroque, as predominantly influenced by the spirit of the Tridentinum, and consequently the manifestation of Tridentine style.[36] As a third example one ought to mention Randall Stewart's book, *American Literature and Christian Doctrine*,[37] where the *geistesgeschichtliche* development of America is interpreted as a progressive development of heresy which, step by step, has passed through Rationalism, Romanticism, and Naturalism. The fact that writers such as Hawthorne, Melville, and James must be excluded from this type of development points to the flaws of this theory.

Next to follow are *geistesgeschichtliche* contributions which, in terms of method, have handled the problem of period style far more convincingly. For the sake of clarity they will be discussed in their proper thematic sequence.

In the field of Spanish studies of literature Américo Castro demonstrates for Don Quixote[38] an undecided *Weltanschauung* on the part of Cervantes, and would like to label as period style the expression of a transition period between two orientations of thought—that of the humanistic Renaissance and that of the counter-reformational Baroque. Castro, it would seem, also recognizes this dichotomy in other writers of the 17th century with whom this dichotomy leads to that precious and rare style which is to be interpreted either as an expression of aggression or as an attempt to achieve some kind of independence from the conflict between the individual and a world no longer secure.

The title *Deutsche Gegenreformation und deutsches Barock in der Dichtung*[39] is already a clear indication of Paul Hankamer's *geistesgeschichtliche* research, but since his interpretation remains close and faithful to the work and his investigation is divided according to genres, he does not set out by repeating the mistakes made by the German school of *Geistesgeschichte*. His book could even be regarded as a precursor to Martini's investigation of "bourgeois realism." However, the solution to the conflict of intellect and nature in the Baroque, apparent to Hankamer, consists only of ascetic self-denial or irony. A consideration of German Baroque in the light of the "unifying" *Zeitgeist* of the Counter-Reformation appears similarly lacking in conviction. Helmut Hatzfeld vigorously upholds the validity of this thesis for Romance Baroque. In the already mentioned *Estudios sobre el Barroco*,[6] he expresses the view that the Baroque is an art of the Counter-Reformation and that it actually received its diffusive impetus and energy from Spain. Although Hatzfeld establishes the *geistesgeschichtliche* inventory inductively and parallel to the stylistic inventory, ultimately his theory seems somewhat too forced.

For the English meditative poetry of the 17th century, Louis Martz sets out to prove a "meditative style,"[40] characterized by the concentration of all psychic energies as an exaltation of current forms of speech. No doubt is to be cast on the findings of an investigation based on intrinsic evidence, but to satisfy the demands of period-style analysis these findings remain too inconclusive, since these style characteristics are also present in the meditative poetry of other periods. Majorie Nicolson has studied the effects on poetry by the scientific discoveries of the 17th century,[41] and she arrives at the conclusion that, on the basis of the new discoveries, the previous symbol of the "circle of perfection" is replaced by the idea of infinity, which then leads to a disintegration of form— i.e., to the period style of the Baroque. As happens so frequently in *geistesgeschichtliche* discussions, the author did not entirely succeed in resisting the hypnotic effect of a central theme.

After an analysis of Romantic poetics and their manifestations in poetry, Meyer H. Abrams successfully employs *geistesgeschichtliche* methods in his book *The Mirror and the Lamp*,[42] to show just how the change from the imitation of nature, exacted by Neoclassicism, to subjective expression is brought about—i.e., "from mirror to lamp." From the standpoint of period style this change is effected as a transition from inductively gained metaphors to metaphors of organic expression. As Abrams offers no sketch of a social background, he is unable to explain adequately the further stylistic development of the 19th century. Along parallels very similar to those of Abrams runs Albert Gerard's treatise on the Romantic period in England.[43] The demand for creative originality, for unity of subject and object and the use of symbol and myth as expressions of an intuitively conceived cosmic unity—for which he offers sufficient documentary evidence—all characterize, to his thinking, the period style of the Romantic epoch.

Through an inductive, almost formal-historical analysis, Gerhard Rudolph[44] succeeds in retracing the poetry of Kleist and Arnim to the same structural principle, the basis of which is to be sought in circumstances where existential awareness courts the danger of losing its naive immediacy. This overriding problem configuration, so apparent in the relationship of the world of the poet and the world of reality, supposedly characterizes the period from 1770 to 1830. Rudolph considers his essay a preliminary study, from which the period style of that epoch could conceivably be determined in its entirety. E. D. Hirsch[45] even goes so far as to pay no attention to national boundaries and to point out an identical Romantic period style for both Wordsworth and Schelling. Substantiating his conclusions inductively, he establishes this style as the expression of identical types of *Weltanschauung*, under the influence of the same *Zeitgeist*.

Possibly the most acutely sensitive and circumspect discussions of the Romantic period, especially with respect to its collectively European character, have been presented by Rene Wellek on "*geistesgeschichtliche*" foundations.[46] In distinguishing between a narrower and a wider concept of Romanticism, he has been able to make a clear cut between German Classicism and Romanticism and still regard them as sharing the common aim of counteracting the influence of the Enlightenment. Wellek arrives at the period style common to the collective European movement from the role assumed by poetic imagination, symbol, myth, and organic nature, to overcome the collectively felt schism of essence between subject and object, the ego and the world, or the conscious and the unconscious. In contrast to so many period-style criteria derived from a *geistesgeschichtliche* orientation, Wellek can, with the help of these criteria, accurately outline the Romantic period, and furthermore, claim their exclusive application to that period.

Among the *geistesgeschichtliche* discussions treating several epochs, one must count Arthur O. Lovejoy's *The Great Chain of Being*.[47] The intellectual development of the whole of occidental culture takes place according to the laws of alternation between two fundamental ideas: the static concept of God as an absolute authoritarian Being, and the dynamic concept of God as a creative Being; this is the perpetual alternation between "classicism" and "romanticism" which is also manifest in the change of period styles. Despite documentary evidence, this type of *geistesgeschichtliche* discussion prematurely appears before the respective streams of thought have been established in all their aspects, and is consequently guilty of increasingly serious generalizations.

The English literary critic David Daiches upholds a much more tangible method in his *Critical Approaches to Literature*;[48] not maintaining that there is indeed such a thing as an entirely fool-proof method, ultimately he wants to have a poetic work of art understood within a historically determined cultural context—i.e., against its *geistesgeschichtliche* background. Period style would reflect this background as an organic unity. But Daiches' own efforts to turn these theoretical guidelines into practice[49] are somewhat disappointing. The *geistesgeschichtliche* back-

ground on which the individual periods have been respectively pro-
jected has been sketched too weakly to allow period style to be derived
convincingly from it.

As the last *geistesgeschichtliche* contribution of this kind one ought to
mention Georges Poulet's treatise, *Les Métamorphoses du Cercle*.[50] In
Poulet's view, the change of periods is expressed in the differing world
image, and as such this change can be read in the various positions occupied by God and Man in the cosmic symbols of circle and sphere.
Man's expanding intellectual horizon—brought about by the upsurge
of the natural sciences —leads to the multitude of Baroque forms with
which the newly created space must be filled. He bases the entire Romantic period on the *geistesgeschichtliche* principle that the opposition of
subject and object expressed in the split between the center and the
perimeter of the circle (in Scholastic philosophy God was both center
and perimeter, and man consequently lived in harmony) is overcome
by a personal act of faith. Apart from all too frequently overworking
the image of circle and sphere, Poulet occasionally finds himself bogged
down in oversimplified generalizations on individual epochs and their
period styles. The risk of sacrificing all literary manifestations to one
idea, a risk to which the *geistesgeschichtliche* method is frequently prone,
is not always avoided in Poulet's work.

THE AESTHETIC CONTRIBUTION

If we are to judge fairly, in this sector we must distinguish once more
between two approaches which both borrow from the arts, especially
from the plastic or graphic arts, but which differ fundamentally in principle. One approach is again based on the Hegelian self-realization of
the *Zeitgeist*, leading in any given period to the same style characteristics in all the arts; actually it is merely a variation on the German *geistesgeschichtliche* school and as such has found its most eloquent support-
ers at the same time; frequently it is impossible to make a clear distinction between the two. The second approach to be discussed here is indirectly based on the criticism of concepts which are automatically and
straightforwardly transferred from the domain of aesthetics into the
realm of strictly literary discussion. This approach accepts aesthetic
categories only after these have been tested as to their validity in literature. Thus the way has been prepared for an intrinsic cultural-sociological discussion of period style.

Heinrich Woelfflin[51] has given the strongest impetus to the profitable application of the categories of style discovered by him in the plastic and graphic arts to scholarly literary interpretation. As representative of the categories basic to a synthetic discussion of an epoch, he establishes for the contrast between the Renaissance and the Baroque five pairs of stylistic antonyms. In order to arrive at a stylistic classification of literary periods, Oskar Walzel, in his address "Wechselseitige Erhellung der Kuenste,"[53] advocates the application of Woelfflin's style categories of linear and picturesque, of two-dimensional and three-dimensional, of closed and open form, or tectonic and atectonic, of diversity and uniformity, and of absolute and relative clarity of substance. Walzel's further works, *Gehalt und Gestalt*[53] and *Das Wortkunstwerk*,[54] are in their methodology more or less the direct consequences of the above hypotheses. The most significant example of a case in which these hypotheses are applied is to be found in Fritz Strich's work *Deutsche Klassik und Romantik oder Vollendung und Unendlichkeit*.[54] As early as 1916 Fritz Strich distinguished as epochal hallmark the exaltedly bloated style of the 17th century from the "linear" style of the poetry of the meistersingers.[56] In true Woefflin fashion Strich outlines the shift from Classicism to Romanticism as the perpetual opposition between an artistic principle of perfection and one of infinity. But Strich simultaneously expands the concept of style to such an extent as to render history of style equal to *Geistesgeschichte*, so that the work of art may in all its stylistic aspects be a manifestation of the *Zeitgeist*. Isolated by their lack of reference to the real sociohistorical factors and to those of the literary works, Walzel and Strich in this respect are as vulnerable to criticism as are the exponents of the school of *Geistesgeschichte*. We must add that, from a scholarly point of view, it is simply not permissible to transfer concepts and categories from the domain of aesthetics to the sphere of literature on the principle of analogy, without finding them confirmed intrinsically and having them revamped so that they are indeed valid as literary concepts and categories. In keeping with the above principle, there appears to be no limit to considering cultural phenomena and literary epochs as analogous and parallel, and as a deterring example one must refer to Oswald Spengler's *Untergang des Abendlandes*,[57] where the concept of an epoch's being subjected to this method becomes completely meaningless.

This vehement criticism might seem superfluous if aesthetic contributions of this kind were not able to cause a stir even today. While in Julius Schwietering's *Die deutsche Dichtung des Mittelalters*[58] we still find a discussion of aesthetics and *Literaturwissenschaft* side by side—the subdivision into categories as vague as Gothic and Romanic has no bearing on the discussion of literature—the series of works by Richard Hamann and Jost Hermand lays bare the problems inherent in this method. Richard Hamann's first attempt (1907)[59] in the field of "reciprocal illumination of the arts" still echoes the familiar ring of the approach of the German school of *Geistesgeschichte*, to say nothing of the organological conception that Expressionism is a style of "exhaustion." In the sequence *Deutsche Kunst und Kultur von der Gruenderzeit bis zum Expressionismus* the first three volumes of which have appeared under the joint authorship of Hamann and Hermand,[60] the change of method seems to have been confined to theory. The respective introductions state as their goal the synthesis of periods on a social and *geistesgeschichtliche* basis without foregoing special tribute to the significance of the masterpiece. But since the respective period syntheses do not meet the minimal requirement of having as their base an inductive style analysis of the literary works, and since, furthermore, period-style categories have not been reassessed as to their vindication in literature, the parallels drawn between the plastic arts, music, and poetry must remain questionable. In establishing major style epochs, Hamann and Hermand are not guided by the inevitable methodological principle of carefully balancing between inductive style analysis and deductive application of insights gained from sciences outside the realm of literature. Thus Hermand's own efforts to rehabilitate the literary period of the Biedermeier as such on the basis of his methodological approach[61] are doomed from the very start.

In the stylistic discussion of epochs, F. W. Bateson unknowingly adopts Woelfflin's categories.[62] He has taken them from Geoffrey Scott,[63] who is directly indebted to Woelfflin. W. T. Jones refers more specifically to Woelfflin's categories in *The Romantic Syndrome*,[64] in which he creates antonyms such as "continuity/discreteness, order/disorder, static/dynamic, soft focus/sharp focus, inner/outer bias, this-world/other-world." With these categories Jones believes he has arrived at a cultural-sociological period-style analysis which is autonomous; in individual cases of the Romantic period, however, he becomes entrenched in superficial conclusions through which can be clearly seen their dependence on Woelfflin. Seen in the same light as the joint undertaking of Hamann and Hermand are Wylie Sypher's two works, *The Four Stages of Renaissance Style*[65] and *Rococo to Cubism in Art and Literature*.[66] Sypher also refers to Woelfflin specifically, and arrives at his period-style characteristics by an analogy of all arts.

In contrast to the above aesthetic contributions there are others which, methodologically sounder, in part tend towards cultural-socio-

logical contributions. Their beginnings reach back as far as those of the
Woelfflin school. Theophil Spoerri was probably the first to transform
Woelfflin's categories into categories of literary style[67] and then to
assess Ariosto and Tasso inductively in comparing their styles, defining
them as to period style. In doing so, he bases his endeavor on antonyms
such as define/dissolve, differentiate/integrate, tie/untie. In his discussion of the Baroque, cited several times previously,[6] Helmut Hatzfeld
includes analyses of works in the domain of the plastic arts to apply the
results thus gained—transformed into literary categories—to the period
style of the Baroque. Very successfully he employs this method in his
previously discussed essay, "Der Barockstil in der religioesen klassischen
Lyrik in Frankreich,"[10] as he does in two later essays on the periods of
the French Rococo[68] and French Naturalism.[69] His works are the most
persuasive evidence for the vindication of the method proposed by us—
i.e., to penetrate to the period style of a major epoch on the basis of a
genuine "reciprocal illumination of the arts."

Marcel Raymond[70] and his pupil Jean Rousset[71] proceed on the
model of Woelfflin, but not until they have revamped his categories to
apply to literature, and together with specific stylistic analyses of individual examples they contribute to a useful description of the period
style of the Baroque. Without foregoing insights gained from aesthetics
as period-style criteria, Imbrie Buffum takes a firm stand against simply grafting Woelfflin's style categories onto literature. In two discussions[72, 73] he draws inductively gained parallels between literature
and the graphic arts, and furthermore, includes the *geistesgeschichtliche*
background.

Although not entirely on the model of descriptive linguistics, Elise
Richter treats Impressionist poetry,[74] and as she deductively includes
results from the domain of painting, she can, with some success, outline
the period style characteristics of Impressionism. Fredi Chiapelli was
able to rely entirely on a formal-aesthetic discussion,[4] as his tutor
Theophil Spoerri had already staked out the period styles of Renaissance and Baroque, depending upon his borrowing from the realm of
aesthetics.

Among the many papers dedicated to our topic and presented in
1951 at the Fifth International Congress of Literature and Language in
Florence, we shall mention only two. Along what are conceivably too
general lines, S. Dresden[75] retraces the parallel style characteristics in
poetry and the plastic arts with respect to conditions of man's environment. Hugo Kuhn, with his lecture "Struktur und Formensprache in
Dichtung und Kunst," achieves more tangible results.[76] In an essay of

1949,[77] Kuhn could prove with unrivalled conviction that all of medieval art represents the exercise of a religious cult which gains from its metaphysical orientation an objectivity which, in terms of period style, becomes manifest as "three-dimensional." In his address of 1951 he expands on his theory. He explains that comparisons between poetry and the plastic arts must be based on three levels of artistic realization: subject matter, language of form, and the finished product; for only "such aspects of works of art as would lead through all three levels to the actual center of its achievement, can in each period make possible a productive comparison of art and literature" (p. 44 f.). In the concept of structure, Kuhn sees the possibility of creating a basis on which the respective levels of the work of art can be compared. Bearing these ideas in mind, Kuhn points to his literary-sociological contributions, discussion of which will follow.

Volker Klotz[78] and Claude David[79] have both attempted to graft onto literature the art-historical concept of Art Nouveau, through intrinsic analyses and comparisons of style. Although both authors proceed very cautiously in drawing conclusions about Art Nouveau in literature, this art-historic concept in particular can be applied to literature only with the greatest of reservations. A possible acceptance of Art Nouveau as a literary period style would have to evolve from a thorough examination along the guidelines we have established.

Finally, we ought to mention the contribution of Karl-Ludwig Schneider. His essay, "Expressionismus in Dichtung und Malerei"[80] continues the period-style analysis of Expressionism begun with an analysis of the metaphor inventory of the Early Expressionist lyric poetry. On the basis of his inductively gained results, Schneider can point to the deliberate destruction of form in both poetry and painting. To be sure, the hypothesis lacks additional substantiation and corroboration by further analyses of individual examples which would put the specific characteristics of Expressionist period style into greater relief. Be that as it may, the efforts of Schneider, Hatzfeld, and Kuhn afford us a glimpse of the "promised land" to which we ought to look for the solution to our problem.

THE CULTURAL-SOCIOLOGICAL CONTRIBUTION

In his *magnum opus, Social and Cultural Dynamics*,[81] Pitirim A. Sorokin has laid the cornerstone for a cultural-sociological discussion of our problem. By setting up "ideational, sensate, and mixed systems of integrated culture," he has outlined the possible cultural-sociological amplitude within which, to his mind, a culture oscillates to and fro. This process is gradual and comprises several of the time units previously treated. Sorokin views the culture of the Middle Ages as the last apogee of the ideational phase, but at the end of the 19th century the manifestations of a "sensate"-oriented culture take precedence; in the 20th century, to be sure, there are definite indications for a revolt along ideational lines. This process is free of any false organological conclusions as to phases of adolescence, maturity, and senility in a culture. Instead, it does allow for the repetition of constituent cultural-sociological components and explains the relationship between the period-style elements of different epochs. Sorokin includes in his investigation all the arts, and maintains that the period-style characteristics of larger epochs ought to be derived from all the arts. While a change in *one* cultural-sociological principal component would indicate a style phase, a change in several components would determine the character of an entire epoch. In individual instances this system still requires detailed follow-ups for the respective epochs and phases, but it should at least serve as a stimulating indication as to how literary investigations of cultural-sociological phenomena—and in our case, period-style analyses—ought to proceed.

Julius Petersen has also attempted to set up cultural-sociological guidelines for literary criticism. In his treatise, *Die Wesensbestimmung der deutschen Romantik*,[82] he has cautiously weighed the various approaches against one another and combined them into a cultural-sociological definition of Romanticism. In the first volume of his broadly based *Die Wissenschaft von der Dichtung*,[83] which he did not complete, Petersen construes an accurately formulated system which, among other aims, has that of determining period style. Within his "co-ordinate" system he distinguishes along the axis of environment the successive markings for individual, habitat, tribe, linguistic community, and race; he then correlates it to that axis on which he has measured the passage of time in segments of age, age group, period, and era. This system appears too contrived to be vindicated by practice, nor can the element of race claim relevance to style periodization.

Erich Auerbach presents a cross-section of occidental culture under the aspect of Realism.[84] He examines works from Homer to Proust in which he interprets individual excerpts from a stylistic aspect, and thus reveals their social, economic, political, *geistesgeschichtliche*, and literary, in short, their cultural-sociological, background. With this synchronic consideration of all style-determining factors he is able to approximate the period-style elements of the individual works. However, Auerbach has not granted sufficient prominence to a mandatory comparison with other contemporary works.

The large-scale *Literary History of the United States*[85] is another work which has as its aim a cultural-sociological discussion of literature. Its editors view literature as an organic expression set against a cultural-sociological background. The development of literature corresponds to the cultural cycle, the first phase of which extends from the period of the first colonial settlements to America's evolution as an autonomous nation; this cycle reaches its apogee in the era of Emerson, Melville, and Whitman, while the second phase comes to a high point in the 20th century, after all cosmopolitan elements in American culture have been realized. Both cycles have been divided into chapters, the titles of which —"The Colonies," "The Republic," etc.—are extraliterary concepts, except for those heading the final phases of the cycles. The last two chapters are then labelled "Literary Fulfillment" and "A World Literature," indicating that literature in its true sense is only possible at the end of a cycle. Nearly all chapters show a parallel structure; only after a cultural-sociological background has been drawn in detail are the literary works of that period discussed. This background then leads to an implied period style and dispenses with stylistic elaboration. In so doing, the discussion resembles in parts the German *geistesgeschichtliche* school of the twenties, a risk run by many of the sociologically oriented investigations. Additionally, the discussion of the literature of the second phase is so much under the compulsive influence of the cyclic theory that this principle must either require that some authors be sacrificed or must lead to erroneous generalizations. Still, this criticism is not intended to detract from the merit of this joint undertaking, which consists of having shown very clearly the dependence of American literature on cultural-sociological factors that are uniquely American.

In order to explain period transitions, the authors contributing to *Transitions in American Literary History*[86] have also availed themselves of the cultural-sociological method. They avoid any reference to the rigid demands of the cyclic process and regard literature as set against a changing cultural-sociological background which may be determined by any number of factors. The first two chapters, entitled respectively "The Decline of Puritanism" and "The Late Eighteenth Century," point out a predominant *geistesgeschichtliche* orientation in these periods, and its precipitation in literature. The period from 1800 to 1860 is discussed from three aspects: "The Decline of Neoclassicism," "The Rise of Romanticism," and "The Rise of Transcendentalism." The internal unity of that epoch does not emerge very clearly, nor does a pertinent, at least cultural-sociological, period style.

In his book *Ursprung und Gegenwart*,[87] the efforts made by Jean Gebser to reduce the entire Modern period in all its manifestations—not only those in the arts—to the common denominator of "aperspective," have the familiar ring of the *geistesgeschichtliche* approach. He does not succeed in progressing beyond purely summary conclusions on the relationship between the arts.

Sir Herbert Read's endeavors must also be counted among the cultural-sociological contributions. A volume such as *The Tenth Muse*,[88] consisting of a variety of essays, shows that Read is equally familiar with literary analysis and the plastic arts, a circumstance which enables him in his discussions to draw on *geistesgeschichtliche*, cultural-sociological, and psychological findings. The cultural-sociological orientation becomes evident in his treatise on the Romantic period, "The True Voice of Feeling,"[89] in which he sees the essence of Romanticism in its quest for a new organic awareness of form, which in Germany inspired Goethe and Schelling, and in England Coleridge and Wordsworth, and which pervaded all sectors of cultural activity. In having the Romantic movement extend into the 20th century, the concepts of epoch and period-style characteristics, however, lose their accuracy and power of conviction.

THE LITERARY-SOCIOLOGICAL CONTRIBUTION

In this sector it is recommended that one distinguish between two streams of literary-sociological trends—i.e., one leaning towards Marxism, and one with an empirical basis. Several traits essential to Marxist literary criticism exert a special influence on the discussions of period style. Hitherto Marxist literary criticism has, though in modified form, clung to the causal determination of the literary superstructure on the basis of socioeconomic conditions. A literary period and its stylistic manifestations are thus more or less directly dependent on the socioeconomic circumstances of that epoch. The work of art itself expresses the bias of objectivity which, on the one hand, is determined by the artist's deliberate objectivity, and on the other is inherent in the material to be treated. As a result, period style is reflected in this bias towards objectivity, but the work of art loses its autonomy under these circumstances. This fact is brought into sharp focus when literature is said to assume the dual role of reflecting class struggle and of assisting in determining the future of the classless society. Thus the methodological approach of the German school of *Geistesgeschichte* is forced into the cul-de-sac of ideology.[90]

Early Marxist literary criticism under Georgi W. Plekhanov already runs along these lines. In his essay, "Die franzoesische dramatische Literatur und die franzoesische Malerei des 18. Jahrhunderts vom Standpunkt der Soziologie,"[91] Plekhanov retraces the form of French classical tragedy and that of contemporary painting to the predominance of aristocratic opinions, endeavors, and orientations of taste. Subsequent political change-overs in France also exerted their influence on the artistic plane. P. N. Sakulin's work has been labeled by later Marxist research as the expression of superficial plebeio-Marxism. In his *Russische Literaturgeschichte*,[92] Sakulin sets himself the goal of pointing out those social and literary aspects which permit Russian literature to appear autonomous. Within the scheme of cultural dialectics, the so-called second cultural epoch from 1650 to 1850 has as its *thesis* Old Russian culture, as *antithesis* Europism, and as *synthesis*, aristocratic culture. The styles of this epoch—i.e., Classicism, Sentimentalism, Maçonism, Romanticism, and artistic Realism, are aristocratic styles: "Pushkin's works, the apogee of aristocratic culture, were an artistic synthesis of the entire literary evolution" (p. 140). There is no doubt as to the significance of aristocratic style for this era, but the stylistic periods are not treated in sufficient detail in terms of literary phenomena.

Contributions to Marxist literary criticism in America have been made by V. F. Calverton and Granville Hicks. In his *Liberation of American Literature*[93] Calverton shows the evolution of American literature as a liberation from the shackles of the "colonial complex" and from "bourgeois ideals" in which the stages of liberation are reflected by period style. Around 1930, optimistic expectancy and trust in the bourgeois ideals turned into despair, thus breaking free of the shackles of society. Hicks portrays the development of a revolutionary literary movement[94] that first makes itself felt with the beginning of the Civil War, and then runs parallel to the progressive decay of capitalism; once again, period style is reflected in the incipient growth of the "Great Tradition." Both Hicks and Calverton prophesy a better future which can be glossed from the evolution of literature.

Christoph Caudwell, an Englishman, attempts to lay bare the basic social structure of poetry in *Illusion and Reality*.[95] To his thinking, poetry evolves out of labor as such, and is the expression of a collective feeling.

With the division of labor, poetry does lose its point of reference, but is still able to express the content of a collective feeling, and in the light of this truth, assumes and fulfills its dynamic role in society. It does not surprise us then that poetry can only be understood in terms of its specific society. Caudwell has English poetry, from 1500 to the 20th century, depend almost exclusively on the bourgeoisie, whose concept of liberty, in his view, rests on an illusion. Hence that poetic content is also the expression of a mere illusion. In a table of the "Movements of Bourgeois Poetry," from 1550 to 1930 he lists for each epoch parallel "general characteristics" and "technical characteristics," wherein the latter reflect the basis evidenced in the former. The radical change-over in society and poetry then takes place with the "final capitalistic crisis" of 1930. Although Caudwell gains sensitive and delicate insights into the essence of poetry in individual instances, his synthetic conclusions cannot claim to be valid.

Hans Mayer almost completely foregoes these primitive causal links in declaring Georg Buechner *the* exponent of his period.[96] This statement of Buechner's representative position results from thorough analysis of the political and social circumstances of Buechner's time and from a detailed scrutiny of his works. Although Mayer's individual interpretations apparently do full justice to Buechner's personality, the claim to consider the poet and politician Buechner as *the* representative of his period is exorbitant, and stems from Mayer's political convictions.

Among the French contributions we ought to mention at this point the works of Lucien Goldmann.[97] He goes so far as to deny a direct determining influence on literature by the basic social structure of which the poet is a part, but dialectical materialism then reveals, to his mind, the connection between the social and historical events of a period that allow for the clarification of the relationship between these processes and the works of art. Period style becomes the expression of a *Weltanschauung* that shapes the literary work out of a diffuse collective awareness. While the novel, for instance, has been based on the ideals of the bourgeoisie until the beginning of the 19th century, since Kafka it has been characterized by stressing the nonexistence of progress in its bourgeois meaning. In their methodology both Goldmann and Mayer move along lines not altogether unlike those of the literary sociological empiricists.

Ernst Fischer was another to abandon the Marxist mirror theory. In his treatise *Zeitgeist und Literatur*[98] he presents art as the poet's immediate awe before the reality of his era. This vision leaves him ample room for individual and supraindividual literary criticism. The over-all manifestation of the new reality in modern art is seen by Fischer under the symbol of the "Angelus Novus," who points to new and better things to come. Still, behind these prophetic criteria almost all other stylistic elements tend to dissolve in ethereal omnipresence.[99]

Georg Lukács is generally regarded as the most prominent exponent of Marxist literary criticism. In his early book on the *Theorie des Romans*,[100] which is not yet Marxistic, he traces the epic back to the unity of a cultural world image, and explains the form of the novel from the increasing lack of trust in that world image. Seen from this angle, epic and novel become period-style criteria. Cervantes's Don Quixote still evidences the crossing of transcendency and monomania, but the process continues via Wilhelm Meister—in whom the reconciliation between inner and outer world is problematic, to be sure, though possible —and ends in the novel of disillusion. Later (1954, 1963) Lukács became the Marxist literary critic to fight most vigorously for the cause of the mirror theory.[101] Unfortunately for this theory, any and all problems of form, being a reflection of objective reality, are eliminated; a dilemma which stems from the logical and consistent application of Marxist literary criticism.[102] Since Lukács, furthermore, walks the path of cyclic evolution of literature, his synthetic consideration carries the chip of the *geistesgeschichtliche* block on both shoulders.[103]

Opposed to this literary criticism proceeding from Marxist ideology, we find empirically based literary sociology, the methodology of which entails fewer self-imposed limitations. As early as 1923 Levin L. Schuecking pointed out[104] that there is present in the form of taste-determining groups indeed more than one *Zeitgeist*. He explains the phenomenon of period style as determined either by literary groups and literary schools or simply by the predominant taste; and while this view is possibly a bit rigid, Schuecking has at least avoided the narrow straits of the *geistesgeschichtliche* school. Finally, he outlines the danger inherent in directly deriving the social structure of an epoch from its literature and in making it a determining factor for that literature—the result of circular reasoning of which Marxist literary criticism is guilty in particular. Albert Guérard confines himself to enumerating literary groups or schools as factors directly determining period style,[105] since, to his thinking, the configuration of the economic, political, and social structure of an epoch can only be pinpointed in period style with great difficulty. In his *Literature and Society*,[106] however, David Daiches has succeeded in presenting concretely based evidence of the reciprocal relationship between literature and society in England, which he examines from the Early Middle Ages to the present day. For the English

Romantic period he cites as one factor the dissatisfaction with bourgeois city society as the basis for literature and the subsequent flight into isolation. Seen in its entirety, Daiches's approach is too general to produce truly definitive period-style characteristics; his concern with detailed stylistic analyses is but slight.

Arnold Hauser[107] demonstrates on a much broader basis the dependence of art and literature on the social circumstances of a given period. Unfortunately he, too, is given to generalizations and foregoes, for example, a conscientious scrutiny of Baroque literature because it defies easy reduction to a common social denominator. His stylistic discussion of medieval courtly poetry is able to yield much more tangible results, since that period is characterized by a firm social coherence.

Hugh D. Duncan[108] has turned his special attention to the social factors which determine the stylistic elements of language. To establish a relationship with society, the form must be understood by at least some part of society and correspond to the content of its respective "situation"; this fact is particularly relevant to the symbol. As long as the social channels of communication remain intact, so does the medium. Conventions of language are fixed in terms of society, because these conventions are considered desirable for the obvious reasons of identification with a social stratum. Period style, then, is determined by a predominant stratum, or authority.

Harry Levin examines those social period-style characteristics that are typical of the 19th-century novel.[109] Well aware of the dangers inherent in generalization, Levin proposes the hypothesis that the novel of the 19th century has its origin in the bourgeois class, and for its topic, material possessions. Society's criticism of these ideals has brought about the disintegration of form so characteristic of the novel of that century.

With his book *Ideal und Wirklichkeit in der hoefischen Epik*,[110] Erich Koehler succeeds in proving that, in terms of form and content, all literary efforts centering on the legend of King Arthur are determined by the universal-historical claim to preeminence on the part of the world of courtly chivalry, and that form and content change when this claim is questioned or challenged. On the loss of the chivalric concept of unity rest the social bases of the pluralistic prose novel on the one hand, and the spiritualized knight-errantry of the legend of the Holy Grail on the other. A very cautious analysis enables Koehler to avoid the pitfall of a circular argument already recognized as such by Schuecking, and consequently to set up valid period-style criteria for the courtly epic. In a later address,[111] Koehler traces the development of the French novel as far as Flaubert, in which he can outline the sociological period-style components in their respective epochs.

Here we ought to mention two essays by Hugo Kuhn which also have as their topic the sociological factors in the poetry of the Middle Ages. Kuhn demonstrates[112] that sociological findings cannot be applied directly to the discussion of poetry; rather, the sociological discussion of literature consists of the characteristic balance of a work between the "historically given real ties of society (concepts and forms) and their meaning as assigned by the poet" (p. 38). From this vantage point Kuhn discovers that courtly poetry does not represent a mirror of medieval society, but has evolved from an "ethic idealism born of a critical view of reality." His other essay[113] shows that in a style analysis of the Middle Ages the epoch—i.e., period style, takes precedence over personal style, since the medieval poet is almost totally committed to the conventions of this style. Medieval style is realized in systems of analogy, so that Kuhn can in the end label this period style as "Analogie-Realismus."

Next to follow is Arnold Hirsch's treatise *Buergertum und Barock im deutschen Roman. Ein Beitrag zur Entstehungsgeschichte des buergerlichen Weltbildes.*[114] From the bourgeois elements in the novel of the second half of the 17th century, so sharp in their contrast to the ascetic interpretation of the world by the Baroque, Hirsch deduced period style criteria of a dual function; these criteria separate the Baroque period from that which immediately follows and which is entirely taken up by a bourgeois awareness of existence, while at the same time a budding bourgeois trend is already apparent in the Baroque period.

The Frenchman Robert Escarpit has submitted a contribution,[115] the principal aim of which is the investigation of the relationship between book and reader. He concerns himself in detail with those sociological factors responsible for the emergence of a new literary group—in our case closely linked to a new period style—and he can furthermore prove that in French literature the appearance of a new group always coincides with a period of political calm or with the end of an authoritatian period, while periods of political tension invariably impede literary development.

THE PSYCHOLOGICAL CONTRIBUTION

While the findings of Freud and Jung have contributed positively to throwing light on the problem of literary analysis, their application in the field of synthetic literary criticism has been far less successful. The reason for this is to be found in the fact that the examination of the psychological make-up of a period must either be determined by the cultural-sociological factors, or proceed from a most careful analysis of its stylistic inventory, if it is not to succumb to the errors of a premature *geistesgeschichtliche* generalization. Jones L. Lewisohn's book, *Expression in America*,[116] in which the development of American literature is conceived of in terms of a liberation from the psychological complex of Puritanism and from that of the "General Tradition," is similar to Calverton's Marxist-oriented endeavor[93] to interpret the evolution of American literature as a liberation from the "colonial complex" and bourgeois ideals. In Transcendentalism Lewisohn sees the beginning of a revolt which expresses the liberation of the creative mind and thus characterizes the transition from poetaster to true poet.

Louis Cazamian upholds the theory that epochs are expressed in the oscillation of literary styles, as marked by the poles of a psychological field-potential. In English Literature[117] the pendulum swings between the poles of emotion and intellect, according to the principle of action and reaction, "convention and revolt." As a period of "sensibility and imagination," English Romanticism is thus a reaction to the previous period of reason, and a resumption of the first Romantic period of the Elizabethan Age. In French literature[118] Cazamian sees a similar law; while the intellectual enthusiasm of the French Renaissance leads to a freedom of thought, the Romantic period is characterized by the psychological quest for freedom of expression. Apart from Cazamian's declaration that the frequency of oscillation between the psychological poles steadily increases as literary development moves closer to the present day (thus procuring a convenient excuse for the collapse of that principle), there is no literary evidence of such a governing principle, unless one were to restrict oneself to the most shallow remarks on periods and period styles. Max Foerster is another scholar to uphold a similar law in literary evolution;[119] "the influence of 'polar reaction' on the psychological structure of our literary periods" (p. 262). The period-style criteria to be gained from it are either erroneous or devoid of meaning.

In contrast, on the basis of inductive analysis, Mario Praz has succeeded in depicting Romanticism under the psychological aspect of erotic sensitivity. The Italian title, *La Carne, la Morte e il Diavolo nella Letteratura Romantica*,[120] expresses the span of sensitivity which gradually takes shape in poetry, predominating around 1800, and aiding in determining the character of the Romantic period. Albert Béguin[121] retraces Romanticism to its three constituent myths: âme, rêve, poésie —the soul, the unconscious (sic), and poetry, which in their interplay characterize Romantic period style.

In the light of the two above studies W. H. Auden's *The Enchafèd Flood*[122] remains somewhat pale. Water and sea are outlined as the central Romantic symbols, since on the level of the unconscious they embody that innocence which man tries to regain in the Romantic period. Auden, however, does not quote sufficient examples, nor does he analyze in a manner detailed enough to derive from his treatise psychological period-style criteria which are exclusively valid for the Romantic period. G. J. Geer's attempt[123] to understand the Baroque as the expression of two psychological conflicts appears slightly exorbitant: "the unconscious irrational fear of freedom and the other, real fear of the reign of terror, the opposing power of society, Church and State" (p. 301).

Leslie A. Fiedler investigates the influence of the 18th century European novel on America[124] and arrives at very extreme results. He states that the American novel of the 19th century represents the flight from physical realities and is consequently unrealistic, negative, sadistic, and melodramatic. The eruption of sexual passions and its manifestation in European literature had a reverse effect in America, where it brought about the exaltation of woman to the point of desexualization. To Fiedler's thinking, this phenomenon may be traced back to the absence of sexuality in American everyday life. Fiedler is guilty of the same error of circular argument committed in part by the literary sociologists.

Although the concept of Walter Muschg's *Tragische Literaturgeschichte*[125] does not initially lead us to expect an investigation of period-style criteria, there are frequent allusions which point to a psychological foundation of period styles. "Renaissance art was created in the awareness that beauty of form is the most profound revelation of the Divine" (p. 21). German Romanticism is explained in terms of youth having subscribed to "the rapture of delirious frenzy, to the unconscious, and the hypersensual" (p. 33). Explanations of this kind lack convincing textual verification and are not sufficiently specific to do justice to the period style of an epoch. In his later work, *Von Trakl zu Brecht*,[126] Muschg shows a more solid approach. Expressionist language and form are first generally outlined on the basis of a psychological interpretation of the *geistesgeschichtliche* background, followed by discussions of the various poets.

One of the most persuasive psychological contributions to our problem has been presented by Walter Abell in his comprehensive treatise, *The Collective Dream in Art*.[127] In combining history and psychology on the plane of "depth analysis," Abell tries to give an explanation for the period style of all the arts. His treatment of Prehistory, Early History, and the Middle Ages leads us to believe that this method constitutes perhaps the most promising application of psychology in determining a period style. Although Abell's concern with literature proper is marginal, he tries to establish in depth psychoanalysis a basis for all arts, which ought to receive proper consideration as cultural-sociological background.

THE EXISTENTIALIST CONTRIBUTION

Existentialist literary criticism would essentially like to include all previous approaches. With respect to our problem configuration its findings, however, are not entirely convincing. Period style is explained in terms of a common space-time experience, but both Theophil Spoerri and Emil Staiger are unable to corroborate their argument with tangible style criteria.

In his essay, "Zur Methode der Stilforschung,"[128] Hermann Pongs has supported existentialist style research, interpreting the folksong of the 16th century as a style of simplicity and as evolving from the co-operative effort of the community. In two books[129, 130] Spoerri transferred Woelfflin's categories, after their metamorphosis into literary categories,[67] to the sphere of existential awareness. The structure of space would then be conceived of as vertical from earth to Heaven in the Middle Ages, as horizontal in its awareness of things terrestrial during the Renaissance, and as diagonal in its tension between the two previous periods in the Baroque.

Taking as period-style basis the differing experience of space and time of Berthold of Ratisbon and Luther, Hannes Maeder has tried to contrast a text of each author against one another stylistically.[131] Since he declares them representative of their time without proper parallel analyses, the experience of space and time is altogether too similar to a *geistesgeschichtliche* concept of *Zeitgeist*. Subsequent descriptive discussions of the grammatical and stylistic inventory are thus already biased from the start and lose their power of conviction.

With his work *Wirklichkeit und Illusion* (1957),[132] Richard Brinkmann has presented a most comprehensive discussion of Realism, which in part moves along existentialist guidelines. To establish the period-style criteria of Realism, he takes as his bases analyses of Grillparzer's "Armer Spielmann," Otto Ludwig's "Zwischen Himmel und Erde," and Keyserling's "Beate und Mareile." He comes to the conclusion that "subjectivism of reality, i.e. the reduction of reality to subjective awareness," represents the fundamental principle of Realism. His argument appears to be all the more persuasive, because he is not totally committed to Existentialist literary criticism.

THE ORGANOLOGICAL CONTRIBUTION

To this approach belong all investigations based on the belief that culture is subject to a biological and organic law of growth. On the principle of analogy, findings of the natural sciences are grafted onto literature, as though literature could be conceived of in terms of genetic material. Since the results of this approach are generally irrelevant to our problem and to literary criticism, they receive only cursory mention, and merely for the sake of completeness.

Richard Hamann based his aesthetic work, *Der Expressionismus in Leben und Kunst*[59] on a cultural-morphological principle, and declared Expressionism to be a style of "exhaustion" which could be proved in all "ageing" cultural organisms. Oswald Spengler then expanded this theory into a morphology of Occidental culture[57] in which the parallelism of all branches of culture and civilization, together with a biological-organological orientation, forced him to abandon the firm ground of results gained by inductive analysis. In *Die Ueberseele*,[133] H. Hamann expresses his view on the development of German literature as corresponding to an organism with the phases of childhood, adolescence, and manhood. Along the lines of this theory, period style is explained in terms of fraternal similarity (p. 22). In these discussions, Herder's concept of the "organic" in culture, to be interpreted metaphorically, has degenerated into biological determinism in its oversimplification.

Josef Nadler's *Literaturgeschichte der deutschen Staemme und Landschaften*[134] must be mentioned in this sequence. To classify individual German tribes as to their stylistic peculiarities and to attribute the Romantic period at all costs to the so-called "new tribes" or "colonial tribes" is to make indeed excessive demands on the element of local color, and to ride it to death.

Robert E. Spiller, one of the principal editors of the cultural-sociologically oriented *Literary History of the United States*[85] has, with his book *The Cycle of American Literature*[135] also made a contribution to the organological approach. To his mind, the development of culture and literature runs along lines to be understood in terms of biological evolution. Spiller's concept is particularly obvious in his periodization and, consequently, in his period-style criteria; terms such as Naturalism, Realism, and Romanticism are conceived of so broadly as to remain without any tangible reference.

The problem of bringing into harmony cultural and biological phenomena has been touched upon by Wilhelm E. Muehlmann in *Homo Creator*.[136] Proceeding from a broad sociological, anthropological, and ethnic basis, Muehlmann concludes nevertheless that all endeavors of this kind must be considered irrelevant.

PERIODIZATION ACCORDING TO GENERATIONS

In this category we ought to refer briefly to the results which periodization according to generations has contributed to the problem of period style. In his 1867 Novalis essay[137] and in his *Das Leben Schleiermachers*[138] Wilhelm Dilthey pointed to the tension between the rising Romantic generation and the achievement of Classical poetry which so frustrated the new generation. In an essay[139] dedicated to this problem, Julius Petersen refers to Dilthey and modifies the latter's hypothesis, but without discarding the concept of German Romanticism as a generation entity. Petersen expands this generation concept in classifying German literature and tries to systematize that principle. He concludes that, for all practical purposes, the concept of generation can be understood in terms of a collective destiny and that it remains rather vague even then. In an essay, "Die Generation als Jugendgemeinschaft,"[140] Eduard Wechsler envisages the birth of a new literary generation from a collective motivation of young people, in contrast to the predominant *Zeitgeist*. Wechsler's concept reflects once more the German *geistesgeschichtliche* school.

The most comprehensive contribution in this respect has been Henri Peyre's book, *Les Générations Littéraires*.[141] A work as carefully planned as his is particularly well suited to illustrate the questionable nature of this kind of methodology. Ultimately Peyre succumbs to the fascination of systematizing literary history through time periods of eight to twenty years, instead of interpreting an epoch or phase in the light of its literary elements. Peyre is another scholar to subject literary evolution to a rhythm which is based on the principle of action and reaction. On the advice of Peyre, Robert Escarpit transformed the concept of generation into the sociological concept[142] of work-team; but in so doing he has admitted that a generation cannot really claim an exclusive inherent rhythm. As a work-team, the generation is determined by social, not biological, factors.

A unit even smaller than that of the generation is established by Hans Otto Burger when he claims to find a relationship characteristic of a period style in works which have appeared more or less at the same time. His contribution to the joint undertaking, *Annalen der deutschen Literatur*,[143] has a comparative basis for individual works determined by the *Zeitgeist* of one year.

THE CONTRIBUTION OF STATISTICS

This contribution is probably the only one to be able to utilize the findings of descriptive linguistics with the aid of the computer in cataloguing period-style elements. At this point, however, we ought not to forget that for the time being we are dealing with a quantitative analysis of grammatical phenomena with which one determines the frequency and distribution of stylistic features, not their density or variation. An impressive achievement, which simultaneously reminds us of the limitations of this method, is the work of Josephine Miles. In the essay "Eras in English Poetry"[144] she examines sentences in English poetry for their nominal or verbal style, and concludes that one can draw a perfect curve which results from the different distribution from generation to generation. While the sentences of around 1500 are predominantly verbal, from 1700 to 1770 they are characterized by a preponderance of nominal style, which then decreases around 1900. The question remains as to what extent this type of quantitative analysis is relevant to period style, since Josephine Miles does not relate it to content. In *Style and Proportion*[145] she demonstrates a refined version of her method, but the result is once more quantitative and for our purposes essentially uninteresting. To arrive at useful period-style characteristics these results would have to be incorporated in a synthetic discussion of literature.

CONCLUSION

No single method of analyzing the phenomenon of period style can claim to be the ultimate one, nor should we subscribe to an eclectic approach. In this paper, we ought to have confirmed our initial hypothesis that the period style of shorter phases can be deduced intrinsically, while for the major style epochs inductively gained results from cultural-sociological neighboring fields should be included to prove the internal unity of a period. The danger of eclecticism may be avoided by pursuing only those methodological approaches vindicated by the literary inventory. Briefly, in order to gain period-style criteria it is advisable to utilize "comparative criticism," if the findings are to be definitive.

Research hitherto has paid practically no attention to one certain methodological approach: The criteria of a period style pertinent to a certain genre must be confirmed by the corresponding style element in another genre; only then can period style definitively prove the unity of an epoch. For example, the metaphor of lyric poetry corresponds to the parable of the epic—in a style period both must rest on the same principle of form and application.

The problem of period style and periodization is closely linked to that of the typology of poets. The types established by Dilthey, van Dam, or even Jung, cannot be starting points for a period-style analysis, however conscientious investigation would probably be able to find them loosely distributed in any period, while the concentrated occurrence of one type could conceivably determine the stylistic character of a period or a phase.

In conclusion one would do well to remember the definition of a period given by René Wellek, as it is based on a convincing literary theory and contains the vindication of the method proposed by us in analyzing period style:[146]

> It should be frankly realized that a period is not an ideal type or an abstract pattern or a series of class concepts, but a time section, dominated by a whole system of norms, which no work of art will ever realize in its entirety. The history of a period will consist in the tracing of the changes from one system of norms to another. While a period is thus a section of time to which some sort of unity is ascribed, it is obvious that this unity can be only relative. It means merely that during this period a certain scheme of norms has been realized most fully.

[*Translated from the German by Dietrich E. R. Koch*]

Notes

1. Leo Spitzer, *Stilsprache. Stilstudien II* (Munich, 1928); pp. 301–364 for Charles Peguy, pp. 208–300 for Jules Romains, and pp. 365–497 for Marcel Proust; see also Leo Spitzer, *Linguistics and Literary History* (Princeton, 1948).

2. Gerhard Fricke, *Materialien und Studien zum Formproblem des deutschen Literaturbarock*. Neue Forschungen, Vol. 17 (Berlin, 1933).

3. Wolfgang Kayser, *Ein Beitrag zur Geschichte der Literatur, Poetik und Sprachtheorie der Barockzeit*. Palaestra, Vol. 179 (Leipzig, 1932).

4. Fredi Chiapeli, "Tassos Stil im Uebergang von Renaissance zu Barock," in *Trivium*, Vol. 7 (1949), pp. 286–309.

5. Ulrich Leo, *Torquato Tasso. Studien zur Vorgeschichte des Secentismo* (Berne, 1951).

6. Dámaso Alonso, *Ensayo de metodos y limites estilisticos* ed. 2 (Madrid, 1952).

7. Willi Flemming, "Die Fuge als epochales Kompositionsprinzip des deutschen Barock," in *Deutsche Vierteljahresschrift fuer Literaturwissenschaft und Geistesgeschichte*, Vol. 32 (1958), pp. 483–515.

8. Herbert Read, *English Prose Style* (New York, 1952).

9. Karl-Ludwig Schneider, *Der bildhafte Ausdruck in den Dichtungen Georg Heyms, Georg Trakls und Ernst Stadlers* (Heidelberg, 1954).

10. Helmut Hatzfeld, *Literaturwissenschaftliches Jahrbuch der Goerresgesellschaft*, Vol. 4 (1929), pp. 30–60.

11. In *Archivum Romanicum*, Vol. 12 (1928), pp. 361–472.

12. Helmut Hatzfeld, *Estudios sobre el Barroco* (Madrid, 1964).

13. Morris W. Croll, "The Baroque Style in Prose," in *Studies in English Philology: A Miscellany in Honor of Frederick Klaeber*, Ed. by K. Malone and M. B. Ruud (Minneapolis, 1929), pp. 427–456.

14. George Williamson, *A Study in Prose Form from Bacon to Collier* (Chicago, 1951).

15. Ian Gordon, *The Movement of English Prose* (Bloomington, 1966).

16. Richard Alewyn, "Vorbarocker Klassizismus und Griechische Tragoedie. Analyse der 'Antigone'—Uebersetzung des Martin Opitz," in *Neue Heidelberger Jahrbuecher*, NS (1926), pp. 3–63.

17. Hans Pyritz, *Paul Fleming's Liebeslyrik*, Palaestra, Vol. 180 (Leipzig, 1932); and *Paul Flemings Liebeslyrik. Zur Geschichte des Petrarkismus*, Palaestra, Vol. 234 (Gottingen, 1963).

18. Joerg-Ulrich Fechner, *Der Antipetrarkismus. Studie zur Liebessatire in barocker Lyrik*. Beitraege zur Neueren Literaturgeschichte, Third Ser., Vol. 2 (Heidelberg, 1966).

19. Rosemunde Tuve, *Elizabethan and Metaphysical Imagery: Renaissance Poetic and Twentieth Century Critics* (Chicago, 1947).

20. Ruth Wallerstein, *Studies in Seventeenth-Century Poetic* (Madison, Wisc., 1950).

21. Eric A. Blackall, "The Language of Sturm und Drang," in *Stil- und Formprobleme in der Literatur. Vortraege des VII. Kongresses der Internationalen Vereinigung fuer moderne Sprachen und Literatur in Heidelberg*, Ed. by P. Boeckmann (Heidelberg, 1959).

22. Karl-Ludwig Schneider, "Anmerkungen zum Antitraditionalismus bei den Dichtern des 'Neuen Clubs'," in *Formkraefte der deutschen Dichtung vom Barock bis zur Gegenwart*, Ed. by Hans Steffen (Goettingen, 1963), pp. 250–270.

23. Paul Boeckmann, in *Von der Sinnbildsprache zur Ausdruckssprache* (Hamburg, 1949).
24. Fritz Martini, *Deutsche Literatur im buergerlichen Realismus 1848–1898*. Epochen der deutschen Literatur, Vol. 2 (Stuttgart, 1962).
25. Karl Viëtor, *Geschichte der deutschen Ode* (Munich, 1923).
26. Friedrich Beissner, *Geschichte der deutschen Elegie*, Grundriss der germanischen Philologie, Vol. 14 (Berlin, 1941).
27. Arthur Huebscher, "Barock als Gestaltung antithetischen Lebensgefuehls. Grundlegung einer Phaseologie der Geistesgeschichte," in *Euphorion*, Vol. 24 (1922), pp. 517–562, 759–805.
28. Emil Ermatinger, *Barock und Rokoko in der deutschen Dichtung* (Leipzig, 1926).
29. Rudolf Unger, "Literaturgeschichte und Geistesgeschichte," in *Deutsche Vierteljahresschrift fuer Literaturwissenschaft und Geistesgeschichte*, Vol. 4 (1926), pp. 177–192; the quote is from p. 188.
30. Max Deutschbein, *Das Wesen des Romantischen* (Koethen, 1921).
31. Hermann A. Korff, *Versuch einer ideellen Entwicklung der klassisch-romantischen Literaturgeschichte*, 4 vols. (Leipzig, 1923–53).
32. Willi Flemming, "Die Auffassung des Menschen im 17. Jahrhundert," in *Deutsche Vierteljahresschrift*, Vol. 6 (1928), pp. 403–446.
33. Paul Kluckhohn, "Biedermeier als literarische Epochenbezeichnung," in *Deutsche Vierteljahresschrift*, Vol.8 (1935), pp. 1–43.
34. Paul Kluckhohn, *Ideengut der deutschen Romantik*. The first edition was in 1941; the fifth (Tuebingen), in 1966.
35. Etienne Gilson, *Les Idées et les Lettres* (Paris, 1932).
36. José Camón Aznar, *Don Quijote en la teoría de los estilos* (Zaragoza, 1949).
37. Randall Stewart, *American Literature and Christian Doctrine* (Baton Rouge, 1958).
38. Américo Castro, *El Pensamiento de Cervantes* (Madrid, 1925); see also "El Don Juan de Tirso y el Molière como personajes barrocos," in *Hommage à Ernest Martinenche* (Paris, 1937), pp. 93–111.
39. Paul Hankamer, *Deutsche Gegenreformation und deutsches Barock in der Dichtung* (Stuttgart, 1935).
40. Louis Martz, *The Poetry of Meditation. A Study in English Literature of the Seventeenth Century* (New Haven, 1954).
41. Marjorie Nicolson, *The Breaking of the Circle. Studies in the Effect of the "New Science" upon the Seventeenth-Century Poetry*, rev. ed. (New York, 1960).
42. Meyer H. Abrams, in *Romantic Theory and Literary Tradition* (New York, 1953).
43. Albert Gerard, *L'Idée romantique de la poésie en Angleterre* (Paris, 1955).
44. Gerhard Rudolph, "Die Epoche als Strukturelement in der dichterischen Welt. Zur Deutung der Sprache von Heinrich von Kleist und Achim von Arnim," in *Germanisch-Romanische Monatsschrift*, Vol. 40 (1959), pp. 118–139.
45. E. D. Hirsch, *Wordsworth and Schelling. A Typological Study of Romanticism* (New Haven, 1960).
46. Rene Wellek, "The Concept of Romanticism in Literary History," and "Romanticism Re-examined," in *Concepts of Criticism* (New Haven and London, 1963).
47. Arthur O. Lovejoy, *The Great Chain of Being* (Cambridge, 1936).
48. David Daiches, *Critical Approaches to Literature* (Engelwood Cliffs, N.J., 1956).
49. David Daiches, *A Critical History of English Literature* (New York, 1960).
50. Georges Poulet, *Les Métamorphoses du Cercle* (Paris, 1961).
51. Heinrich Woelfflin, *Kunstgeschichtliche Grundbegriffe* (Munich, 1915).
52. Oskar Walzel, in *Philosophische Vortraege veroeffentlicht von der Kantgesellschaft* (Berlin, 1917).

53. Oskar Walzel, "Gehalt und Gestalt im Kunstwerk des Dichters," in *Handbuch der Literaturwissenschaft*, Ed. by Oskar Walzel (Wildpark-Potsdam, 1923).

54. Oskar Walzel, in *Mittel seiner Erforschung* (Leipzig, 1926).

55. Fritz Strich, *Deutsche Klassik und Romantik oder Vollendung und Unendlichkeit* (Munich, 1922).

56. Fritz Strich, "Der lyrische Stil des 17. Jahrhunderts," in *Abhandlungen zur deutschen Literaturgeschichte. Festschrift fuer Franz Munker* (Munich, 1916), pp. 21–53.

57. Oswald Spengler, *Untergang des Abendlands* (Munich, 1923).

58. Julius Schweitering, "Die deutsche Dichtung des Mittelalters," in *Handbuch der Literaturwissenschaft*, Ed. by Oskar Walzel (Wildpark-Potsdam, 1932).

59. Richard Hamann, *Der Impressionismus in Leben und Kunst* (Cologne, 1907).

60. Richard Hamann and Jost Hermand, *Deutsche Kunst und Kultur von der Gruenderzeit bis zum Expressionismus* (Berlin, 1959, 1960, 1965).

61. Jost Hermand, *Die literarische Formenwelt des Biedermeier Beitraege zur deutschen Philologie*, Vol. 27 (Giessen, 1958).

62. F. W. Bateson, *English Poetry and the English Language* (Oxford, 1934), pp. 76–77.

63. Geoffrey Scott, *Architecture of Humanism* (London, 1914).

64. W. T. Jones, *The Romantic Syndrome* (The Hague, 1961).

65. Wylie Sypher, *The Four Stages of Renaissance Style* (Garden City, 1955).

66. Wylie Sypher, *Rococo to Cubism in Art and Literature* (New York, 1960).

67. Theophil Spoerri, *Renaissance und Barock bei Ariost und Tasso* (Berne, 1922).

68. Helmut Hatzfeld, "Rokoko als literarischer Epochenstil in Frankreich," in *Studies in Philology*, Vol. 35 (1938), pp. 532–565.

69. Helmut Hatzfeld, "Discussion sur le naturalisme français," in *Studies in Philology*, Vol. 39 (1942), pp. 696–726.

70. Marcel Raymond, *Baroque et renaissance poétique* (Paris, 1955).

71. Jean Rousset, *La Littérature de l'âge baroque en France*, (Paris, 1953).

72. Imbrie Buffum, *Agrippa d'Aubigne's Les Tragiques. A Study of the Baroque Style in Poetry* (New Haven, 1951).

73. Imbrie Buffum, *Studies in the Baroque from Montaigne to Rotrou* (New Haven, 1957).

74. Elise Richter, "Impressionismus, Expressionismus und Grammatik," in *Zeitschrift fuer Romanische Philologie*, Vol. 47 (1927), pp. 349–371.

75. S. Dresden, "La Notion de style en Littérature et dans les Beaux-Arts," *Atti del Quinto Congresso Internazionale di Lingue e Letterature Moderne*, Mar. 27–31, 1951 (Florence, 1955), pp. 11–19.

76. Hugo Kuhn, "Struktur und Formensprache in Dichtung und Kunst," *Atti del Quinto Congresso Internazionale di Lingue e Letterature Moderne* (Florence, 1955), pp. 37–45.

77. Hugo Kuhn, "Zur Deutung der Kuenstlerischen Form des Mittelalters," *Studium Generale*, Vol. 2 (1949) pp. 114–121.

78. Volker Klotz, "Jugendstil in der Lyrik," in *Akzente*, Vol. 4 (1957), pp. 26–34.

79. Claude David, "Stefan George und der Jugendstil," in *Formkraefte der deutschen Dichtung vom Barock bis zur Gegenwart*, Ed. by H. Steffen (Goettingen, 1963), pp. 211–228.

80. Karl-Ludwig Schneider, "Expressionismus in Dichtung und Malerei," in *Gratulatio. Festschrift fuer Christian Wegner* (Hamburg, 1963), pp. 226–243. This essay, together with the previously mentioned "Themen und Tendenzen der expressionistischen Lyrik" (see Ref. 22) and further contributions to Expressionism, appeared under the title *Zerbrochene Formen* (Hamburg, 1967).

81. Pitirim A. Sorokin, *Social and Cultural Dynamics* (New York, 1937–41).
82. Julius Petersen, *Die Wesensbestimmung der deutschen Romantik* (Leipzig, 1926).
83. Julius Petersen, *Die Wissenschaft von der Dichtung* (Berlin, 1939).
84. Erich Auerbach, *Mimesis* (Berne, 1946).
85. *Literary History of the United States*, Ed. by R. Spiller *et al.* (New York, 1948).
86. *Transitions in American Literary History*, Ed. by H. H. Clark (Durham, N.C. 1953).
87. Jean Gebser, *Ursprung und Gegenwart*, enlarged ed. 2 (Stuttgart, 1966).
88. Sir Herbert Read, *The Tenth Muse. Essays in Criticism* (London, 1957).
89. Sir Herbert Read, "The True Voice of Feeling," in *Studies in English Romantic Poetry* (London, 1953).
90. A good summary of Marxist literary criticism is given by Hans Norbert Fuegen in "Die Hauptrichtungen der Literatursoziologie und ihre Methoden. Ein Beitrag zur literatur-soziologischen Theorie," in *Abhandlungen zur Kunst-, Musik-, und Literaturwissenschaft*, Vol. 21 (Bonn, 1964).
91. Georgi W. Plekhanov, *Ueber Kunst und Literatur, Studienmaterial fuer die kuenstlerischen Lehranstalten*, Notebook 4 (Dresden, 1955), pp. 102–127. The essay itself dates from 1905.
92. P. N. Sakulin, in *Handbuch der Literaturwissenschaft*, Ed. by Osker Walzel (Wildpark-Potsdam, 1927).
93. V. F. Calverton, *Liberation of American Literature* (New York, 1932).
94. Granville Hicks, *The Great Tradition. An Interpretation of American Literature since the Civil War* (New York, 1933).
95. Christopher Caudwell, in *A Study of the Sources of Poetry* (New York, 1947); ed. 1, 1937.
96. Hans Mayer, *Georg Buechner und seine Zeit* (Wiesbaden, 1946).
97. Lucien Goldmann, *Recherches dialectiques* (Paris, 1959); *Sociologie du roman* (Paris 1965); "Le structuralisme génétique en sociologie de la littérature," in *Littératur et Société. Problèmes de méthodologie en sociologie de la littérature*, Edition de l'Institut de Sociologie de l'Université Libre (Brussels, 1967), pp. 195–222.
98. Ernst Fischer, in *Gebundenheit und Freiheit der Kunst* (Vienna, 1964).
99. In the most recent works of Mayer, Goldmann, and Fischer, Peter Demetz sees definite tendencies to shrug off orthodox marxist literary criticism; such was indeed the central theme of the address delivered on Apr. 24–25, 1969, at the Third Annual Conference on Comparative Literature, University of Southern California. In the area of period-style analysis, the trends of Mayer, Goldmann, and Fischer lead to results based on an empirical approach.
100. Georg Lukács, *Theorie der Romans* (Berlin, 1920).
101. See *Die Eigenart des Aesthetischen. Aesthetik Teil I* (Berlin, 1963).
102. As evidenced by the following quote from *Beitraege zur Geschichte der Aesthetik* (Berlin, 1954), p. 425: "The form? It is not much of an enigma, I believe, to him who regards artistic form as a reflection of objective reality—although it be abstract in terms of reflection of content—just as Lenin, in the realm of logic, explained the final realization of that form."
103. Lukács conceives of literary evolution in terms of three highlights: Homer, Goethe, and the superachievement of Socialist Russia still to come; see *Goethe und seine Zeit* (Berne, 1947); this scheme, however, is already evident in *Theorie des Romans*.
104. Levin L. Schuecking, *Soziologie der literarischen Geschmacksbildung* (Munich, 1923).
105. Albert Guerard, *Literature and Society* (Boston, 1935).

106. David Daiches, *Literature and Society* (London, 1938).
107. Arnold Hauser, *Sozialgeschichte der Kunst und Literatur*, 2 vols. (Munich, 1953).
108. Hugh D. Duncan, *Language and Literature in Society* (Chicago, 1953).
109. Harry Levin, "Society as Its Own Historian," in *Contexts of Criticism* (Cambridge, Mass., 1957), pp. 171–189.
110. Erich Koehler, in *Studien zur Form der fruehen Artus- und Gralsdichtung. Beihefte zur Zeitschrift fuer Romanische Philologie*, Notebook 97 (Tuebingen, 1956).
111. Erich Koehler, "Les possibilités de l'interpretation sociologique illustrés par l'analyse de textes littéraires français de différentes époques" in *Littérature et Société* (Brussels, 1967).
112. Hugo Kuhn, "Soziale Realitaet und dichterische Fiktion am Beispiel der hoefischen Ritterdichtung Deutschlands," in *Dichtung und Welt im Mittelalter* (Stuttgart, 1959), pp. 22–40.
113. Hugo Kuhn, "Stil als Epochen-, Gattungs-, und Wertproblem in der deutschen Literatur des Mittelalters," in *Dichtung und Welt in Mittelalter* (Stuttgart, 1959), pp. 62–69; the essay dates from 1957.
114. Arnold Hirsch, ed. 2, *Literatur und Leben*, New Series, Vol. 1 (Cologne and Graz, 1957); ed. 1, 1933.
115. Robert Escarpit, *Sociologie de la Littérature* (Paris, 1958).
116. Jones L. Lewisohn, *Expression in America* (New York, 1932).
117. E. Legouis and L. Cazamian, *History of English Literature* (London, 1926–27).
118. L. Cazamian, *History of French Literature* (Oxford, 1955).
119. Max Foerster, "The Psychological Basis of Literary Periods," in *Studies for William A. Read*, Ed. by N. Caffee and T. Kirby (New Orleans, 1940), pp. 254–268.
120. Mario Praz (Milan, 1930); pub. in English as *The Romantic Agony* (London, 1933).
121. Albert Beguin, *L'âme romantique et le rêve*, 2 vols. (Marseille, 1937).
122. W. H. Auden, *The Enchafèd Flood* (New York, 1950).
123. G. J. Geer, "Towards the Solution of the Baroque Problem," in *Neophilologus*, Vol. 44 (1960), pp. 299–307.
124. Leslie A. Fiedler, *Love and Death in the American Novel* (New York, 1960).
125. Walter Muschg, *Tragische Literaturgeschichte* (Berne, 1948).
126. Walter Muschg, in *Dichter des Expressionismus* (Munich, 1961).
127. Walter Abell, *The Collective Dream in Art. A Psycho-Historical Theory of Culture Based on Relations between the Arts, Psychology, and the Social Sciences* (Cambridge, Mass., 1957).
128. Hermann Pongs, in *Germanisch-Romanische Monatsschrift*, Vol. 17 (1929), pp. 256–277.
129. Theophil Spoerri, *Die Formwerdung des Menschen. Die Deutung des dichterischen Kunstwerks als Schluessel zur menschlichen Wirklichkeit* (Berlin, 1938).
130. Theophil Spoerri, *Die Struktur der Existenz. Einfuehrung in die Kunst der Interpretation* (Zurich, 1951).
131. Hannes Maeder, *Versuch ueber Zusammenhang von Sprach- und Geistesgeschichte*. Zuericher Beitraege zur deutschen Sprach- und Stilgeschichte, No. 1 (Zurich, 1945). [A comparison of texts of Berthold of Ratisbon and Luther as to their space-time experience.]
132. Richard Brinkmann, *Wirklichkeit und Illusion*. Ed. 1, (Tuebingen, 1957); ed. 2, Tuebingen, 1966.

133. H. Hamann, in *Grundzuege einer Morphologie der deutschen Literaturgeschichte* (Leipzig, 1927).
134. Josef Nadler, *Literaturgeschichte der deutschen Staemme und Landschaften*, 3 vols. (Ratisbon, 1912–18).
135. Robert E. Spiller, *The Cycle of American Literature. An Essay in Historical Criticism* (New York, 1955).
136. Wilhelm E. Muehlmann, *Homo Creator. Abhandlungen zur Soziologie, Anthropologie und Ethnologie* (Wiesbaden, 1962).
137. Wilhelm Dilthey, *Das Erlebnis und die Dichtung*, ed. 8 (Leipzig and Berlin, 1922), pp. 268–348; the essay dates from 1867.
138. Wilhelm Dilthey, *Das Leben Schleiermachers* (Berlin, 1870).
139. Julius Petersen, "Die literarischen Generationen," in *Philosophie der Literaturwissenschaft*, ed. by E. Ermatinger (Berlin, 1930), pp. 130–187.
140. Eduard Wechsler, in *Breysig-Festschrift* (Breslau, 1927), pp. 66–102.
141. Henri Peyre, *Les Générations Littéraires* (Paris, 1948).
142. Robert Escarpit, *Sociologie de la Littérature* (Paris, 1958), p. 12, footnote 2.
143. Hans Otto Burger, in *Annalen der deutschen Literatur* (Stuttgart, 1952).
144. Josephine Miles, "Eras in English Poetry," in *PMLA*, Vol 70, pp. 853–875.
145. Josephine Miles, *Style and Proportion. The Language of Prose and Poetry* (Boston, 1967).
146. René Wellek, *Theory of Literature*, ed. 3 (New York, 1956), p. 265. From the universal aspect of comparative criticism Wellek discussed the present–day difficulty of the period styles of the Baroque, of Romanticism, and of Realism so comprehensively as to make any critical commentary superfluous; see also René Wellek, *Concept of Criticism* (New Haven and London, 1963), pp. 69-255.

LIST OF CONTRIBUTORS

BARTHES, ROLAND
Born November 12, 1915 in Cherbourg, France.
Studied at the Sorbonne. Licence-ès-lettres, Diplôme d'études supér
ieures.
Present position: Directeur d'études á l'Ecole Pratique des Hautes
Etudes, Paris, Sorbonne.

Books: *Le Degré zéro de l'ecriture*, Paris 1953; *Michelet par lui-même*, Paris 1954; *Mythologies*, Paris 1957; *Sur Racine*, Paris 1960; *Essais critiques*, Paris 1964; *Critique et vérité*, Paris 1966; *Le Système de la Mode*, Paris 1967.

DIÉGUEZ, MANUEL
Born May 2, 1922 in Saint Gall, Switzerland.
Studied at the College Pierre Viret, Lausanne, Gymnase classique de
Lausanne, the Universities of Lausanne, Geneva, Paris, Santander and
Madrid. Licence ès sciences politiques; Licence en droit; Licence ès
lettres.
Present position: Freelance writer and critic.

Books: *La Barbarie commence seulement*, essai de politique et de morale sur l'avenir de l'Europe, Paris 1948; *De l'Absurde*, essai sur le nihilisme, précédé d'une lettre ouverte à Albert Camus, Paris 1948; *Les murs de notre ciel*, récit, Paris 1949; *Le Paradis*, récit, Paris 1953; *Dieu est-il américain?* essai satirique, Paris 1957; *Rabelais par lui-même*, Paris 1960; *L'écrivain et son langage*, essai, Paris 1960; *Chateaubriand ou le poète face à l'histoire*, Paris 1963; *Essai sur l'avenir poétique de Dieu*, Bossuet, Pascal, Chateaubriand, Claudel, Paris 1965; *De l'Idolâtrie*, Discours aux clercs et aux derviches, Paris 1969; *Science et Nescience*, Paris 1970.

FALK, EUGENE H(ANNES)

Born August 10, 1913 in Czechoslovakia.

Studied at the Sorbonne and Charles University, Czechoslovakia, 1938.
Ph.D. Victoria University, England 1942.

Present position: Professor of French and Comparative Literature,
University of North Carolina, Chapel Hill.

Books: *Renunciation as a Tragic Focus*, Minneapolis 1954; *Types of Thematic Structure*,
Chicago 1967.

FUCKS, WILHELM

Born June 4, 1902 in Leverkusen, Germany.

Studied at the University of München.

Present position: Professor and Director of the I. Physics Institute at
the University of Technology, Aachen since 1941 and Director at the
Institute for Plasmaphysics of the "Kernforschungsanlage Jülich"
(atomic research center).

Books: *Energiegewinnung aus Atomkernen*, Essen 1948; *Formeln zur Macht*. Prognosen über
Völker, Wirtschaft, Potentiale. Stuttgart 1966; *Nach allen Regeln der Kunst*. Diagnosen
über Literatur, Musik, bildende Kunst. Stuttgart 1968.

GUIRAUD, PIERRE LOUIS ROGER

Born September 26, 1912 in Sfax, Tunisia.

Studied at the Sorbonne. Docteur en lettres.

Present position: Professor at the University of Nice.

Books: *Les sources médiévales de la poésie formelle: la rime*, Groningen 1952; *Langage et
versification d'après l'oeuvre de Paul Valéry. Etude sur la forme poétique dans ses rapports avec la
langue*, Paris 1953; *Les caractères statistiques du vocabulaire*, 1954; *Index du vocabulaire du
symbolisme*, Paris 1953–1954; *Bibliographie de la statistique linguistique*, Utrecht 1954;
Index du vocabulaire de la poésie classique, Paris 1955; *L'aroot*, Paris 1956; *La stylistique*,
Paris 1957; *La grammaire*, Paris 1958; *La sémantique*, Paris 1959; *Les locutions françaises*,
Paris 1960; *Problèmes et méthodes de la statistique linguistique*, Dordrecht-Paris 1960;
La syntaxe du français, Paris 1962; *L'ancien français*, Paris 1963; *Le moyen français*, Paris
1963; *L'étymologie*, Paris 1964; *Les mots étrangers*, Paris 1965; *Le français populaire*, Paris
1966; *Patois et dialectes français*, Paris 1966; *Les mots savants*, Paris 1967; *Structures éty-
mologiques du lexique français*, Paris 1967; *Le gay savoir de la Coquille ou la clé des ballades
en jargon de Villon*, Paris 1968; *Problèmes et méthodes de la stylistique*, Paris 1970; *Les
grands textes de la stylistique*, Paris 1970; *Le testament de Villon ou le gay savoir de la Basoche*,
Paris 1970.

MARTINI, FRITZ

Born September 5, 1909 in Magdeburg, Germany.
Studied at the Universities of Zürich, Graz, Heidelberg and Berlin.
Ph. D. Berlin 1933. Ph. D. habil. Hamburg 1938.
Present position: Professor at the Technische Hochschule in Stuttgart.

Books: *Deutsche Literaturgeschichte. Von den Anfangen bis zur Gegenwart*, Stuttgart 1949; *Deutsche Literatur des bürgerlichen Realismus*, Stuttgart 1962; *Kleines Literaturlexikon* (Deutsche Autoren seit 1600), 4th edition, Bern 1968.
Editor: *Das Wagnis der Sprache*. Interpretationen deutscher Prosa von Nietzsche bis Benn, Stuttgart 1954; *Klassische Deutsche Dichtung*. Erzählkunst, Autobiographien, Schriften zur Dichtkunst, 14 vols. Freiburg i. Breisgau 1962; *C. M. Wieland, Werke* (Nach den Erstdrucken), München 1964.
Coeditor: *Der Deutschunterricht*. Beiträge zu seiner Praxis und wissenschaftlichen Grundlegung, Stuttgart 1949. (with: R. Ulshöfer, F. Maurer, G. Storz); *Jahrbuch der Deutschen Schiller-Gesellschaft*. Stuttgart 1957. (with: W. Muller-Seidel and B. Zeller).

McSPADDEN, GEORGE E.

Born February 25, 1912 in Albuquerque, New Mexico.
Studied at the University of New Mexico, Stanford University, and the University of Chile. Ph.D. Stanford University 1947.
Present position: Professor and Head of the Department of Romance Languages, University of North Carolina at Greensboro.

Books: *Spanish Spoken in Chilili New Mexico*, Albuquerque 1935; *The Spanish Prologue Before 1700*, Stanford; *An Introduction to Spanish Usage*, New York.

NICHOLS, MARIE H(OCHMUTH)

Born July 13, 1908 in Dunbar, Pennsylvania.
Ph.D. University of Wisconsin 1945.
Present position: Professor of Speech, University of Illinois.

Books: *Rhetoric and Criticism*, Baton Rouge 1963; Editor: *American Speeches*, 1954; *A History and Criticism of American Public Address*, 1955.

THORNTON, HARRY AND AGATHE

M. A. Edinborough.

Present position: Senior Lecturer, Department of Philosophy, ABPsP, ANZAsS University of Otago.

Books: *Time and Style*, Dunedin, New Zealand 1962.

TIMPE, EUGENE F.

Born September 24, 1926 in Tacoma, Washington.

Ph.D. University of Southern California 1960.

Present position: Associate Professor of German and Comparative Literature, The Pennsylvania State University.

Books: *American Literature in Germany, 1861–1872*, Chapel Hill 1964; *Thoreau Abroad*, editor and contributor, Hamden, in press.

UITTI, KARL DAVID

Born December 10, 1933 in Calumet, Michigan.

Studied at the Universities of Nancy and Bordeaux. Ph.D. University of California (Berkeley) 1959.

Present position: Graduate Representative (Director of Graduate Studies), Princeton.

Books: *The Concept of Self in the Symbolist Novel*, Gravenhage 1961; *La Passion littéraire de Remy de Gourmont*, Paris 1962; *Linguistics and Literary Theory*, Englewood Cliffs (New Jersey) 1969.

ULLMANN, STEPHEN

Born June 13, 1914 in Hungary.

Ph.D. Budapest 1936, D. Litt. Glasgow 1949.

Present position: Professor of Romance Languages, Oxford University.

Books: *Words and their Use*, New York 1951; *The Principles of Semantics*, Glasgow 1951; *Précis de sémantique française*, Berne 1952; *Style in the French Novel*, Cambridge 1957; *The Image in the Modern French Novel*, Cambridge 1960; *Semantics: An Introduction to the Science of Meaning*, New York and Oxford 1962; *Language and Style*, New York and Oxford 1964.

WEISSENBERGER, KLAUS H. M.
Born November 15, 1939 in Sydney, Australia.
Present position: Assistant Professor of German, University of Southern California.

Books: *Formen der Elegie von Goethe bis Celan*, Bern 1969; *Die Elegie bei Paul Celan*, Bern 1969.

INDEX OF NAMES